SWAMP MONSTERS

SWAMP MONSTERS

TRUMP VS. DESANTIS—

THE GREATEST SHOW ON EARTH (OR AT LEAST IN FLORIDA)

MATT DIXON

LITTLE, BROWN AND COMPANY

New York | Boston | London

Little, Brown and Company
Hachette Book Group
1290 Avenue of the Americas, New York, NY 10104
littlebrown.com

First Edition: January 2024

Little, Brown and Company is a division of Hachette Book Group, Inc. The Little, Brown name and logo are trademarks of Hachette Book Group, Inc.

The publisher is not responsible for websites (or their content) that are not owned by the publisher.

The Hachette Speakers Bureau provides a wide range of authors for speaking events. To find out more, go to hachettespeakersbureau.com or email hachettespeakers@hbgusa.com.

Little, Brown and Company books may be purchased in bulk for business, educational, or promotional use. For information, please contact your local bookseller or the Hachette Book Group Special Markets Department at special.markets@hbgusa.com.

Print book interior design by Bart Dawson.

ISBN 9780316397223
LCCN 2023943647

Printing 1, 2023

LSC-C

Printed in the United States of America

To the circumstances that led me to want to write this book, and the people whose support helped make it happen. Especially Ana.

CONTENTS

CONTENTS

PART III: FLAME WAR

INTRODUCTION

FROM SWING STATE TO "FREE STATE"

FLORIDA FLORIDA FLORIDA.

Tim Russert held up the whiteboard with an impish smile, tapping it for effect. It was past three in the morning on November 8, 2000, and the host of *Meet the Press* had run out of words— save for these three.

Earlier that night, election night—a long-awaited face-off between the Democratic presidential candidate, Al Gore, and his Republican opponent, George W. Bush—it had seemed clear that Gore was going to be the next president of the United States. The 2000 election cycle had been a bruising one; everyone expected it to be one of the closest presidential races in the nation's history. But Russert's cohost for the NBC News election coverage that evening, the legendary anchor Tom Brokaw, had announced that Gore had won Florida's twenty-five electoral votes and in the process likely given himself the inside track to beat Bush, whose brother was, coincidentally, the state's governor.

"Turns out that Governor Jeb Bush was not his brother's keeper," Brokaw intoned in his trademark deadpan style.

But the Gore presidency did not last long.

In a moment that would go down as a black eye for political media and a turning point in world affairs, a short time later, NBC, like other national news outlets, had to announce it had spoken too soon. With egg smeared all over their faces, networks and wire services admitted they had called Florida prematurely.

"The networks giveth; the networks taketh away," Brokaw said. "NBC News is now taking Florida out of Vice President Gore's column and putting [it] back in the too-close-to-call column."

The madness of the moment, as the White House hung in the balance, gave way to one of the most iconic moments of broadcast-era election coverage. As lawsuits were being filed and recounts openly being discussed, a likely sleep-deprived Russert did just one thing when asked how it all might come to an end.

On live television, with much of the nation watching, he reached for a whiteboard that had three words scribbled on it: the name of the Sunshine State written three times for emphasis.

The message was clear: the country's future would come down to Florida and Florida alone.

Ultimately, Russert was right. Bush would go on to win the state by a 537-vote margin—the very margin that would be cited in a legal battle that went all the way to the Supreme Court and, ultimately, won him the nation. But the implications went beyond one hotly contested election: the event also ushered in an era of politics in which razor-thin margins are the norm rather than the attention-grabbing exception.

"Back in the day, there weren't a lot of close elections," John Lapinski, the director of elections at NBC News, told the *Today Show* in 2020, recalling an election night two decades earlier. "[The year] 2000 started a new trend where we've seen tons of almost-tied elections. People weren't prepared for what would happen if it was a tie, and I don't think people expected that in 2000."

The impact of the 2000 recount was undeniable—think about the more than two decades spent in Iraq and Afghanistan, the effects of No Child Left Behind, and the sweeping $1.3 trillion tax cut. But policy aside, it also marked the start of a new role for Florida, one at the forefront of American politics. Though the constant spotlight of 2000 eventually faded, every four years since then, the lights and cameras have returned as the nation watches to see which candidate will clinch the state—and perhaps the country. Indeed, the infamous, chaos-filled recount has come to define Florida, whose elections have developed their own sort of mythology—one of overlong polling lines, voting irregularities, and other shenanigans, real and imagined. Inevitably, some politico, somewhere, will shrug and say the three words that capture the eye-rolling nature of the whole affair: "Florida gonna Florida."

This reputation, though at times exaggerated, was not completely undeserved at first. For years, Florida was not only the nation's largest swing state—the biggest, most politically important state that could be won by either party—but also its most mercurial one, prone to swinging right or left based on the slimmest of margins. The five presidential elections after 2000 were collectively settled by 1.1 million votes out of nearly forty-five million cast. The average margin of victory for the successful candidate was 2.6 percent—an already low number that drops to two percentage points if you remove George W. Bush's comparatively massive five-point win over John Kerry in 2004. The state's volatile political destiny, seemingly, had long been written.

Then came Donald Trump.

Of all the surprises that occurred in November of 2016, Trump's three-point-plus margin in Florida was particularly eye-popping, not least because Hillary Clinton had a much larger, better financed operation in the state. But the outcome of their epic contest in Florida, as shocking as it was, was a mere prelude for everything else to come. For unbeknownst to anyone at the time, Trump's performance that November night would mark the start of a new Florida, one destined to be the cultural nerve center of the new Republican Party. It would make the state a battleground for a new sort of political showdown: one between two presidential aspirants from the same side of the aisle.

It would set the stage for the rise of a then political unknown: a congressman by the name of Ronald DeSantis.

For months, Hillary Clinton had a sense of inevitable victory.

This was a conviction shared by the nation's top political prognosticators and pundits—the conviction that surely voters would view Donald Trump's bid for the presidency with the same disdain the Democratic Party did; the conviction that they knew American politics, that they knew the American people. Ultimately, of course, that perspective, through the all-knowing lens of hindsight, left many with the realization that they didn't know nearly as much as they thought they did.

On election night that year, I was in Palm Beach Gardens attending the watch party for Patrick Murphy, the Florida Democratic Senate candidate who was widely expected to (and did) lose to Senator Marco Rubio. While there was a clear understanding in the room regarding Murphy's fate, the mood was buoyed by the fact that Clinton was going to defeat Trump—or so everyone thought. That race was the main focus of those milling around the ballroom, slurping up every politico's favorite beverage: free election night booze.

The room was generally upbeat throughout the evening, and Murphy's concession, at 8:45 p.m., did little to dampen the mood. The crowd's focus was on bigger things. I joined the throng as it transitioned to the hotel bar, sitting by myself and sipping a Miller Lite, watching returns roll in as I polished my final story of the night.

Then Ohio was publicly called for Trump.

Then North Carolina, another key swing state, was going in Trump's column.

What had been nervous laughter over the clinking of drinks and the background sounds of MSNBC transformed into something darker as, for the first time, the possibility of a Trump presidency began to sink in for a room of hard-core Democrats in one of the Sunshine State's bluest counties.

Then it was announced. Trump had won Florida.

The room fell apart.

There were no physical altercations, but the alcohol-fueled crowd suddenly looked less like a group of well-dressed operatives out of a James Bond movie and more like an the motley crew of bounty hunters and misfits who filled the Mos Eisley Cantina in *Star Wars*.

That particular evening, I was covering election night as POLITICO Florida's bureau chief, a job that had brought me to my fair share of watch parties. And under normal circumstances, I considered this a perk: the buzz and energy at these events are enough to give any political junkie a high. But as the mood quickly soured, it became clear that it would be best if I finished the night in my hotel room.

"The fucking media and their obsession with [Clinton's] emails," screamed one supporter from a high-top table.

This was a common theme in the wreckage that was now the Palm Beach Gardens Marriott. Democrats were upset at one another for not doing enough to dim the Trump campaign's spotlight on Clinton's infamous use of a private email server during her time as secretary of state. Even more than that, they were furious at the media for repeatedly covering the issue. "What about her emails?" later became the sarcastic battle cry of wounded Democrats who continue to blame the press for a Trump administration that was more extreme than many of them could have imagined. The irony occurred to me as I surveyed the increasing chaos: the Democratic watch party had developed the same antimedia vibe as a Trump rally. My election-night buzz fading, I returned to my room to try to make sense of the evening's events.

Florida had long been known as the nation's largest swing state. But in the years following that fateful November night, that political identity has been upended and a new, perhaps more consequential identity has replaced it—that of a haven for one-party rule. This transformation sets up a perplexing dynamic: Florida's reputation as an unpredictable, must-win state in national elections is slipping, but its status as the nation's new Republican headquarters has ensured that its overall influence remains. This designation means it's not just the best representation of the new world order of American politics; it also predicts where the country will go next.

All the while, the Republican Party's mascot has of course remained the elephant, but the new party could just as easily be represented by a shirtless man from Florida wearing Mickey Mouse ears while riding an alligator through the Everglades, a Pub Sub in one hand, a cafecito in the other, and a half-smoked cigar clenched between his teeth.

It is now the party of Florida Man.

If Trump's three-point win in 2016 laid the foundation for the New Florida, another set of election results cemented it.

In the fall of 2022, Ron DeSantis clinched the state's gubernatorial election for a second time, beating Democrat Charlie Crist, a political chameleon and Florida's former Republican governor, by nearly twenty percentage points. It is a staggering margin whose importance is hard to overstate. At that point, decades of Republican control had made even casual national-level observers see Florida as slowly moving out of the swing-state column. The 2022 midterms, and DeSantis's subsequent rise, however, cast the state in a totally different light. Across the nation, President Joe Biden's approval ratings were slipping, bolstering the battle-tested idea that the party that controls the White House is fated for a bad midterm election cycle. Memorably, that idea was proved wrong in most corners of the country, as Democrats held the Senate and lost the House by a much slimmer margin than anticipated. The predicted red wave had largely fizzled—that is, everywhere but in Florida.

In the Sunshine State, DeSantis and his fellow Republicans wiped out Democrats up and down the ballot. The midterms gave the governor supermajorities in the state legislature as he headed into his second term, during which he was widely expected to announce his 2024 bid for the presidency. Bolstering his chances was his famously hands-off approach to the COVID-19 pandemic, which transformed him into the national conservatives' new gubernatorial ideal. By the time he'd declared victory in the 2022 midterms, he was a household political name with generally high approval ratings and more money in the bank than any governor in American history.

As DeSantis's status as a mythical figure in the new conservative movement has become impossible to ignore, Florida's influence, too, has drastically increased. The state has become ground zero for a new Republican Party that was remade by Trump and that has been carried forward by DeSantis. The governor has used his massive platform within the party to usher in right-wing populist reforms that have breathed life into once-fringe extremist views. He has strengthened and defined a political movement forged by Trump, and he's achieved this by—among other things—banning discussion of gender identity in his state's classrooms, criminalizing medical care for trans minors, giving a conservative overhaul to the state's education system, making immigration a top-tier issue in a state hundreds of miles from the Mexican border, labeling corporations as "woke" and "evil" rather than political allies who fund Republican politics, and, above all, making the art of "owning the libs" and the manufacturing of mass outrage the point of politics rather than its occasional by-product.

It's a strategy that his supporters have embraced.

"Ever since Jeb [Bush], for me, Florida has long been a place for Republican conservatives to look toward as the ideal state," said Alex Stroman, the former executive director of the South Carolina Republican Party. "It has been a Disney World for Republicans. Things are run well there, and you have good leaders. Then COVID came, and all that was amplified. It was a continuation of good leadership in the state of Florida that we all saw from the outside looking in."

This is not something that people elsewhere in the country are merely talking about: Americans have been moving to the state in droves since the pandemic subsided. In 2022, 318,855 people moved to Florida from other states, more people than moved to any other state during the same period—a statistic DeSantis regularly touts when framing Florida as ahead of the curve on important policy fights.

"By keeping Florida free and open, we have created a positive economic environment and invested in our state's workforce and communities," DeSantis said in November of 2022. "As a result, Florida is leading the nation in net migration and talent attraction. As other states continue to struggle at the hands of poor leadership, people and businesses are flocking to Florida."

DeSantis drawing conservatives to Florida is tied to the message that his policies represent a push toward freedom. On paper, it's an objective philosophy that benefits all, but in practice it is anything but: DeSantis's political foes point to the fact that the newfound freedom often only goes one way as the governor champions policies strongly opposed by many racial and ethnic minorities, trans residents, and other marginalized communities. But on the conservative side of the political spectrum, the script has been written. Florida is no longer just a state: it is the Free State of Florida, or so the DeSantis campaign swag says.

"Florida is now the new pinnacle for freedom. The pinnacle of the Republican movement. No state is more important in post-MAGA Republican politics," said Nick Iarossi, a prominent Florida lobbyist and one of the few in the state's GOP establishment who backed DeSantis in the 2018 primary. "It is the epicenter because of what Governor DeSantis has done. Conservatives across the country say, 'I wish he was my governor.' There is no better example than the huge number of people coming here from

Democratic-led states. People are leaving all these blue states to move to Florida. It's a huge wave."

During a lunch at the La Gorce Country Club, in Miami Beach, early in his first term, DeSantis, in a display of political prescience, echoed this sentiment, telling longtime lobbyist and ally Slater Bayliss that he thought conservatives from across the country would start moving to Florida in response to policies instituted in Democratic states. Bayliss told him that he agreed with "conventional wisdom" that people move to the Sunshine State because of warm weather and low taxes—and the fact that there's no personal income tax—but that for the most part they come from the Northeast and do not vote Republican. DeSantis was insistent that this was changing and that people now see "Florida as a beacon of freedom."

"I am not sure I bought it or thought it was true at the time," Bayliss joked later. "But he has made it that way, and post-COVID, there is no question Florida is a conservative destination."

Indeed, in 2021 alone, Florida hosted several major national conservative conferences, including those held by the Conservative Political Action Coalition, which has been hollowed out and remade as a pro-Trump political organ; Turning Point USA, the conservative education reform group led by Charlie Kirk, who in 2018 was dubbed "Trump's man on campus" by POLITICO; the Faith and Freedom Coalition, a group formed by Ralph Reed, the former George W. Bush adviser who underwent a makeover in order to remain relevant to the remade Republican Party; and smaller events such as the Million Maskless March, which was organized by antimaskers and amplified by Trump-world creatures such as Roger Stone, a Nixon-era trickster now best known for serving as Trump's political ride or die.

"We kind of started looking at states that were open. We looked at Georgia, Florida, Texas, [and] South Dakota, and Florida by far made the most sense," said Reed of his decision to bring the thousands of conservative activists that make up his membership to the state. Further, he added, because conservative Florida mainstays Rubio and DeSantis were both on the 2022 ballot, the choice "was just natural for us."

As Florida became the host for conservative megaconferences while the rest of the nation grappled with pandemic-driven shutdowns, DeSantis was the star, billed as the keynote speaker at most events, even as other top-tier national Republicans tried to carve out their own niches within Trump's political base. DeSantis dominated a Trumpless straw poll taken at CPAC's Orlando event in 2022, racking up 61 percent support, a figure no one else came close to. Senator Rick Scott, who during the 2022 election cycle led Senate Republican campaigns, and Senator Marco Rubio, who was trounced by Trump in Florida during his failed presidential run in 2016, received less than 1 percent of the vote at the same event. The results further instilled the sense that DeSantis had become the dominant force not only in Florida politics but also within his party nationally.

Conversely, over the same period, Democrats in Florida have been in free fall. The national party apparatus has started to abandon a state it no longer needs to win the White House in favor of other, more feasible battlegrounds, and the state-level Democratic infrastructure is in shambles, leaving the future of the party bleak and raising inevitable questions about whether Florida can ever return to its former role as a swing state or if that long-standing political designation has been replaced with a sign at the Florida-Georgia border that reads: WELCOME TO FLORIDA, HOME OF THE NEW REPUBLICAN PARTY.

The 2022 midterms, of course, hugely amplified the state's already noticeable shift to the right. For the second election cycle in a row, Democrats were successful nationally but bludgeoned in Florida, a feat punctuated by the GOP's takeover of the Democrats' long-held voter registration advantage. This effectively washed away any swing-state residue left behind from past political eras, signaling to Democratic organizations that their money would be better spent in states such as Arizona, Georgia, and North Carolina, where they might have a fighting chance.

For Democrats, then, Florida's role can be compared to the once ubiquitous pandemic-era Peloton purchase: at one point, it may have seemed like a good investment; now, it looks like nothing more than an expensive mistake one should ignore.

The complete collapse of a political party in a state where it once had a strong foothold is a self-perpetuating phenomenon. As national money dried up, transactional donors—who will give to whoever is in control as a means to remain close to political power—no longer had any reason to fund Democrats. And when those checks stopped, it became harder for Florida's Democrats to combat DeSantis's rise, even with basic initiatives such as nonstop voter registration drives and other types of so-called permanent infrastructure. These initiatives are the political equivalent of eating your vegetables—the basic building blocks of political campaigns. But in recent years, Democrats have been unable to afford them.

"One of the by-products of Republicans being in charge for twenty-five years and our being in a desert for so long is that we have much fewer resources," said Sean Shaw, a former Democratic state representative and the party's nominee for state attorney general in 2018. "Registration costs money. Building infrastructure costs money."

The GOP takeover of the state has been facilitated by the rise of DeSantis as a national conservative powerhouse. Democrats in

Florida have been unable to slow his political ascent in any meaningful way. This is the equivalent of being Mike Tyson's sparring partner: you're destined to emerge from each fight bloodied and bruised rather than victorious. Florida Democrats now serve as the punching bag for the likes of DeSantis, Scott, and Rubio as those ambitious politicians build their reputations as nationally significant Republicans who at this point have spent years planning for a 2024 bid for the White House.

It's against this backdrop that a new, clearly increasingly far-right environment has emerged. In very Floridian fashion, however, its defining feature remains chaos and the power of influence. And at its heart is the feud between DeSantis and Trump.

The relationship started out as one of political mentor and mentee after Trump's endorsement fueled DeSantis's 2018 upset win in the Florida Republican gubernatorial primary, in which he defeated an opponent who had the firm support of the state's entire Republican establishment. But this alliance quickly and publicly unraveled as it became clear that DeSantis was developing into a threat to Trump—most crucially, to his ambition to return to the White House in 2024.

As the 2022 midterms progressed, a wave of media attention, on top of the organic rivalry that was growing behind the scenes, fueled the sense that there had been a clash, and perhaps an inevitable one, between two politicians whose former bromance helped them become the biggest figures in Republican politics. Trump started taking overt potshots at DeSantis, workshopping nicknames such as Meatball Ron and Ron DeSanctimonious and putting almost all his focus on trashing his former mentee, whom he has all but acknowledged is his chief 2024 rival.

It was at that same time, during the 2022 midterms, that Trump once again began holding rallies, amping up a political machine that would take aim at the ten Republican incumbents who voted to impeach him—none of whom, notably, are from his adopted home state of Florida. DeSantis, meanwhile, spent months brushing off questions about 2024, even as he openly orchestrated a run, scoffing in his typical arrogant style at reporters who had long been told behind the scenes by the governor's allies that he was eyeing a White House bid. The comments, of course, came as DeSantis routinely fled to fundraisers and keynote events that just happened to be situated in early general election states.

During a meeting in 2020 on the balcony of Mar-a-Lago, the now infamous Palm Beach County resort and Trump's permanent residence, Trump made his distrust of DeSantis clear to a close circle of advisers. He touted all he had done for DeSantis as president and bemoaned the meager return on his investment. This is one of Trump's consistent gripes with DeSantis: a nagging sense that although Trump had been essential to making DeSantis a national political figure, the governor had done nothing to help his magnanimous benefactor in return.

And so, with his signature offhand enmity, Trump aimed his political cannon at the man he had once called an ally.

"He is a good governor and a tough cookie," Trump told his advisers. "But some people are just not that grateful."

PART I

THE CREATURE FROM THE BLACK LAGOON

CHAPTER ONE

THE WILDERNESS

R on DeSantis was not in total political purgatory, but he could have been excused for thinking he was.

It was the fall of 2016, and the three-term Florida congressman was fresh off a miserable failed bid for a seat in the US Senate. DeSantis, like other Republicans vying for the spot, had dropped out of the race when Marco Rubio returned, tail between his legs, to run for reelection after Donald Trump turned Rubio's bid for the White House into nothing more than a punch line about presidential hand size—or something like that. Still, even before Rubio returned to Florida, DeSantis was not breaking through. His campaign had struggled to hit the 5 percent mark, even in what most acknowledged was a lackluster GOP primary field.

According to people who know him best, when DeSantis looked in the mirror, he saw a president looking back. Now, however, he was merely a politician without a campaign. In just a few short years, he would inject right-wing orthodoxy into all Florida's major institutions. He would be branded America's Governor by conservatives across the country and try to wrest from Donald Trump a Republican Party that the former president had remade in his own image. But in 2016, all that was but a blip on the horizon.

For now, DeSantis was out in the wilderness.

DeSantis and a small group of advisers, including Nick Iarossi, Scott Ross, and Brad Herold, were essentially wandering around Tallahassee like the city's last door-to-door encyclopedia salesmen trying to sell DeSantis's political viability. But the moment was not totally void of direction, even if outward appearances implied otherwise.

DeSantis was not yet a real political player, but even from an early age he held political ambitions. After growing up in the working-class suburb of Dunedin, near Tampa, he graduated from Yale, where he was famously the captain of the school's baseball team. He then went on to Harvard Law before being assigned to the navy's JAG Corps, with stints at Guantánamo Bay and in Iraq, as a legal adviser.

In 2016, still smarting from his unceremonious exit from the Senate race, and with his legal background in hand, DeSantis calculated that running for state attorney general in the 2018 midterms would be a good way to chart a path out of political exile. And indeed, there are few nonfederal posts better suited to building a reputation beyond Florida's 1,350 miles of pristine coastline than top attorney in a hugely important swing state, where you could fire off lawsuit after lawsuit.

After the state senate president, Joe Negron, also an attorney, assured him that he was not pursuing his own bid, DeSantis's path seemed much clearer. He and his team had a lunch at the Edison, an old Tallahassee electric plant turned restaurant in the shadow of Florida's state capitol. There they etched out a plan to meet with the Tallahassee-based lobbyists whose offices lined Adams Street and who comprised the core of the Florida Republican Party. These lobbyists are key to fueling costly statewide races and have long influenced which candidates are able to run a viable campaign and which are not. DeSantis was then hard at work trying to earn the support of transactional lobbyists, who care less about policies than access—the same lobbyists whom, in a few short years, he would publicly deride as slimy swamp creatures when padding his populist bona fides.

But while he and his team were in agreement about the importance of transactional lobbyists, DeSantis was distracted by an idea that everyone around him brushed off as a delusion of grandeur: he was certain that he could get the endorsement of President Donald Trump.

The New York billionaire had just ascended to the White House, a process that saw him steamroll over a sixteen-person GOP primary field chock-full of career politicians and notch a victory over Hillary Clinton—a victory that included, of course, a shocking win in Florida, where the Democrat had been the heavy favorite. Trump emerged from the fight with a cultlike following every bit as loyal to his nascent Make America Great Again movement—no matter what it stood for—as it had been to any political ideology espoused by the Grand Old Party. At that point, Trump had fully hijacked a huge swath of the Republican base, in the process disempowering mainstays such as Jeb Bush and Marco Rubio, having convinced many former supporters that "those old-school Republicans" were more worthy of their scorn than their votes.

As DeSantis was quietly feeling out support to make a run for Florida attorney general, he was also a regular presence on Fox News. He ably used his perch on the House Foreign Affairs Committee to become the cable-news defender of Trump, fending off allegations that his election had been the result of Russian meddling.

"I think the media is definitely trying to sow doubts about Donald Trump's legitimacy. I don't think there's any question about that. I'm not sure that that's necessarily going to have legs," DeSantis told Fox News's Neil Cavuto in December of 2016. "I mean, he is going to take the oath of office on January twentieth. And he is going to pursue policies."

At that point, DeSantis was a three-term congressman but a relative unknown outside the Fox News bubble. However, his attack-dog style had indeed caught Trump's attention—and appreciation. As DeSantis's reputation grew, in moments of particular intensity, the White House would even reach out to Fox News to make sure DeSantis was booked, especially as the Russia investigations drew an increasing amount of scrutiny. DeSantis expertly played to Trump's vanity and, one conservative news hit at a time, slowly carved out a permanent place on the president's radar.

DeSantis rightly understood that the number one consideration Trump used when picking allies was whether they said nice things about him. And DeSantis said a lot of nice things about Trump.

As DeSantis's campaign began to pick up momentum, he hired his own TV booker and started speaking on Fox News more frequently. As a creation of the Tea Party movement in the mid-2000s, he spoke the language of the conservative base, and with these appearances, his aptitude for communicating with Trump's core supporters was on full display.

DeSantis had been honing these skills for a while, and not always in the most obvious ways. Before law school, before his time in the navy, he had briefly gone into teaching: from 2001 to 2002, he taught history and government at the Darlington School, an elite private school outside Atlanta. He made an impression on students both for his attempts to ingratiate himself with them—he attended parties at which high school seniors were present and once even challenged a student to a milk-drinking contest—and for his questionable ideas about American history and politics, especially the hot-button topics of abortion and the Civil War, which he allegedly claimed was "not about slavery!" The echoes of the early days of DeSantis's philosophical and political development, including those specific to slavery, are evident in the policies he would put forward two decades later, when he was at the helm of Florida. The journey he took from the rural Georgia boarding school to the governor's mansion, however, was paved with experiences that would only harden his far-right worldview. But it wasn't until he left the navy, in 2010—two years before his first election to the US Congress—that his star really began to rise.

DeSantis's first major moment in the political spotlight came in 2011 while he was hitting the Tea Party circuit hard, hawking copies of his self-published book, *Dreams from Our Founding Fathers,* a title born out of a desire to troll Barack Obama's *Dreams from My Father.* The Tea Party—a movement led by a growing legion of self-proclaimed disaffected conservatives trying to reshape the Republican Party—laid the foundation for the sort of populist politics Trump would later bring roaring to life and DeSantis would use to build his brand. The movement aimed to buck traditional political institutions by pushing Republican leadership further to the right and injecting libertarian ideals into the conservative moment.

As DeSantis described it, his book was a critique of modern Democratic politics centered on the teaching and writing of the nation's founding fathers. It was a hit with conservative groups and Tea Party organizations, springing DeSantis from the relative obscurity of the political rubber-chicken dinner circuit, the only space in conservative Florida politics where he was well known at the time.

DeSantis had been plucked from obscurity during a speaking engagement to hype his book at a meeting of the West Orange County Tea Party, a since disbanded Orlando-area group. And it was here that his political career got its true start; he emerged having resolved to run for Congress.

"I met Ron at a Tea Party meeting," said a GOP consultant who played a role in persuading him to run for office. "I had folks suggest to me that we might be similar in characteristics, which, as I look back on who he's become, makes me feel like an asshole."

After filing to run for Congress, DeSantis won a six-person GOP primary, after which he easily won the general election race for a conservative-leaning seat just south of Jacksonville. One term quickly turned into three, and during his tenure, he built a résumé impressive for any politician trying to find a home on the GOP's right flank. He cofounded the überconservative Freedom Caucus, a collection of lawmakers who often quarreled with their party's own leadership. He was openly and staunchly pro-Israel, a stance that caught the early attention of the late Sheldon Adelson, a Las Vegas casino magnate and major longtime donor to the Republican Party. DeSantis also supported efforts to repeal the Affordable Care Act—commonly referred to as Obamacare—and voted for a symbolic budget resolution that would raise the age for Medicare and Social Security to seventy. (That vote would later become the subject of a TV ad Trump ran against DeSantis implying that he wanted to water down popular long-standing programs. These attacks came as DeSantis was preparing his run for president, a time he used to walk back his previous votes on the issue: in 2023, DeSantis said he was "not going to mess with" entitlement programs.)

DeSantis had taken a circuitous path, and while it had brought him far, he still hadn't achieved anything close to the success he felt he deserved. But the Fox News appearances, his biggest platform up to that point—essentially, auditions for a place on the new MAGA stage Trump had built—remained promising. And DeSantis was nailing them.

As his presence grew in the Trump orbit, DeSantis found himself in the Washington offices of the business intelligence company Morning Consult the day of Trump's inauguration, in late January of 2017. It was the location of a celebration hosted by the 45Committee, a dark-money group that spent $20 million in support of Trump late in the 2016 election cycle. The effort helped one of its funders, Joe Ricketts—whose family owns the Chicago Cubs—return to Trump's good graces after being one of the early leaders of the Never Trump movement. The event put DeSantis in the same room with some of the Republican Party's biggest movers and shakers at a time when Trump's brand of populism was becoming the party's main ethos. Crucially, the group included Sheldon Adelson, the major GOP rainmaker. In just a few years, Adelson would prove to be a big factor in DeSantis's rise and even chair his splashy 2018 finance committee.

"He got to shake the hand of the big guy—Sheldon," recalled a Republican consultant who had been in attendance. "As I look back on what DeSantis has become today, the moment seems even bigger."

It was moments like this that had DeSantis's ad hoc group of advisers wonder, as one told me, whether he was "running for the wrong office."

For it was becoming increasingly apparent that DeSantis was a political unicorn. He had the ability to tap into national Republican donor money, funds that were out of reach for any other state-level candidate. He had near unfettered access to the Fox News airwaves, infamous for converting backbench congressmen into national stars. And, most crucially, he had the approval of Donald Trump.

DeSantis, his advisers thought, could easily assume the conservative role in the Florida GOP primary that had been long filled by

Richard Corcoran, the Republican Speaker of the Florida House of Representatives, who had served as Rubio's chief of staff when *he* was Speaker of the Florida House, from 2006 to 2008. Corcoran was seen as a pugilistic, rock-ribbed conservative and longtime Tallahassee insider, albeit one who could never achieve the national political capital that DeSantis had already secured. The largest obstacle in his way, then, was the agriculture commissioner, Adam Putnam, the baby-faced scion of Florida political and citrus royalty. Putnam had been elected to the Florida House in 1996, at the time the youngest member ever, then served a decade in Congress, a tenure that included two years as chair of the House Republican Conference. He had returned to Florida in 2009 to run for agriculture commissioner, but most observers believed that his ultimate destiny lay in one place: the governor's mansion. Putnam was well known and well liked among the state's Republican establishment, which was preparing to fully fund his 2018 gubernatorial campaign.

As he headed into 2017, with his eye on the governor's seat, DeSantis was increasingly insistent that he could convert his reputation as one of Trump's staunchest defenders into an endorsement from the man himself. However, despite his team's growing understanding of DeSantis's political dexterity, the suggestion still fell on incredulous ears. A sitting president with an incredibly intense national following was not going to endorse a relatively little-known congressman, much less one who was not supported by most of the power brokers in his own state. But flashing his brand of unshakable self-assurance, DeSantis brushed off his advisers' concerns, doubling down on his insistence that he had Trump's ear. If he did, he knew, it would unleash a tidal wave of momentum that could swamp even Putnam and his well-heeled donors.

"That's exactly the conversation we [were] having," one DeSantis adviser recalled when I brought up the stakes that had been at hand.

"Adam Putnam would have had to have five thousand barbecues to match the sort of attention and free media you get on Fox News."

Meanwhile, the hope that the DeSantis team would have access to money that other Florida Republicans did not had indeed become reality: DeSantis turned out to be a billionaire whisperer.

That dynamic was on full display in October of 2017, when DeSantis and his still small group of advisers walked into the Venetian, a Las Vegas hotel and mainstay that, at the time, was owned by Adelson. Ever since their fateful handshake the morning of Trump's inauguration, DeSantis had forged strong ties with the billionaire, strategically growing his reputation as one of the staunchest pro-Israel members in Congress. Of all the causes Adelson championed during his life, this was the one he was most passionate about—one that, every four years, prompted Republican presidential hopefuls to align themselves with the casino magnate and his mighty checkbook, which had a reputation for floating Republican presidential campaigns. This process was so well known that the primary had been dubbed the "Sheldon Adelson primary." While Adelson's backing was generally reserved for presidential runs, DeSantis knew he would need the billionaire's support to win the governorship; presidential candidate he was not, but he was trying to build a fundraising base largely from scratch.

"They were talking...like...Bedouin tribes of Israel [in the] pre-biblical era," an aide said in early 2020. "I'm not even sure I'm saying it right—it was just so esoteric. Sheldon knew exactly what [DeSantis] was saying, but everyone else in the room was lost."

Adelson eventually agreed to lead DeSantis's finance team, a largely ceremonial role that did not require him to work on the campaign but only lend his name to it as a clear sign of legitimacy. However, that arrangement reeled in other big-fish GOP donors such as David Bossie and Rebekah Mercer, both of whom were close Trump allies. This was an impressive coalition, not simply for its ties to Trump but also for what it signaled: a group of people who did not normally play in nonfederal elections would show up in a big way for this gubernatorial hopeful.

The Adelson meeting made things feel very real for DeSantis, who would soon secure a victory that made even the mighty billionaire's backing pale in comparison.

On December 22, 2017, Donald Trump sat on Air Force One preparing to light Florida politics—and, unbeknownst to him, his own political future—on fire. The forty-fifth president was set to use his hugely influential Twitter account to play kingmaker in Florida's GOP gubernatorial primary.

As Air Force One approached Palm Beach International Airport, Trump tweeted, "Congressman Ron DeSantis is a brilliant young leader, Yale and then Harvard Law, who would make a Great Governor of Florida. He loves our Country and is a true FIGHTER!"

I just so happened to be in my sweatpants nursing a whiskey and Coke while wrapping Christmas presents in my hometown of Denmark, Wisconsin, a farming town of roughly two thousand people just outside of Green Bay. I was visiting from Florida, where I'd lived since 2008, covering the state's influential and cutthroat politics. The years that passed had given me a front-row seat to DeSantis's rise from a self-published Tea Party author to US congressman. But even my years as a close witness could not prepare me for DeSantis's next stop.

The swampy peninsula known as Florida has long served as a refuge for other states' drifters and outcasts, many of whom proudly wear the badge of Florida Man or Florida Woman. The state's political status could, perhaps, be best compared to that of wealthy eccentric family members: throughout the year, they serve as punching bags for their scoffing proper relatives, but come Christmas, those same scoffers will be lining up for what they know will be the best gifts under the tree.

Florida's gift, for those lucky enough to receive it, is twenty-nine electoral votes—often the difference maker between four years in the political wilderness and four years in the White House. Although the state's comic Florida Man image is irresistible for national headline writers, it masks a serious political ecosystem: Florida is home to more than sixty billionaires who fund candidates and organizations across the country. It is home to key voting demographics—most notably, the nation's largest bloc of Hispanics and a huge collection of senior-citizen voters—that campaigns target in presidential races and that politicians otherwise message-test year-round. And, of course, Florida has long been held up as the nation's largest swing state.

This last moniker in particular is precisely what drew Trump to focus on its political landscape and to make a man he had little personal relationship with its governor.

The fight for Trump's endorsement was fierce. There were warring camps, conflicting arguments, and heavy lobbying appeals to anyone with the slightest influence.

The Washington-based brain trust that hashed out whom Trump should endorse in the Florida gubernatorial election included Marc Short, chief of staff to Vice President Mike Pence; Marty Obst, one of Pence's top political advisers; Brad Parscale, who served as Trump's 2016 digital director and 2020 campaign manager and who was also a Pence adviser; Justin Clark, an attorney who served in the Trump administration and led the legal effort to try to overturn the 2020 election; David Bossie, who served as deputy campaign manager in 2016 and has since remained in Trump's orbit; Bill Stepien, who served as White House political director and replaced Parscale as Trump campaign manager in July of 2020; Corey Lewandowski, the 2016 campaign manager and longtime Trump orbit creature; and Brian Jack, who also had a stint as White House political director.

The process started with most of the group set on backing Putnam—or at least staying out of the fight. Slowly, however, the pro-DeSantis camp, led by Bossie and Representative Matt Gaetz, who thought Putnam was a "goober" and who functionally ran DeSantis's campaign, especially in the early stages, started to make progress.

"That was mostly Bossie and DeSantis," said a DeSantis political adviser familiar with the inroads the gubernatorial candidate was making within Trump's camp. "I can't really think of anyone else who had significant play in that. Nobody was playing at that level with Trump to have gotten something like that done. That was mostly brute force from DeSantis with an assist from Bossie."

Bossie appealed to what the two men saw as Trump's "instincts," framing Putnam as a pre-Trump establishment Republican who would never truly fit the Make America Great Again mold. DeSantis, they argued, was much better attuned to Trump, and there were scads of Fox News video clips to help make their point: for weeks, DeSantis had praised Trump and trashed special counsel Robert Mueller, who had been tasked with investigating alleged Russian election meddling and who was the focus of Trump's considerable scorn.

"I knew inherently and personally that Ron DeSantis was more in sync with the president's agenda than what I considered the establishment candidate, Adam Putnam," said a Trump aide involved in the Putnam-DeSantis debate.

Fox News's role in the process cannot be overstated. The network not only gave DeSantis nearly unfettered access to its airwaves, it also largely blocked Putnam from making substantial appearances, even though Putnam's campaign spent hundreds of thousands of dollars to run ads on Fox. And in August of 2018, when Putnam was granted a rare appearance on the network, his slot came in the early morning hours, considered the cable news desert. The first question he was asked was about a Trump rally held in Tampa the previous night, where the president had brought DeSantis onstage and called him a "brilliant cookie."

Putnam responded to the loaded question by talking about his campaign's focus on vocational education, a dry response that crystallized how foreign his brand of establishment politics was to the MAGAverse, which required its people to be able to throw punches at a moment's notice and focus on the "red meat" politics of the moment rather than the dry minutiae of policymaking.

All the while, it was becoming ever clearer that the path to winning Trump's endorsement was not for the faint of heart. As one adviser wryly put it, "There were different tones for different times." During one meeting at the Pennsylvania Avenue office that was home to many pro-Trump super PACs, things grew testy. Bossie exploded, yelling at the conference room, "We are wasting everyone's time. The president is going to be with Ron DeSantis. What are we doing here?" It was not a reference to the meeting Bossie was in but rather to the contention that Trump was set to put his political brand behind DeSantis's candidacy.

The crescendo came as Putnam was in the ear of Pence, who in turn was lobbying Trump to refrain from endorsing anyone altogether. Pence and Putnam had served in Congress together and were friends. At the same time, Putnam advisers were in the ears of Short and Obst—the two Pence aides—hoping that, if Trump had to endorse a candidate, it wouldn't be DeSantis.

"We were talking directly with Marc Short," said a former Putnam adviser. "Both Marc and Vice President Pence were trying really hard to keep Trump out of it. I don't think they were fans of DeSantis, and they knew how big Trump's endorsement would be."

They were joined in their effort to block Trump's interest in DeSantis by then Florida governor Rick Scott, who has since become the state's junior senator. Scott made his abrupt emergence onto Florida's political scene by dropping more than $70 million of his own money to unexpectedly win the 2010 gubernatorial race. Scott's takeover of Florida politics was arguably another catalyst for Florida's lurch to the right.

Since 2010, Scott has spent $100 million of his personal wealth to go 3–0 in Florida statewide races and was one of the first establishment-type Republicans to back Trump, penning a USA Today op-ed in January of 2016 saying that Trump had "America's pulse." During the 2016 election cycle, he ran a pro-Trump super PAC that raised $20 million. Despite the fact that Scott's disciplined, robotic speaking cadence could not be further from the president's brawling demeanor, he'd thrown in his lot with Trump. He had some sway in the Trump universe, including working closely with him during the 2022 midterms while running the National Republican Senatorial Committee—which, under his watch, lost virtually all its top races in humiliating fashion. Mostly, though, Scott was a ruthless politician in his own right, someone who had long dreamed of being in the White House one day. And he realized early on that Ron DeSantis's ascent could pose a threat to what he hoped would be a national political career—a complication that did not come with Putnam, who, everyone knew, had a state-level ceiling.

"It had nothing to do with Putnam; Rick Scott just wanted to be the belle of the ball," said a former DeSantis aide. "He knew full well that Adam Putnam was never going to be competitive with him on the national stage. He was smart enough to know Ron DeSantis could."

But even Scott did not prove to be enough of a Trump whisperer to persuade him to steer clear of DeSantis. Trump knew when he sent the tweet praising DeSantis that he had run afoul of Scott's wishes; he just didn't care.

"When Trump called DeSantis to talk after the tweet, he basically said, 'Well, did you like my tweet?'" said a former DeSantis aide. "He told him, 'Rick Scott is going to be pissed at me for doing it, but I don't care. You're my guy.'"

The first tweet was not a direct endorsement, but it was as close to a promise of one as DeSantis could get: Trump was clearly signaling to the political world where his preferences lay. Trump's official endorsement, also via Twitter, did not come until July of 2018. And in true Floridian fashion, it came after a dramatic showdown: an even more covert lobbying war that pitted the biggest names in the state's politics against one another.

In May of 2018, Matt Gaetz, who had established a national reputation as one of Trump's biggest supporters, snagged an Oval Office meeting with the president and his daughter-in-law Lara to talk about rescue dogs, an issue that was near and dear to Gaetz's heart. However, in the opinion of those aware of the meeting, this topic was a mere cover: it was widely believed by both camps to be a chance for Gaetz to lobby Trump to officially endorse DeSantis. Upon getting word of the meeting, Brian Ballard, one of Florida's most influential lobbyists and a Trump ally, and former Florida attorney general

Pam Bondi, another longtime Trump ally and soon-to-be leader of a pro-Trump super PAC, made a direct request to White House officials: block the Gaetz meeting.

Gaetz was waiting in the Roosevelt Room for the start of his 6:00 p.m. meeting with the president, an appointment he really did think would be about rescue dogs. Despite the suspicion swirling around his White House visit, Gaetz had no ulterior motives. But as time wore on, he began to wonder if there was a problem. Eventually a junior White House staffer arrived and told Gaetz the president could not see him that night. A confused Gaetz was escorted out of the White House and later that night received a call from an equally confused Lara Trump.

"Where were you?" she asked Gaetz.

"A staffer told me I had to leave," Gaetz said.

"Well, we did not get to talk about rescue dogs," Lara Trump said of her unexpected later meeting with Ballard and Bondi. "All they wanted to do is show...why [the president] should not come to Florida and why he backed the wrong guy and could still back off."

Once Gaetz realized he had been played by Bondi and Ballard, he calmed down. "Game respects game" was his general demeanor as he regrouped with DeSantis's inner circle to plot his next move. The opportunity presented itself when then *New York Times* reporter Jonathan Martin reached out to Todd Harris, a veteran Republican consultant working with DeSantis's campaign. Martin wanted to see if DeSantis's camp had a comment about Pence working behind the scenes to persuade Trump to stay out of the race. Ironically, this was set to read like a victory lap for Putnam's team, who'd worked to get the story placed; but when Harris informed the campaign that the story was coming, the DeSantis team resolved to upend the Putnam narrative.

"We determined the best move was to show [the *New York Times*] all the evidence in the world to change the narrative [and say] that Trump is being managed by Pence. Trump hates being managed," said a former staffer who was involved in this slice of political espionage. "That was the strategy, and it worked. When it came out, Trump was furious."

The hope was to play on Trump's notorious stubbornness. If he got it into his head that people thought he was someone's puppet, especially a puppet of his vice president, it would steer him in the direction of endorsing DeSantis. Trump can be driven by a "no one tells me what to do" mentality, and in this case if he thought Pence was trying to "manage" him, that would work in DeSantis's favor.

That was followed up days later by a Gaetz-authored op-ed on the Breitbart website laying out the instances in which Putnam had said negative things about Trump and underscoring the idea that the president should instead trust DeSantis.

"Adam Putnam's 'Never Trump' attitude has been overtaken only by his ambition to be governor. After Trump secured the nomination, Putnam was asked if he would endorse Trump," Gaetz wrote. "His snarky reply: 'I don't envision a scenario where I would endorse Trump prior to the convention, and we'll see what the convention yields.'"

The op-ed was the final salvo. It landed during what had been a lengthy and brutal lobbying fight waged on several fronts, from private DC conference rooms to the front page of the *New York Times*.

Trump had heard enough.

"Congressman Ron DeSantis, a top student at Yale and Harvard Law School, is running for Governor of the Great State of Florida," Trump tweeted on June 22, 2018. "Ron is strong on Borders, tough on Crime & big on Cutting Taxes—Loves our Military & our Vets. He will be a Great Governor & has my full Endorsement!"

A memorable example of Trump's takeover of Florida, and its implications for DeSantis, occurred late in the 2018 GOP primary during a campaign bus stop in the Villages.

A sprawling retirement community just north of Orlando, the Villages is home to a huge collection of die-hard Republican voters. It's also one of the fastest-growing regions in the country, drawing an endless supply of Republican voters from working-class communities in the Midwest and Northeast. Built into a massive community and political player by GOP megadonor Gary Morse, who was a so-called Bush Ranger (meaning that he raised more than $200,000 during George W. Bush's reelection campaign), it often attracts national political attention: in 2008, it was the first rally spot for John McCain's newly picked running mate, Sarah Palin, and even drew stops from Trump in both 2019 and 2020. More modestly, though, the Villages also happens to be where I got my start in journalism.

My introduction to Florida came when I was a brand-new college graduate moving from the bar-lined streets of downtown Milwaukee, where I attended Marquette University, to the golf cart–lined streets of the Villages. Being a twenty-two-year-old living and working in a retirement community assured me of two things: there was always a rousing game of shuffleboard to be had and there was always a grandmother eager to introduce me to her visiting granddaughter.

When I graduated from college, I was ready to join a bustling newsroom, breaking big stories and holding politicians accountable. Instead, I ended up at the *Villages Daily Sun*. It is a publication owned by the developer of the community, a situation that came with certain editorial hurdles: as the saying goes, "No bad news happens in Florida's friendliest hometown."

And so it was that I found myself in the Villages on the morning of Palin's visit—September 22, 2008. To this day, the Palin rally might be the biggest one I've ever attended. Nearly fifteen thousand people were packed onto Lake Sumter Landing, the Villages' answer to a town square. It was a shoulder-to-shoulder crowd as far as the eye could see. The newspaper, eager to make the Palin rollout in its backyard seem bigger than it actually was, reported the crowd at sixty thousand, a number it had plucked from thin air. (As the paper's "political reporter," I was present when the publisher, Phil Markward, and the executive editor, Larry Croom, stared out the window of the second-story newsroom and discussed how big a crowd the newspaper should report the next day. They landed on sixty thousand, and into the story it went.)

"A day after Sarah Palin visited The Villages, the community was still basking in the national spotlight of a GOP rally that drew 60,000 supporters to Lake Sumter Landing Market Square," read the beginning of my day-after dispatch.

The rest of the article was written in the PR style you would expect of a newspaper merely trying to play the part. The *Villages Daily Sun,* after all, is akin to the alien trying to blend in as a human in the movie *Men in Black.* To covertly meld into society, the alien covered itself in a disguise that made it look humanoid, but only in the most generous of assessments. That is the *Villages Daily Sun:* a marketing rag masquerading as a big-time newspaper, desperately trying to convince you of its respectability.

A decade and several presidents later, Adam Putnam's campaign bus rolled through the Villages. It was 2018, and he and his team were visiting the retirement community of more than one hundred thousand people—easy pickings for the folksy redhead from nearby Polk County during most periods of Florida political history. But as Putnam talked to people in a farmer's market, he began to run across die-hard Trump supporters who had clearly gotten the signal from Trump's December 2017 tweet: DeSantis good; Putnam bad.

"We were walking through one of the Villages squares. You know, shaking hands and kissing babies. That sort of thing," said one former Putnam adviser. "A woman came up to us and said, 'I really like you a lot,' but when Adam asked, 'Do I have your vote?' her answer was no."

Putnam was surprised. The woman knew who he was; she was clearly a supporter, and it turned out that before moving to Florida's friendliest hometown, she'd even lived in Putnam's congressional district.

"She told him, 'I've voted for you in the past but just can't now,'" the aide recalled. "She said she was just such a Donald Trump supporter, and that he was the best thing that happened to the country, so if he said she had to vote for DeSantis, that's who she was voting for.

"It was one of the weirdest conversations I've ever had," the Putnam aide added. "[I] kind of knew at that point—it was just different."

The "it" in this case was what had been seen as the modern Republican Party in Florida, an overwhelmingly powerful organization that turned Florida into a national political behemoth and effectively built a machine that allowed for decades-long one-party rule in the nation's largest swing state. Florida had long been purple in national races but red at the state level.

Trump World would never love Putnam, but his campaign still raised $40 million in donor money trying to engineer a round peg into a square hole. Putnam met with the best consultants and advisers that the state and national Republicans had to offer in his attempts to erase the daunting shadow Trump cast on the race, but it was all for naught.

"He was asking me a lot of questions and if I was interested in working for him. The first question, and the one that kept coming up in various ways, was, 'All right, how do I beat a guy that is running as Donald Trump when people don't see me as aligning with Donald Trump?'" said a longtime Florida GOP consultant who met with Putnam in the Tallahassee offices of Meredith O'Rourke, one of Florida's most prominent GOP fundraisers and a longtime ally of both Putnam and Trump.

"I looked at Adam Putnam across the table," the adviser recalls, "and I told him, 'You probably don't.'"

DeSantis went on to trounce Putnam by nearly 20 percentage points, ensuring in the process that both he and Trump would be on the general election ballot.

DeSantis was one of the highest-profile Trump-backed politicians in a state the president would need to win to secure reelection just two years later. It was an implied part of the deal that, functionally, it was a DeSantis-Trump ticket, something Democrats tried to use to their advantage. They tried to put DeSantis's association with Trump front and center, framing DeSantis as "too extreme" for the nation's largest swing state.

"The Ron DeSantis endorsement has the genetic code of Trump politics, of Trumpism. It's going to be the most clear-cut revelation of the value of the president's support and standing in the state," Michael Caputo, a Trump adviser on the 2016 campaign, told POLITICO at the time. "Everything that's measurable in a national race is measurable in Florida. You want to know about the deplorables? Northwest Florida, baby. How does Trump play with Puerto Ricans? Look at the I-4 corridor. How does he play with upper-class Jewish intellectuals? Look at Palm Beach. White suburban retirees? Look at the Villages."

Ron DeSantis and Donald Trump were, for the moment, great political allies. The two were even developing a friendship that, impressively, seemed to transcend the campaign trail. What was on the horizon, though, was not so idyllic.

Much of that, at least early on, was driven by DeSantis's wife.

Casey DeSantis was born in Ohio in 1980 and met her future husband on a driving range at the University of North Florida. The two were married in 2009, less than three years before DeSantis's congressional run. Hindsight, and anyone with even a cursory understanding of modern Florida politics, will tell you that this fact provides a snapshot of the politically ambitious mindset of the couple. And anyone who understands DeSantis's thought processes will divulge that Casey—a former Jacksonville television personality—is the most influential adviser and powerful force in DeSantis's universe. This force was put on display during the general gubernatorial election as DeSantis's campaign prepared the now infamous "Build the Wall" ad.

Few things during DeSantis's 2018 campaign got more attention—and triggered more outrage among libs, another desired outcome—than the Trump-worshipping TV spot that featured Ron and Casey's daughter Madison paying tribute to Trump's southern border wall. The ad shows DeSantis using gleeful baby talk, encouraging Madison to "build the wall" as she plays with building blocks. In the same ad, he reads to his then infant son, Mason, from a book meant to evoke Trump's former reality show, *The Apprentice*. "You're fired!" DeSantis reads before noting to Mason, "That's my favorite part." The ad concludes with DeSantis using a Make America Great Again campaign sign to teach Madison to read.

The ad was narrated by Casey DeSantis, who played the main role in the ad but who was anything but supportive behind the scenes. Though she was a lifelong conservative and DeSantis's most trusted adviser by a long shot, she had never been a natural Trump supporter. She thought the TV ad was at best silly and at worst humiliating and was completely opposed to running it. And Ron DeSantis would not green-light the spot without her approval.

"Casey was apprehensive about the wall commercial," said a former DeSantis campaign staffer. "She did not have a great deal of comfort in [Ron's] marrying himself to Trump. But the ad was not going to run without her approval, and they had to convince her to agree. There were direct conversations on this."

Despite her initial protests, Casey finally relented. She understood that Trump's power with the Republican base was at its peak. He could make political fortunes and end them, all in a single tweet. If Ron DeSantis was to continue on the promising political trajectory he and Casey had laid out, she knew she had to swallow her pride and play the part.

"She values winning and destiny way more than love, or hate, or however you want to say it," the former campaign staffer said. "It was part of a winning strategy. [DeSantis] needed Trump in many ways, and Trumpism was winning Republican primaries at that point. Just look at how Adam Putnam begged to be accepted into Trump's world even after Trump endorsed DeSantis."

In an interview conducted shortly after the ad started airing, Casey DeSantis said it was designed to push back on an onslaught of negative ads targeting their campaign, most of which came from Putnam-backing Republican establishment types.

"There was seventeen—I think it was $17 million in attack ads up against Ron. Special interest, and so that is kind of where we were," she told Jacksonville TV station First Coast News in 2018. "And we said, 'Well, how do we respond?' We responded with humor, and we had fun. I think a lot of people liked it, and they got the joke."

Eventually, word started getting back to Trump that Casey and, by extension, Ron were less than enthusiastic about the ad and had even mocked the idea in the middle of the shoot.

The idea that the DeSantis duo was smirking at Trump's immigration masterpiece—the border wall—was, to Trump, an early example of DeSantis's lack of gratitude. Fanning the flames was persistent chatter that the production company behind the shoot had an outtakes reel that showed video of Casey and Ron speaking about the spot in disparaging terms.

"It somehow got back to Trump, and he apparently said, 'Get me the fucking tape,'" said Rick Wilson, who was a veteran Republican ad maker before cofounding the anti-Trump group the Lincoln Project. "I doubt he or his team ever actually saw a tape, but apparently it showed the two laughing about the idea for the ad, and even hearing about that did not sit well with Trump."

A Trump campaign aide acknowledged they were aware of the outtakes and said of Trump himself, "I know he knew."

It was 2017, and storms were beginning to brew.

On September 20, Hurricane Maria made landfall in Puerto Rico, devastating the community and many of its surrounding islands. The storm reached category 5 status, sustaining winds of 157 miles per hour and higher—the most extreme classification meteorologists have to offer.

A year later, Trump erupted into a rage.

At the time of the storm, Puerto Rico's infrastructure was so crippled that accurate death tolls could not be determined. A study conducted the following year put the number at nearly three thousand. Trump tweeted his disagreement with the figure, writing "3,000 people did not die" and erroneously blaming Democrats for the release of the study.

Trump's assertion, without evidence, that death tolls were inflated sent shock waves through Florida's Republican ecosystem. It was in the middle of the 2018 midterms, and the GOP was in the process of wooing Florida's significant pool of Puerto Rican voters, a group made larger by the many Puerto Ricans who'd moved to the state following the devastation of Hurricane Maria. Then governor Rick Scott, who may have won his US Senate recount that year because of a Puerto Rican base, joined several high-profile Florida Republicans in taking the rare step of disagreeing with Trump. The president, however, directed most of his ire in that moment at DeSantis, who had won the GOP primary just months earlier, largely thanks to Trump's support—and who had just released a statement that Trump was not happy with.

While DeSantis's public statement did not denounce his benefactor's claims directly, it made clear that he did not think fuzzy math was involved: "Ron DeSantis is committed to standing with the Puerto Rican community, especially after such a tragic loss of life," a DeSantis campaign spokesman said. "He doesn't believe any loss of life has been inflated."

That was enough for Trump to paint DeSantis as disloyal. As one Trump adviser at the time told my POLITICO colleagues Alex Isenstadt and Marc Caputo, the comment represented a "divorce."

Some Trump advisers, even years later, saw DeSantis as disloyal simply for siding with a scientific study rather than Trump's factless assertions. Brad Parscale, the longtime Trump supporter who was preparing to serve as his 2020 campaign manager, relayed to the DeSantis team that Trump was furious that the governor hadn't backed his unfounded claims.

"It was told to us by Brad that Trump was ticked because he did not respond well to the Hurricane Maria stuff," said a former DeSantis campaign adviser. "That was a pretty tangible example of the petty early disdain DeSantis had for [Trump]."

The Trump-DeSantis relationship is defined by that sort of duality. For years, the two were seen as close allies and, to some degree, friends, but in reality, there has never been total ease in the relationship. Far from idyllic even at its best, their friendship ultimately came down to political expediency. This is emblematic of how both men operate: Trump has long been seen as a real estate mogul with limited loyalty, known well outside of politics for a reality show centered on the idea of firing the powerless and for showing no ability to connect with people who cannot do anything for him in return. DeSantis, for his part, has many of those same traits. In a 2022 interview conducted outside DeSantis's boyhood home in Dunedin, Florida, his father, also named Ron, told *New Yorker* writer Dexter Filkins that even as a kid, his son had a well-established reputation for being "stubborn." DeSantis, he said, was smart and focused, particularly on baseball; his team had even gone to the Little League World Series in 1991, a by-product of years of intense practice his dad said happened on the street in front of their home.

DeSantis would go on to Yale, where he earned straight As and was captain of the baseball team. But his reputation for being ornery and self-righteous only grew.

"Ron is the most selfish person I have ever interacted with," a former Yale baseball teammate told *The New Yorker* in June of 2022. "He has always loved embarrassing and humiliating people. I'm speaking for others—he was the biggest dick we knew."

Meanwhile, John Stuper, his baseball manager at Yale, told POLITICO for a 2020 magazine profile that after D, as he called DeSantis, was about to get his first college hit, he instructed him to execute a hit-and-run. That meant that if DeSantis got on first base, which he did, he was to start running for second base as soon as the next batter made contact with the ball.

In a display of neglect, DeSantis would instead be picked off at first base, an unfortunate outcome that, under normal circumstances, would serve only as a bad memory, one that would fade away with time. But sitting in his office, talking to a handful of POLITICO reporters more than two decades later, DeSantis blamed the umpires.

"I was like, 'Coach, he balked,'" DeSantis recalled.

This statement, made without a hint of self-awareness, was emblematic of DeSantis as a child, as a baseball player, and as a politician: never apologize and never take the blame. These personality traits would one day come to define his political persona.

CHAPTER TWO

THE PERFECT STORM

There is no way to understand DeSantis's rise to dominance in Florida, or Trump's reshaping of the state's political landscape, without first understanding two corresponding developments: the near-total collapse of the Florida Democratic Party and the ascent of the Florida GOP to the position of one of the most dominant political parties in the country.

That is a blunt assessment, of course, but even a cursory look at election results since 2014 shows that Democrats have been outmanned and outfinanced in a state that once elected Barack Obama in back-to-back presidential elections. To put it into shocking perspective, Democrats have not held the Florida governor's mansion since *Titanic* was the world's top-grossing film. They have not held the Florida House since the Monica Lewinsky scandal broke. And they have not held the Florida Senate since the late great Coolio's "Gangsta's Paradise" topped the charts.

Losing is nothing new for Florida Democrats, but as the unsuccessful election cycles pile up, the depressing sense that things will never change increases.

"The only ones of us left here are the stubborn and the stupid. I like to think of myself as the former, but who knows?" said Beth Matuga, a longtime Democratic consultant. "It does make me get up every day in the morning and wonder what we are even doing here. But I do always fall back on the idea that what are we supposed to do? Throw our hands up and cede the whole state to Republicans? I live here. I would like it to be better."

Under DeSantis, however, things seem likely to get worse for Florida's Democrats.

Democrats had been losing ground in Florida for years, but few moments encapsulate the path to rock bottom more than election night in 2016.

The booze-soaked conference room in the Tampa Marriott Water Street was filled with an all-too-familiar sadness. Clinton's exhausted Florida operation, desperate for a win, was slowly realizing that it was about to endure yet another stinging defeat.

Election day was turning into night, and members of the inner circle of Clinton's Florida campaign were huddled over a table littered with data sheets, half-empty cups of brown liquor, and a growing pile of Stella Artois bottles—the elixirs of choice as the news grew increasingly dire. Staffers could do nothing but sit in stunned disbelief as they watched years of hard work burn to ashes, destroyed by a chaos-driven former reality show host they feared would soon turn his flamethrower onto democracy itself.

Scott Arceneaux, the former executive director of the Florida Democratic Party and, that year, a senior Clinton adviser, knew he had to say something. It was hours after Trump had been informed by his Florida team that he had won the state and shortly before the race would be officially called.

A cell-phone video of the moment shows Arceneaux addressing a dozen or so staffers in the war room. He stood before them in an understated black jacket and blue shirt—no necktie, as was his wont.

"If this guy wins tonight," he said, "we are not going to fucking lay down and let [him] tear down this country. It's going to be a lot of guys like you who are going to have to pick up the ball and run with this," he added, referring to the populist wave that Trump had ridden to the White House and that threatened to swamp the entire country.

"We should've never thought it was going to be a blowout," Arceneaux continued, growing somber. "I think a couple months ago, a couple weeks ago, we thought probably things were going to be different."

He acknowledged that the conservative rural white voters who turned out in record numbers had made the difference. Clinton's campaign had focused elsewhere, essentially running a three-county race and working to effect a huge turnout in the Democratic strongholds of Miami-Dade, Palm Beach, and Broward Counties. And while they had indeed run up big numbers there, it was not enough to overcome Trump's "angry white" wave.

"We all know who those voters are," Arceneaux said in his remarks to the Clinton team. "Those voters we are just…we are not going to get. Those were a lot of angry white voters that we've talked about a lot in this campaign and at the end of the day, [they] broke the other way."

Other Florida Dems were similarly stunned. Bill Nelson, the seventy-three-year-old Democratic US senator who at the time was the de facto head of the Florida Democratic Party, had spent the day pestering professional staffers to check numbers reporting from various precincts, trying to game out whether Democratic Senate nominee Patrick Murphy would knock off incumbent Republican senator Marco Rubio. He would not.

"Nelson, as he did in 2012, was having folks look up random precincts in random counties that he considered important," said one staffer who had been in Clinton's war room. "We started seeing places like North Florida, where Murphy was leading Clinton by a decent amount, and we knew sure as shit those folks did not know who Patrick Murphy was. It was at that point that we kind of knew [Clinton] was in trouble."

After it was clear that Trump was going to win Florida, Nelson slipped out the back door with his family but without addressing the crowd assembled down the hallway, something he normally enjoyed doing: anyone who has even a casual relationship with Florida Democratic politics has heard Nelson, who lost his Senate seat two years later to Rick Scott, say winkingly, in his slow, deliberate cadence, "If you want to go in reverse, you put the car in R."

For many Florida Democrats, the moment wasn't just another political loss; it was also a grim indication that the state's electorate was turning into something they had long feared. They saw Trump as running on hate, division, and xenophobia—and winning.

"Donald Trump did not make any bones about what he was running on, and voters here said they wanted more of that," said Ray Paultre, executive director of the Florida Alliance, a collection of progressive fundraising groups. "That is disheartening."

Besides Obama's back-to-back wins, Florida Democrats' closest taste of victory since the mid-1990s came in 2010 with the passage of the Fair Districts amendments to the state constitution. These were antigerrymandering initiatives that passed with 63 percent of the vote, initiatives that should have upended Florida's future redistricting processes.

Getting 63 percent of voters to support antigerrymandering language that had been fiercely opposed by Florida's Republican leaders and their deep-pocketed donors was a major accomplishment, one that should have left a huge imprint on the state's politics. And indeed, for some time, things were looking up for the Democrats. A lawsuit filed after Florida's 2012 redistricting uncovered a covert scheme in which Republican operatives planted maps they had drawn that favored their own candidates but that were officially filed under other people's names. After a multiyear legal battle, the Florida Supreme Court ultimately tossed these out, instead approving maps drawn by the plaintiffs, which included left-leaning groups such as Common Cause and the League of Women Voters of Florida. It was the break Florida Democrats thought they needed to finally harness political momentum and start clawing their way back to relevance.

The new maps gave the state's Democrats the ability on paper to get to a 20-20 state senate split by the 2020 election cycle, which would have given them their first sniff of power in the state in nearly thirty years. Things, they thought, were finally looking up. And yet they saw as they headed into the 2024 election cycle that maps drawn since then are much better for Republicans, virtually enshrining GOP legislative dominance for another decade and giving Democrats a 28-12 disadvantage in the state senate.

"Of course there was disappointment," said Ellen Freidin, a progressive attorney who helped lead the Fair Districts effort. "You have to have good districts, you have to have good candidates, you have to have lots of funding, and you have to have a good strategy. My role was limited to the districts. We got that done. You have to focus on what you can control."

Beyond some disappointing antigerrymandering efforts, Fair Districts also spurred the creation of the Florida Alliance, founded by Christopher Findlater to create a progressive political infrastructure outside the formal Florida Democratic Party. The party had angered some of the state's biggest liberal donors and union groups by backing conservative-leaning Democrats in an effort to win the large swaths of the state that were up for grabs but not necessarily open to progressive candidates. However, in true Florida Democrat fashion, the group has brought its own share of complications.

In early 2008, Freidin was in Orlando, in the middle of a trip through the state trying to drum up support and money for Fair Districts, when her phone rang. The call was from Findlater, who, she said, "enthusiastically" wanted to help with the Fair Districts effort—and to prove it, he'd written her a five-figure check, funding her early push to add antigerrymandering language to the state constitution. This was the Florida Alliance's introduction to Florida Democratic politics, even if at that time it remained off the public radar. The group, which initially shrouded itself in secrecy and dubbed its onetime headquarters the Fortress of Democracy, started as a collection of fewer than ten super-wealthy progressive donors. Since that time, it has expanded to nearly seventy donors and has created a multipronged organization that focuses on nearly every aspect of political campaigns.

The emergence of the Florida Alliance should have been a boon for Florida Democrats: tapping into a wealthy progressive community that was not yet active in donor circles was, in theory, exactly what the underfunded party needed. However, it quickly became clear that things would not be so simple. The emergence of a second well-funded Democratic group has led to a tense dynamic between it and the Florida Democratic Party, even if on paper the two groups have similar political goals. Although there have been attempts to mend fences over the years, their relationship has remained fraught at best: both sides have blamed the other for Florida Democrats' continued failures, and turf wars over a split in party staffers, donors, and voter messaging, along with debates over who should focus on registration, voter contact, and overall strategy, are a regular occurrence.

The heart of the fight is over donors. Many of Florida Democrats' biggest sources of campaign finance, both individuals and organizations, now either split their contributions or will not give money to the formal Florida Democratic Party. This, in turn, exacerbates perception problems for the group, which remains the face of the party's efforts in Florida but only gets a fraction of the money that moves through the Democratic ecosystem. This, they feel, puts them in the position of getting most of the blame for bad election cycles, even if they have control of just a fraction of the resources.

"All these fucking [political nonprofit organizations] have no accountability," said Beth Matuga, the veteran Florida Democratic operative who has a reputation as one of the most vocal defenders of formal state parties. "They portray themselves as doing field operations, [but] they can't show you any record of what they do. I have sent dozens and dozens of people into the field to knock on doors and do [literature] drops for our state candidates. You know how many times they have ever encountered a paid field operation? Not once. It's because they do not exist."

"Absolutely," added Natalie Kato, a Democratic attorney and political consultant when I asked her whether the rift between the Florida Alliance and the party has hurt Democrats in Florida. "They sucked out all the donors. I represent liberal clients, and I saw this firsthand in 2020. I said, 'I need money for Democrats,' and [my clients said they] would give money but [I couldn't] give it to the party.... This kind of thing happens all the time."

Meanwhile, Ray Paultre, the Florida Alliance's current executive director, says the solution lies in creating a system in which each group has its own set of responsibilities rather than relying on one group that may not be best situated to do everything.

"Where at times there is disagreement with the party, [it's] over the fact they can't do everything," he said. "The fissure is not as large as some people think, but it's there and can be a problem because that's not how Republicans operate. The chamber [of commerce] is in lockstep, generally, with what Republicans want. So are groups like Americans for Prosperity. There is no fissure at all on that side; they just want to win. We need to get to that level."

One could argue that, in the war between the Democrats, Florida Alliance backers have largely won out: the organization has grown dramatically and now has offshoots—called donor tables—that focus on messaging, opposition research, fundraising, and outreach to specific subsets of the Democratic base, including Hispanic, LGBTQ, and Black voters. But in the big picture, it's clear that little has changed since the Florida Alliance's emergence on the state political scene: Democrats have lost their one US Senate seat, control just eight of the state's twenty-eight seats in the US House of Representatives, have won just one statewide race since 2018, and have seen Republicans build on supermajorities in the state legislature.

To rub salt into the wound, the DeSantis administration is not content with a Florida political map covered in red: it wants to erase Fair Districts altogether—the Florida left's only major non-Obama achievement in decades.

In March of 2022, Ron DeSantis deliberately vetoed GOP-drawn congressional maps that gave Republicans sixteen seats, forcing lawmakers in a subsequent legislative special session to pass a map with twenty GOP-leaning seats. This move—an echo of the Democrats' Fair Districts loss—proved key to helping Republicans flip the US House after their disappointing 2022 midterm season. It also dissolved a longtime Black-performing congressional district in North Florida, a region of the state that was once a key hub for slave trading and that since 2018 had been held by Democrat Al Lawson.

In response to DeSantis's challenge, voting rights groups filed a lawsuit alleging that eliminating the Black-performing district violated the Fair Districts amendments. Attorneys for DeSantis responded in court filings in a way that confirmed the worst fears of those groups: his map was intended to prompt a court challenge that would overturn Fair Districts completely. They argued that the so-called nondiminishment clause of the Fair Districts amendments violated the United States Constitution. In a March 2022 memo, DeSantis's general counsel said the governor's legal team thought the clause was in violation because "it assigns voters primarily on the basis of race but is not narrowly tailored to achieve a compelling state interest."

In the end, Democrats and progressive groups spent untold sums passing the Fair Districts amendments, which should have been their biggest win in decades—but ultimately gained little more than an increase in intraparty tensions. It's the story of Florida Democrats: one step forward, three steps back.

Republicans in Florida couldn't have been in a more different position from their Democratic opponents. Since the early 2000s, the state GOP's wins have been consistently piling up, with no end in sight.

Republican dominance in Florida is most obvious—and most dramatic—in voter registration statistics. When Obama won Florida in 2008, Democrats had a roughly 700,000-person registration advantage in the state. Largely thanks to that massive margin, Obama beat his opponent, John McCain, by 2.8 points. This win, and his subsequent victory in 2012, were the only serious feathers in the Democrats' caps since 2000, and even that took the emergence of a generational candidate with a strong national following—one largely based outside the state. And indeed, Florida's Democrats couldn't count on that sort of support in every election, as they soon learned the hard way.

In 2010, Democrat Alex Sink, a well-liked, well-connected, state-elected CFO, lost the governor's race to Republican Rick Scott by just 61,570 votes, or around 1.2 percentage points. At the time, Democrats had a 568,202-person voter registration advantage. Four years later, Scott won reelection over Democratic challenger Charlie Crist by 64,145 votes, or one percentage point, only 0.2 percentage points off his previous margin of victory. By contrast, Democrats then had just a 457,728-person registration advantage, a nearly 20 percent drop-off compared to 2010.

Four years after that, Ron DeSantis beat Democrat Andrew Gillum, the former Tallahassee mayor, by 32,463 votes (around 0.4 percent) in a race that went to a recount. The close margin belied the still-sinking status of the Democrats, who then had only a 257,175-person registration advantage, a more than 40 percent decrease from 2014 and a nearly 55 percent drop-off from Scott's first victory, in 2010.

Then, in 2022, DeSantis beat Charlie Crist by nearly twenty points, a staggering, historic win that came as Republicans had built a roughly 300,000-person voter registration advantage.

These numbers make a simple point: in the years following Obama's first election, Florida's political reality has changed in a way that has inflated Republicans' power—and doomed Democrats' prospects in the state.

"Florida has broken my heart so many times. Four of the last five elections, we went into election day being sure Democrats were going to win and getting the rug pulled out from underneath us," said Carlos Odio, a former executive director of the Florida Alliance who also served in the Obama White House. "I was on a private plane going to Crist's victory party in 2014. I was the guy on the plane saying, *I don't know if we are going to win this.* I was getting ridiculed and booed. We lost. To see it happen again and again and [to see us] not learning our lesson is really hard."

Crist's first bid for governor, in 2014, raised the highest hopes; the Democrat was up in most public polls in the final weeks of the campaign. Ultimately, though, he was bested when Rick Scott sunk $15 million of his personal cash into the race. This and the Republicans' ensuing barrage of late-cycle attack ads helped Scott win reelection, albeit by the slimmest of margins. And by the time Crist's 2022 effort rolled around, the atmosphere had drastically shifted, a reflection of Democrats' wilting hopes in the state: no one really thought he could win, and his general election campaign did little to excite even loyal party insiders.

"What campaign?" joked veteran Democratic consultant Ashley Walker, who helped run Obama's 2012 Florida race. "I don't think anyone really saw that race as viable, and no one is surprised he lost big."

Florida Democrats, though, have a much bigger problem than what happens in any one election cycle. National donors and party organizations increasingly see the state as a bad investment. They've spent hundreds of millions of dollars in several election cycles and have little to show for it: meanwhile, states such as Arizona, North Carolina, and, most notably, neighboring Georgia are becoming winnable for Democrats—and are much, much less expensive than Florida. Historically, in the heat of an election, Orlando, Tampa, and Miami alone have been three of the most expensive media markets in the country, and unfortunately for campaigns' wallets, getting on TV is an imperative in a state of nearly twenty-two million people. While retail politics—door knocking and one-on-one voter contact—is cheaper, the reality is that Florida is much too big for that, and thus such tactics are not how its statewide races are won.

Those problems are all exacerbated by the Republicans' sense of urgency—and the Democrats' learned helplessness. The Republicans not only own Florida at the state level, they also continue to need it to win the White House, while Democrats can get there through the Midwest. Winning states such as Wisconsin, Michigan, Pennsylvania, Minnesota, and Illinois hand Democrats enough state-level wins to snag the presidency, even if they lose Florida. Simply put, national Democratic donors no longer see Florida as a priority, and their donations—or lack thereof—reflect this stance. During the 2018 midterms, national Democratic groups such as the Democratic Governors Association, the Democratic Congressional Campaign Committee, and the Democratic Senatorial Campaign Committee spent roughly $60 million in Florida: in 2022, they spent only $2 million.

In a strange turnabout, then, cheaper states turning blue has exacerbated Democrats' "Florida problem": because national Democrats see Florida as a tough investment, the resources needed to try to rebuild in the Sunshine State have moved elsewhere, including places such as Georgia.

"It's been so much money here," said Republican consultant Stephen Lawson, who works in Georgia but spent much of his career in Florida, where he worked on the campaigns of Ron DeSantis and Marco Rubio. "It's an exorbitant sum. [And] I think Georgia Democrats get, like, 80 percent of their money from out of state."

The inability to woo national donors is one of the largest financial difficulties facing Florida Democrats. However, there have also been issues with the überwealthy Democratic donors within the state. Though Florida boasts more than sixty billionaires total, they vote across the political spectrum, and the vast majority of the state's richest Democrats don't much care about Florida politics. Most come from other states and view Florida as a vacation home, a place they visit to play, relax, and dodge income tax. Many of them care much more about high-profile federal races and perhaps could not even find Tallahassee on a map. Trying to secure the support of these big Democratic donors is akin to trying to entice a toddler away from a cookie jar with a steaming bowl of broccoli.

During the 2020 cycle alone, Democratic donors with homes in Florida spent more than $30 million on federal races that did not directly or specifically focus on Florida—a troubling statistic that only covers visible funds. There exists a growing network of nonprofit organizations, including so-called dark-money groups, that are becoming the favored vehicle for donors. These, too, tend to skip over Florida. The Florida Democratic Party, for example, might see only between 5 and 20 percent of all the money that flows through the Democratic ecosystem each election cycle. Florida Republicans, however, are largely fueled by in-state transactional donors who care far more about influencing legislative majorities than joining partisan-based culture wars. Those donors have a huge influence in legislative races in the state and give almost exclusively to Republicans because they see little need to support powerless Democrats.

"We talk about tactical advantages Republicans have in progressive fantasia," said Odio, the former director of the Florida Alliance. "Nationally, they think the Koch brothers run everything, but if you have any experience in Florida you know there are a few industries that totally control the process. It's big sugar, utilities, Publix, Disney, those sorts of guys."

Getting their donors to focus on state-level party building is a nationwide problem for Democrats. Nationally, Republicans control fifty-eight state legislative chambers compared to the Democrats' forty. The GOP also has twenty-three trifectas—a term that denotes control of both chambers of the state legislature and the governor's mansion—compared to the Democrats' fourteen. Republicans have convinced their donors and political infrastructure that winning states is just as important as federal races, if not more so, for achieving their policy goals, something Democrats have been unable to do.

"Our donors are only focused on federal races, and Republicans know that," said Paultre, the Florida Alliance's current director. "They study our spending habits, just like we study theirs. They know one thing: a national Democratic donor does not give a fuck about its states."

Republicans and conservative groups, on the other hand, see talking to voters as a never-ending task needed to build political and messaging power. The effort in Florida is largely led by Americans for Prosperity, which has a massive Florida chapter that continually has people in the field. In the last six months of 2021—notably, not an election year—the group knocked on 350,000 doors talking to voters about their conservative, often libertarian-leaning policy priorities, including school choice, lower taxes, smaller government, and ending taxpayer incentives for private companies. "Because Democrats don't do it all the time, it means they do not have a preseason," said Skylar Zander, AFP's Florida state director. "When trying to drive political outcomes outside of policy outcomes...we are already warmed up, and they are just starting."

Odio, who was executive director of the Florida Alliance, said that getting some of the state's biggest rainmakers to care about regional legislative races in the past has been difficult. He summed up the Democrats' decades-long predicament in just a few brusque words.

"You don't understand how hard it is to get them to give a shit about state legislative races."

CHAPTER THREE

"IT DOES NOT HAPPEN WITHOUT TRUMP"

With Trump's endorsement paving the way, DeSantis would go on to dominate Putnam in Florida's 2018 gubernatorial primaries. By the time election night rolled around, DeSantis had an overwhelming lead in public polling and ultimately won by huge margins, a victory that gave way to a huge party in the bar at the Rosen Shingle Creek, in Orlando.

DeSantis supporters and advisers clinked glasses, plotting a path forward as they celebrated. Quietly, however, many of them fretted about the upcoming general-election fight against Andrew Gillum, the Tallahassee mayor and Democratic nominee, who had just notched an upset win over Congresswoman Gwen Graham, the party's establishment pick.

Few observers had gone into election night thinking that Gillum would win his primary. I certainly didn't. As reporters often do, I had prewritten a shell of a story before the results came in, saying that Graham had won her heated five-person primary and explaining what that meant for the general election. As the night dragged on, however, it became clear that that long-held narrative was collapsing and that Gillum would eke out a three-percentage-point victory. I had to scurry out of the ballroom at the Rosen Shingle Creek, where I was covering DeSantis's election night event, to sit on the floor in the hotel hallway, hurriedly rewriting my story about a Democratic primary that had upended everyone's expectations.

Though no one would say so publicly, the prospect of running against Gillum in a general election was worrisome even to DeSantis's biggest supporters. Gillum had intense, near Trump-like support from the Democrats' grassroots base. He was an incredibly dynamic speaker and was trying to become Florida's first Black governor. He was instantly seen as a surprise thirty-nine-year-old rising star in the party, someone who would stir up a general-election buzz—a threat that Graham, a traditional establishment politician, had not posed. Juxtaposed with DeSantis's gruff, humorless style, which could come off as mean and inaccessible, Gillum's leading-man persona looked formidable.

After the race, however, Gillum would go on to face massive scandal. In April of 2020, pictures of him naked on the floor of a Miami Beach motel emerged. Paramedics responding to a suspected methamphetamine overdose had been called to the room, in which were reputed male prostitutes. Two years after that, Gillum was indicted on corruption charges related to his time as Tallahassee mayor. In May of 2023, he was acquitted, but the incidents severely damaged his public and political brand.

As the 2018 general election kicked off, though, Gillum was still seen as a rising star, not just in Florida but also in national Democratic politics. He was without question more charismatic than DeSantis, and when the time came for both candidates to audition in front of Florida voters, DeSantis's team feared, these differences would be painfully obvious.

Even to those closest to him, DeSantis came off as a charmless battering ram of a man. A former adviser was fond of telling people, "Ron DeSantis does not have any old fishing buddies." This was not so much commentary on DeSantis's hobbies (he has none) so much as a reflection of his lack of traditional social graces and lifelong friends. DeSantis in 2018 was seen as at best socially awkward and at worst as someone with absolutely no interest in other people, even when he was in the middle of a one-on-one conversation.

His social awkwardness was legendary—and at that stage of my career covering Florida politics, I was already well acquainted with it.

The first time I met DeSantis was relatively unremarkable—partially because I didn't know I was sitting across the table from a guy who one day wanted to be president but mostly because of the personality that he brings to his every interaction. We were tucked into a booth at Jacob's, a downtown Tallahassee eatery on the first floor of a DoubleTree hotel blocks from the state capitol. It's frequented by political types visiting Tallahassee from out of town, and during the state's two-month legislative session it's littered with lawmakers and lobbyists doing the people's work—one plate of eggs, one pot of coffee, and one campaign check at a time.

It was the summer of 2011, and I was there as a favor to Tim Baker, a Republican consultant I had known for a while who also happened to be the general consultant on DeSantis's then nascent congressional campaign. At that time, few really knew who DeSantis was. He was strapped into what would be a brutal six-way GOP primary in the ruby-red Sixth Congressional District, an affluent coastal area just south of Jacksonville where the primary winner easily wins the general election. To boost his chances, he hired Data Targeting, a legendary Gainesville-based GOP firm led by Pat Bainter, a sort of mythical creature in Florida Republican circles.

Nondescript can be a trite way to describe an office space, but in Pat's case, no word fits better. The epicenter of most of the state's Republican political maneuvers, from redistricting to plotting the strategy for $40 million–plus Florida Senate campaigns, is an office in an unassuming strip mall.

The firm's point person on DeSantis's race was Baker, a Marine who brought that military style and mindset to campaigns. He quickly burst onto Florida's political scene by showing an aptitude for dabbling in the dark arts of opposition research. Baker is a nice guy, but he's also the sort of person who leaves the impression that he has somehow obtained access to ten years of your tax returns along with your high school transcripts when you sit down with him.

On an otherwise quiet summer morning, seated across from Baker and DeSantis in a booth at Jacob's, I sensed from the get-go that DeSantis had no interest in being there but was just checking a box on a list put in front of him by his political handlers. At the time, I was the Tallahassee-based reporter for the *Florida Times-Union,* the daily Jacksonville-area newspaper that was closely covering the race. DeSantis's agenda, which included flirting with the donors and political influencers who call the city home, also included meeting with a lowly reporter from the local newspaper. DeSantis sat quietly on the inside portion of the booth, staring at his phone and occasionally chiming in in a way that barely hid his apathy. He would catch the audible clues that signaled his attention was needed at that moment in the conversation—but only just barely.

The arrogance-laced political style of the guy the nation now knows was very much on display during that meeting. DeSantis was a dime-a-dozen congressional candidate from a quiet region that rarely gets national play, but he carried himself like someone who knew he would be running for president one day.

Some politicians flood the zone with charm in a stereotypical brand of baby-kissing politics. That's not Ron DeSantis. His most noticeable personality trait is his inability to have an unstrained social interaction with someone he doesn't want to be around. He's not good at hiding this disinclination, nor do I think he cares to.

Seven years later, the aloof man I awkwardly drank coffee with was set to prove that his team's concerns about running against a dynamic candidate such as Gillum were warranted. He then faced a much larger post-primary audience of Republicans who needed to make the tricky transition from being longtime Putnam loyalists to being staunch DeSantis supporters. These people needed to back a politician few of them knew well but nonetheless wanted to get behind in order to ensure that Democrats did not elect a new Florida governor for the first time since 1991. To begin that process, the morning after the election, lobbyists and political types had to make a long, hungover drive from Tallahassee to Orlando for a brief meeting with DeSantis. It was, as they say in campaign parlance, the check-drop moment.

Along with my wife, Ana Ceballos, who was covering the election for the *Naples Daily News,* I was in one of Rosen Shingle Creek's many restaurants the day after the primary election, witnessing the scene firsthand. One by one, the familiar faces of Putnam supporters passed us on their way to DeSantis—and just a few minutes later came by us again in the other direction, meeting apparently over. In their brief time with DeSantis, each would-be donor had been handed a baseball-themed document that outlined contribution levels: a "single" was a certain dollar amount, a "double" a higher dollar amount, and so on.

For Putnam allies, driving to Orlando with their tails between their legs for the post-primary check drop was an exercise in humiliation, exacerbated by the fact that DeSantis is not the sort of warm, charming personality who can disarm a tense situation.

"It was just a strange experience, one like I'd never had with a politician at really any level. It was...just a few minutes [that] I was in the room with him," said a longtime Florida Republican operative who stopped to chat with us in the restaurant after the awkward DeSantis encounter. "It's like he did not want to be there. I was bringing him a check, and...the entire time we were trying to have a conversation, he was looking over my shoulder just waiting for the exchange to end."

DeSantis did little to assuage the fears of advisers concerned about his aloofness. The day after his primary win, he said in a TV interview that Florida should not "monkey this up" by electing Gillum in the general election. The comment was immediately seen by Democrats as a racist dog whistle and was just the sort of misstep they needed to frame DeSantis as racist early in the campaign. It was a theme they would try to pin on him frequently, including after an October debate in which Gillum said, "Now, I'm not calling Mr. DeSantis a racist. I'm simply saying the racists believe he's a racist."

"Yeah, that was frustrating. Tough way to start things," said a DeSantis adviser. "We were kind of freaking out behind the scenes, but DeSantis never was. He knew what he meant and thought the whole thing was overstated.

"But we knew Gillum was going to do whatever he could to get people to see DeSantis through a racism lens," he added. "We just didn't know we were going to hand them a path to doing it fifteen minutes after we won the primary."

The comment was a precursor to even more trouble. Early on, DeSantis's campaign struggled to raise the sort of money needed to run for governor in a state of twenty-two million people and ten expensive media markets. All the while, Matt Gaetz, who would make regular unannounced stops at DeSantis's headquarters in Orlando, was less than subtle about the fact that the campaign, in his mind, was inadequate.

At his persistent urging, DeSantis began to give real thought to a shake-up. His staffers at the time were insistent that the concerns were overblown, but at that point Gaetz "*was* the campaign," one adviser said, and Gaetz was the recipient of basically "every other call" DeSantis made, said another. Gaetz had huge sway over all decisions, including staffing.

Eventually, Gaetz persuaded DeSantis to bring in Susie Wiles, the veteran Republican consultant who had helped Rick Scott become governor in 2010 and who had led Trump's 2016 Florida campaign. She would eventually become among the chief protagonists in the Trump-DeSantis rivalry, but in 2018 she was still in the good graces of both camps and was sent in to ensure that a Trump ally would occupy the governor's mansion in a state that was a crucial part of the Republicans' presidential math.

Along with that hire came a revamped communications strategy led by Tallahassee-based Republican communications veteran Sarah Bascom and a boost of renewed energy from former Trump staffer Justin Caporale. The shape of the campaign at that point varies depending on whom you ask. Some say it needed a reshuffle and an injection of new blood; others argue that without the change of pace, Florida would have elected Gillum and forever changed the state's political trajectory.

"I was dumbfounded," said an adviser who was part of the team that came in to resuscitate the campaign. "There was no infrastructure. Not only were there not defined departments with processes, but there was no long-term staff there to enact the governor's preferences. It was clear to me there was no inner circle.

"I asked simple things like, 'What is the process for paying invoices?' and they looked at me and said, 'What do you mean?' I immediately took six credit cards out of my pocket, personal and business, and handed one to each person who I thought needed one. That's how things were handled initially."

Meanwhile, the team was heading into the first debate with Gillum, in mid-October. Congressman Byron Donalds, a Black Republican from southwestern Florida, was involved in debate prep; Gaetz, a skilled debater with a unique ability to get under people's skin, often played Gillum during practice. No one pulled punches to spare DeSantis's ego during these sessions but instead tried to get him to lash out in the hope that if he did so in rehearsal they'd be able to avoid a bad moment onstage. Once DeSantis was under the spotlight, though, things weren't so easy.

"I remember being in the conference [room] with Gaetz and with Susie watching debate preparation, and we all thought it was going well," said a campaign adviser. "And then that first debate with Gillum came, and Ron got flustered onstage. Once Ron left his safe space, it was a very different DeSantis we saw."

CNN's Jake Tapper, who moderated the nationally televised debate, asked questions about DeSantis's "monkey it up" comment and why he did not return campaign contributions from Steve Alembik and his company, SMA Communications, after it came out that Alembik had used the N-word in a tweet about former president

Barack Obama. While DeSantis parroted earlier statements, saying he would not return the money because it had already been spent during the primary, he did acknowledge that he'd "made a mistake." It's these moments that show just how far DeSantis has evolved since then: the DeSantis most of the political world knows today would never apologize for anything—by design. The political ecosystem he helped create is relentless in its insistence that politicians should never apologize but instead double down on whatever their perceived sins happen to be. Contrition is weakness, according to the ethos of the modern political news cycle.

But 2018 was a different time, and Ron DeSantis was a different politician. He still abided by the script and long-standing political norms. He apologized because, at that moment, an apology was what was required.

Then, to his team's surprise, after a tough first debate, DeSantis performed better in the second debate, later that month, and finished the campaign on a relatively high note, winning or coming close in late-cycle public polling. The surprise recovery was just a sign of bigger things to come.

Election night—November 6, 2018—found DeSantis holed up in a suite at the Rosen Shingle Creek, an Orlando hotel that is a mainstay of Florida's political convention circuit. He and Casey had been trying to get the media to call the race in his favor, a task easier said than done: the race was neck and neck, and most large media organizations have a strict protocol as to who can formally call a race and when, though many campaigns don't know this.

First the DeSantises tried to get the Associated Press to call the race. When that was unsuccessful, I got a text message from communications staffer Sarah Bascom. She asked me to come meet some people in the main room at the hotel, where everyone was watching the returns. Much to my surprise, out walked Susie Wiles, the campaign manager, and Mike Grissom, a longtime Republican operative and former executive director of the Republican Party of Florida—someone who was a well-known figure in the state's politics but whose role in the DeSantis campaign I had been unaware of until that moment.

Both asked me to call the race on behalf of POLITICO, my then employer, which of course I could not do on my own. They walked me through the math and their thinking amid the hum of election night anticipation, and while their reasoning made sense to me, I had no ability to unilaterally call the election. I'd known both Wiles and Grissom for years, so although they seemed slightly annoyed that I was unable to help, the exchange remained friendly.

What came next, though, caught everyone off guard. Despite the continued confidence of DeSantis's team—hence their calls to the press—the race had been a nail-biter, and Gillum had very much remained within striking distance during the early part of the evening. Gillum's team, however, was apparently less confident and reached out to concede far sooner than DeSantis's brain trust had expected. It surprised many in the VIP area when Wiles went running through the hallway of the hotel and into an elevator to head up to the suite and hand DeSantis the phone. By the time she got there, she was trailed by Gaetz and Kent Stermon, a Jacksonville-area defense contractor, major GOP donor, and one of the few people who could rightfully claim to be a close friend of DeSantis.

"They had a good conversation, but brief," said a person in the room on election night. "It was kind of weird they called it when we were not ready to, but we took it."

DeSantis won by roughly forty thousand votes, which plunged

the race into a recount, but the outcome was never in jeopardy. A few failed court challenges later, DeSantis had officially pulled off the impossible: in two short years, he'd gone from near political purgatory to Florida's governor's mansion.

"It does not happen without Trump," said a former campaign staffer. "That's all that mattered. It's what made DeSantis who he is today, for better or worse."

DeSantis was on his way. But while mostly free from political baggage, would he be able to leave behind the personal issues that had raised red flags among some voters—and even some staffers? DeSantis, after all, was an egoist and an anti-charmer, something that even those closest to him had winced about since that first congressional campaign.

Later, some would recall a conference call between DeSantis and his top campaign staffers: Tim Baker; Brian Huges, a longtime Florida GOP operative; and Patrick McQuillen, who handled the campaign's finances. The campaign had just bought its first TV spot, but much to the staffers' chagrin, DeSantis informed them that he had spent the entire day watching TV so he could see it. Surely his time would have been better spent knocking on doors or raising money, doing any sort of campaign work, but the staffers brushed it off—until DeSantis revealed that he hadn't seen the ad anywhere and became noticeably upset. He started to read the veteran political operatives the riot act, accusing them of being at least idiots, at most criminals. Though he never came out and said it, DeSantis seemed to imply his advisers had taken the money and not placed the ad, thereby stealing from the campaign.

As things grew increasingly heated, Casey DeSantis, who was also on the call, realized what was happening. The ad buy was on cable, but the couple had satellite TV in their condo. It wasn't his staffers' ineptitude that had caused DeSantis to miss the ad.

"We have DirectTV, Ron," Casey said. "Comcast is our internet."

CHAPTER FOUR

A MOVABLE FRAT HOUSE

Ron DeSantis's gubernatorial administration sprouted from a condo just south of Jacksonville, where he and his family lived while he finished out his term in Congress.

After DeSantis's victory, Susie Wiles and future chief of staff Shane Strum, a figure who would eventually go down as one of the biggest backstabbers in the DeSantis story, sifted through reams of applications for top administration posts. An almost complete political outsider with little connection to Tallahassee, DeSantis initially had neither the Rolodex nor the instincts to build an administration on his own. As the new gubernatorial reality solidified, though, waves of résumés rolled in, some from people who would go on to be administration stalwarts, others from people who had solid credentials but did not make the cut, and still others from people who could only be described as state fair–type oddities who mistook money and connections for real political talent. Among the candidates in this final category was Jason Pirozzolo, an Orlando hand surgeon who had morphed into a fairly significant GOP donor and fundraiser. Pirozzolo's reputation was that of half surgeon, half frat boy. He was known for hosting huge Republican fundraisers, including at least one DeSantis attended at an Orlando home that was a cross between Millionaires' Row mansion and college party pad.

"He spared no expense when it came to anything he did, particularly his house. It looked and felt more like a frat house inside than [the home] of a distinguished hand surgeon," said a Republican lobbyist who attended soirees there. "[There are] neon strobe lights in his house gym with techno music blaring. And a giant bar room… in which he always had young [women] bartending for political fundraisers."

Pirozzolo's ability to raise money for Republican candidates, paired with his flashy persona, granted him access to high-profile Republicans, one of whom was Matt Gaetz. The two would go on to play starring roles in a 2021 Department of Justice investigation centered on the party culture allegedly involving Gaetz and his close circle of associates, including Joel Greenberg, a former elected tax collector in Seminole County, just outside Orlando.

In just a few short years, Greenberg would plead guilty to six federal crimes, some of which were related to public corruption and sex trafficking, for which he was sentenced to eleven years in prison. For more than a year after his May 2021 guilty pleas, he would cooperate with federal investigations targeting Gaetz—investigations that focused especially closely on a September 2018 trip to the Bahamas that involved, among others, Gaetz, Pirozzolo, and five women, one of whom Gaetz was alleged to have had sex with when she was a minor. Greenberg was not on the trip, which involved the use of private planes owned by Pirozzolo and former state representative

Halsey Beshears, a close friend of Gaetz who was later appointed by DeSantis to be his administration's top business regulator. Gaetz and Greenberg were regularly seen together and developed a reputation as partyers; at one point, Gaetz referred to Greenberg as his "wingman." It was reported in February of 2023 that Gaetz would not face federal charges, an announcement that once again made him a mainstay at Trump political rallies and immediately put him on the short list of Republicans who might run for Florida governor in 2026.

In 2018, though, Gaetz and Greenberg were in DeSantis's Orlando headquarters in a condition staffers thought was akin to two guys who had just come off a hard night of partying.

"I remember Matt Gaetz, unannounced, coming into the office in Orlando and looking like he had been on a three-day bender. Bloodshot eyes, just looking like shit and kind of walking into the office," recalled a former DeSantis campaign staffer who said Gaetz came to meet with then campaign manager Brad Herold. "He brought this other guy who I had never seen. Later [I] found out it was Greenberg, but [I] had no idea who it was at the time."

Another former aide said the two were wearing board shorts and T-shirts and left the meeting in the campaign office conference room "barking orders."

"Matt was like, 'Get so and so on the phone,'" the staffer reported. "'Let's call them.' They were talking about surrogate calls and stuff. It was clear that he felt empowered to do whatever he wanted. He was there for three or four hours."

Gaetz's power was clearly felt when the transition team gave Pirozzolo a day-one interview in the conference room at the Marriott in Ponte Vedra Beach, where early transition screenings were being held. These screenings, attended by a handful of top DeSantis aides, were heavily influenced by Gaetz, who remained at the time one of DeSantis's most trusted advisers.

In a story I wrote in May of 2021, in the middle of Gaetz's sex trafficking investigation, a half dozen former campaign staffers outlined the extent of Gaetz's involvement in guiding the general-election campaign as well as in building the early administration. Gaetz functionally helped make DeSantis a viable state-level Florida politician and used that as leverage in the early days to install his allies in key administration posts. This included trying to make Pirozzolo DeSantis's first surgeon general.

"Man, I can't tell you how much by the end of the election [Gaetz] was in the campaign," said a former DeSantis adviser who worked on the race. "By the time we were in heavy general-election mode, DeSantis was not doing anything without Gaetz being in on it."

During Pirozzolo's one-on-one sit-down with DeSantis on the first day of transition interviews, the governor-elect was polite but brushed off the idea of picking the doctor as surgeon general because of a handful of red flags, including his well-known reputation as a party guy and his questionable financial ties to the medical marijuana industry.

Gaetz also secured his father, Don Gaetz, former president of the Florida Senate, an interview for the position of DeSantis's education commissioner. While this attempt also struck out—DeSantis had already settled on Richard Corcoran, the former Florida House Speaker and onetime political rival—the interview was another demonstration of just how much Gaetz had worked his way into DeSantis's inner circle.

"It was a testament to how much he thought he owed Matt," said a transition official. "I'm not sure Don would have ever been the guy, but the governor thought he needed to do this favor."

Gaetz also tried to install in the administration someone who would go on to be what DeSantis considered an enemy, a person who was for a time blackballed by his administration: me.

Early in the transition process, I started getting text messages from Gaetz about becoming DeSantis's communications director. It was an exceptionally strange moment for me. The recruiting effort was twofold: Gaetz first felt me out, then Chris Dorworth, a former Republican state representative and early DeSantis adviser, went in in earnest.

I met Dorworth in person during a Republican Party of Florida event at Orlando's Rosen Centre hotel. As we sat at a small table near the hotel's Sam & Bubbe's bar, the scene of many liquor-fueled bits of Florida political history, Dorworth made the pitch.

It didn't last long. I love my side of the game; the idea of leaving journalism to work for a campaign did not and does not appeal to me in any way. The pitch was not specific: the men only said that they thought someone with a relatively high profile who knew Florida politics and its press corps would have been a good fit. I immediately told them I was not interested and was insistent that they shut down these talks immediately; the last thing I wanted was for word to get out that I was being courted by an administration I was about to cover. If the story was going to get out, I at least wanted to tell it.

The great irony of the situation is that I would go on to have epic battles with DeSantis's administration, to the point where Shane Strum, its first chief of staff, not only openly decried me to DeSantis and anyone who would listen but also blackballed me.

In September of 2020, roughly two years after I'd turned down Dorworth's pitch, I joined fellow POLITICO reporters Michael Kruse and Gary Fineout in writing a lengthy profile of DeSantis, one of the first to appear just as it was becoming clear that DeSantis was poised to be a national MAGA-fueled Republican rock star. We were able to snag one of the first interviews with DeSantis, who is notoriously media-averse and was known for doing few interviews outside the conservative-media ecosystem. I did meticulous research and had a series of questions ready to go for the interview, to be held in DeSantis's office. It was an exciting moment I was looking forward to, in large part because I knew we were likely to be one of the only traditional media outlets to have this opportunity.

The day before the interview, however, I was told it was not going to happen... for me.

On a planning conference call ahead of the meeting, I was told that our editors had agreed to a stipulation put in place by Strum: they would offer the interview, but only if I was not there. POLITICO agreed to the condition without telling me ahead of time; I only learned about it in passing while on the call.

In retrospect, this made the administration's attempt to hire me that much stranger. In a relatively short period of time, I'd gone from someone who was recruited to coordinate their messaging to someone who was forbidden to interview the governor. In other ways, though, it was not so surprising. Part of the early administration fallout I and several other reporters had with the DeSantis administration stemmed from fights with Helen Aguirre Ferré, the woman they settled on after I expressed no interest in the communications director job. Ferré was a former *Miami Herald* columnist whose partisan approach should have disqualified her from a taxpayer-funded position. Ferré and I had fought both publicly and privately before she was sent off to be executive director of the Republican Party of Florida, a job much better suited for her skill set.

Strum and his team pretended to care about the fast and public deterioration of the administration's relationship with the media—

at first. One afternoon in the summer of 2020, I got a call from a person who was friends with both me and Strum. He said that Strum knew things were bad between Helen and me, so he wanted to have a meeting with me to try to resurrect the administration's relationship with POLITICO. Though I was very much annoyed with the state of the DeSantis camp's press relations, I was not about to turn down the meeting. So off I went to a mostly empty Beef 'O' Brady's near my old house in Tallahassee's Midtown neighborhood to spend the afternoon drinking beer and eating nachos with Strum. He now holds a very consistent dislike for me, but at the time, was still trying to pretend he did not.

It was the middle of the dead season in sports, so as we drank light beers and picked at our nachos, the bank of TVs over the bar showed lawn mower racing. It was a convenient icebreaker as we felt each other out. Eventually, Strum got down to business and suggested that if Ferré was giving us too much trouble, he could serve as a "back channel" and help us get information we needed.

I was aware that the communications office worked for Strum, so the covert nature of his offer didn't much make sense, but at that point I was still willing to take him at his word. If he said he wanted to help make things better, I was going to trust that. I left that Beef 'O' Bradys, which shut its doors shortly thereafter, with a feeling of optimism. I thought the relationship was salvageable and that I had just opened us up a new door into DeSantis's world.

Strum never answered one of my phone calls again, though several administration officials at the time—and since—have told me that he continued to speak ill of me, functionally poisoning the well for me with DeSantis. By the time Strum departed the administration, in February of 2021, he left in his wake several unhappy staffers.

"I had always felt it was a strange work situation. I often just kind of tried to play dumb to try and stay off his radar," said a former administration staffer.

Another influential person in DeSantis's orbit was Kent Stermon, the Jacksonville defense contractor who had been with DeSantis when he'd gotten the news about Gillum's concession—but who, in addition to being one of DeSantis's closest associates and donors, had proved to be something of a millstone around his friend's neck.

Stermon had been close with DeSantis going back to his days in Congress. When DeSantis decided to drop his failed Senate bid, in 2016, he returned to the Jacksonville area to run for reelection—in a district that had been redrawn and no longer included his home. To make sure he lived in the newly configured district, he moved into a condo co-owned by Stermon, at the time an executive at the defense contracting firm Total Military Management. When I first reported this arrangement, during the 2018 race, it opened DeSantis up to scathing criticism from his opponents, who were eager to point out that DeSantis, despite having positioned himself as a populist, was a sitting congressman living in a condo owned by a donor whose company actively lobbies Congress. Yet Stermon remained in DeSantis's orbit, and in 2019 the governor appointed him to the board of governors of the state university system. "He really wanted that," a former DeSantis staffer recalled.

Stermon remained in DeSantis's inner circle until his death in 2022, itself a moment of great sadness and scandal. He was found dead in his parked pickup truck, and autopsy reports later revealed he died as a result of a self-inflicted gunshot wound. His sudden demise came amid persistent rumors that he was under investigation because of accusations that he had sexually assaulted an underage babysitter. In April of 2023, the *Daily Mail* corroborated these rumors, reporting that he killed himself after having had an inappropriate relationship with a minor and alleging that he had, bizarrely, offered Taylor Swift tickets to the girl in return for pictures of her breasts. He later offered a reported five-figure sum to the girl's father. Shortly after the father refused, Stermon put a bullet in his own head.

DeSantis never addressed Stermon's death, although the two men had been very close. The scandal passed without dragging in the then governor in any material way—though it confirmed misgivings that many in his circle had long harbored about Stermon's predatory nature.

"He was very creepy at times," said a female former DeSantis staffer in an interview before Stermon's death. "I would not say [he and DeSantis] were best friends at all; I think the governor sees him as a useful tool. Beyond that, I think Kent is just one of those guys who likes to feel important…he is always around power. DeSantis does not have a lot of friends, and Kent saw himself as one. He would call staff sometimes, all dramatic if the governor would not call him back."

When she was preparing to leave the administration, the former staffer added, Stermon elevated his "creepy" demeanor, feeling he could be more open given that she was no longer officially involved in the governor's team.

"The worst example is a call I had with him when leaving the administration. It was very inappropriate," she said. "He said that I should make an OnlyFans account now that I was leaving…he said he could get together a group of donors and they would support it and buy naked pictures or whatever. I didn't know how to respond.

"He tried to keep it light and play off like it was a joke," she added. "It did not feel like it."

After Stermon's suicide, other former staffers said the events added another layer of concern—he had had so much sway in DeSantis's orbit and operated relatively unchecked.

"It's terrifying looking back at it, after what we know now," said a former staffer after Stermon's death. "I'm kind of [shook] up, to be honest."

DeSantis's transition team was gradually coming together in the helter-skelter way common to the campaigns of many newly elected governors: things were frenetic but generally headed in the direction needed to build an administration from scratch. This included a January 2019 event in Miami replete with donors and well-heeled supporters basking in the afterglow of a successful election. Among the guests were Lev Parnas and Igor Fruman, two naturalized US citizens born in the former Soviet Union—Parnas in Ukraine and Fruman in Belarus. They would later be found guilty in federal court of illegally sending hundreds of thousands of dollars from a Russian oligarch to the Trump campaign in an attempt to tip the 2016 presidential race in Trump's favor. Their ties to Trump earned them national notoriety, but they also had a favorite gubernatorial candidate: Ron DeSantis.

Parnas and Fruman had become central players in a scheme to funnel money to state and federal politicians, in part to try to sprout a medical marijuana business—an unrelated but uncanny parallel with Jason Pirozzolo's ties to the market. The federal government initially withheld the identity of the Russian oligarch behind the cash but made the name Andrey Muraviev public in March of 2022, when it unsealed an indictment outlining his attempts to influence US elections by channeling cash through Global Energy Producers, a fake company set up by Parnas and Fruman. Ultimately, federal authorities found that Muraviev had "attempted to influence the 2018 elections by conspiring to push a million dollars of his foreign funds to candidates and campaigns."

Trump's ties to the duo at that point had gotten much of the attention, but without question, for years, they'd also had DeSantis's ear—and he had their money.

According to the unsealed indictment, on election night in 2018, Muraviev congratulated Parnas and Fruman on the "victory in Florida." It was an apparent reference to DeSantis's win over Gillum. Global Energy Producers had given $50,000 to Friends of Ron DeSantis, money the governor eventually handed over to the US Treasury after Parnas's and Fruman's subsequent arrest, but the stain of the two had already covered DeSantis's campaign and the early days of his administration. Fruman pleaded guilty to campaign finance–related crimes, while Parnas went to trial and was found guilty of six counts of campaign finance violations. He was sentenced to twenty months in prison. According to a November 2019 report in the *Orlando Sentinel,* DeSantis met the men on six separate occasions, going back to a May 9, 2018, event hosted by the pro-Israel Zionist Organization of America, which took place when DeSantis was still in Congress.

In January of 2019, as DeSantis's transition team was coming together, the two attended a Miami event held to congratulate the new governor and complained that they were stuck in the back of the room, something they had not expected. The "peasant treatment" would not last, however. At DeSantis's swearing-in, outside Florida's historic capitol, in Tallahassee, the two were allowed entrance to the VVIP section, an area set aside for major campaign donors and those close to the governor. But in a race in which Friends of Ron DeSantis—a committee that under Florida law can raise unlimited sums—collected nearly $40 million, Parnas and Fruman's $50,000 check was not exactly a top-end contribution. In fact, the committee had brought in eighty-one contributions of more than $50,000 each, according to campaign finance records.

So how did Parnas and Fruman secure prime real estate at DeSantis's inauguration?

The answer is a handwritten note from DeSantis himself.

"There was a note—it had to have come from Ron," said a transition staffer. "I do not know where it would have come from otherwise. I saw it, and it was the governor's handwriting. I do not know why he wanted them there so badly, but he did."

Two other staffers I interviewed said they also saw the note.

Once Parnas and Fruman became central figures in the House Intelligence Committee's investigation into whether Donald Trump withheld $400 million in aid from Ukraine—a move prosecutors alleged was intended to pressure the Ukrainian president, Volodymyr Zelensky, into investigating the Biden family—their presence in Florida was put under renewed scrutiny. Documents unearthed by the House committee reveal that Parnas was a key player in the scheme, which led to Trump's first impeachment. It implicated Parnas in a scandal quickly enveloping the presidency, and that moment cast his many interactions with DeSantis and the DeSantis campaign in a different light. Headlines quickly began to emerge tallying the number of times DeSantis met with Parnas and Fruman, and the *Tampa Bay Times* was the first to report that the two men were at DeSantis's inauguration.

What has never been reported, though, was the handwritten stamp of approval from DeSantis himself.

During the transition period, Parnas directly reached out to DeSantis in an effort to land on his Transition Advisory Committee on Public Safety, focused on law enforcement and holding government institutions accountable. Parnas did not ultimately get a spot on the forty-five-person panel, but it was not for lack of trying: his dogged efforts included directly lobbying DeSantis after he had won the election and asking his assistant, Deanna Janse van Rensburg, to to reach out to transition staff directly.

"She would always want updates, like, 'What's the latest on getting him on the committee?'" said a transition staffer who had fielded the calls. "She was nice but pushy. She had this assumption that we would do what she told us to do, and [she] would not take no for an answer.

"I could overhear the governor and Lev on the phone in the transition office; they definitely talked," the staffer added. "I do know Lev called directly about the transition when he did not get the answer he wanted. DeSantis, though, kept a fairly normal tone. It was like he sounded with any lobbyist or donor."

When news broke of the Parnas and Fruman indictments—and their roles in the Ukraine scheme—it was late 2019, and DeSantis had not yet become the partisan knife fighter that he is today. Throughout that year, he'd enjoyed approval ratings in the low to mid-sixties, an extremely high number in the anti-incumbent era of politics. News that he had direct ties to both men, who had, notably, attended his inauguration, left DeSantis staffers, especially Strum, scrambling to figure out a way to distance the governor from the political land mine. This immediately bred a sense of paranoia in DeSantis's first-floor capitol offices as staff members who worked on the campaign but were not considered close to DeSantis thought the news would be "weaponized" against them: they feared that, as people who had worked the inauguration and remained in the administration, they were going to be tossed under the bus by Strum and Helen Aguirre Ferré. Their fears largely came true. Ferré said publicly that Justin Caporale, at the time DeSantis's external affairs director and subsequently a top Trump staffer, was responsible for seating at the inauguration event, functionally blaming him for the presence of two men embroiled in an impeachment-inducing national scandal.

DeSantis has often declined to comment on specifics about Parnas and Fruman, and there was no indication that the two ever received any favors from the administration, though they tried. In October of 2019, my former POLITICO colleagues Arek Sarkissian and Natalie Fertig reported on the duo's rebuffed attempts to use a flood of cash to break into Florida's medical marijuana business. Industry insiders who spoke to POLITICO at the time said they met with Parnas and Fruman several times as federal investigators were zeroing in on their campaign finance scheme, but no one really took them seriously.

"They just want to be that cool investor that goes home to their family on the holidays and is like, 'Hey, I own a cannabis business,'" one executive told POLITICO. "They were very concerned about perception."

DeSantis escaped the several news cycles focused on his relationship with the two Soviet-born scandal artists, but it did mark the start of the erosion of his relatively popular image. The high approval ratings he had enjoyed up to that point would remain, but the drubbing he took over his association with Parnas and Fruman offered a glimpse of the rigid, cutthroat politician he would soon become.

CHAPTER FIVE

THE PURGE

Tensions were growing high in the George Bush Republican Center.

This is what the Republican Party of Florida calls its Tallahassee headquarters, a three-story building nestled among the downtown lobbying and law firms just north of the state capitol. In the few years before DeSantis took office, the building had been home to a relatively weak party apparatus that had come off years of disconnect from then governor Rick Scott, who refused to raise money for the party or interact with it in any way. It's rare for a governor to ignore the party he or she is supposed to lead, but that's exactly what Scott did, retaliating after the party rejected his handpicked candidate for party chairman in favor of state senator Blaise Ingoglia, whom Scott did not like.

DeSantis was not planning on staying as hands-off as Scott, and he set that tone as soon as his administration began.

In April of 2019, three months after DeSantis took office, Strum, the chief of staff, and DeSantis's wife, Casey, made the quick jaunt to party headquarters in what would be the first step in DeSantis's quick consolidation of power over the Republican Party of Florida.

Notably, Casey's role was so prominent in these efforts that she'd been assigned an office in the governor's suite, an unusual move in and of itself—even more so because this room was generally used by governors' chiefs of staff.

With DeSantis's victory in the rearview mirror, the party was beginning to set its sights on 2020 and Trump's reelection. They were led by the executive director, former Trump White House staffer Jennifer Locetta, and hugely influenced by Susie Wiles, who along with helping fix DeSantis's campaign in 2018 had run Trump's 2016 Florida campaign and was expected to lead his 2020 Sunshine State effort. Wiles's presence, and that of her handpicked executive director, Locetta, was a clear signal that their focus was going to be Trump's reelection—unwelcome news to a governor who thought the party should always work for him.

"Susie and her team were viewed like hall monitors for Trump," said a staffer who was among the many Wiles-aligned people who would later be targeted for dismissal by Strum and Casey. "The easiest way to do that was for him to discredit us and eventually remove us."

Casey DeSantis and Strum gathered the staff for the forthcoming purge, quizzing them in what came off as a ham-handed attempt to use the get-to-know-you meeting as cover for an interrogation. People in the conference room later said that Casey and Strum displayed a noticeable fascination with "Susie people," a reference to operatives who had been planted in the party by Wiles, who in turn was slowly becoming aware that team DeSantis was preparing her for an unceremonious exit. A round of people would eventually be fired, including Locetta, who learned she was being let go while undergoing cancer treatment.

Until that moment, though, there was no sense that anything was amiss. A focus on elbowing out Wiles and her political associates, former aides recall, should not have been as surprising as it was. Things only seemed clearer in retrospect: in the months after the 2018 election, Strum had asked Wiles about things that happened on the campaign, including whether she'd received money that she was not entitled to.

"I think in that moment, she took it too cavalierly," said an aide involved with the Florida GOP at the time. "She did not understand where the questions were coming from—probably naively—or what was happening until it happened."

The shoe did not drop right away, but when it did, things happened fast.

In early September, nearly five months after Casey DeSantis and Strum's visit to the Republican Party of Florida headquarters, Steve Contorno, then with the *Tampa Bay Times*, obtained a memo outlining a golf-themed fundraising strategy for Friends of Ron DeSantis. For $25,000, you could golf in a foursome with the governor, catch a ten- to fifteen-minute meeting with him, or attend an "intimate and high-dollar gathering" at which he was present. Meanwhile, a one-on-one golf game with DeSantis would set you back $100,000, and a dinner event required $150,000, according to the *Times*-reported memo.

It is hardly out of the ordinary for a governor's political team to set up expensive fundraisers, but what the memo's leak did was shine a massive spotlight on a traditionally behind-the-scenes process and expose some of the DeSantis committee's overall fundraising strategies. Most damningly, the memo had been written by Wiles, making her the perfect fall person after it ended up on the front page of the *Tampa Bay Times*. She played the good soldier, telling the newspaper that the baldly wallet-targeting plan was never implemented and that DeSantis upheld the "highest standards of ethics," but it was the final straw and helped crystallize just how sour the relationship between her and DeSantis had become.

The *Tampa Bay Times* story broke on September 12, 2019, and soon after, Wiles was "unemployed and unemployable," a former DeSantis aide said. Five days later, my POLITICO colleague Alex Isenstadt and I broke the news that Wiles had officially been booted from Trump World, a place she had effectively helped create. That same day, Wiles also left her job with Ballard Partners, the lobbying shop run by Brian Ballard, which has long been one of the most influential political organizations in Florida but greatly expanded its reach outside the state during the Trump administration. Wiles cited health reasons publicly, but in reality, her ousting was part of a sustained lobbying effort mounted by Kent Stermon, the Jacksonville defense contractor and DeSantis donor who died by suicide while under state investigation; Brad Parscale, the former top Trump digital strategist who at that time was angling hard to get into DeSantis's political orbit; and DeSantis himself. Just before the September 2019 firing, the three had started reaching out to Ballard clients, especially those associated with the Wiles-run Jacksonville office, with a very clear message: get rid of Wiles.

"The governor put pressure on Brad Parscale," said one former aide. "Parscale thought he was going to come in and run DeSantis World. I don't know if he said, 'Have [Ballard] fire her,' but DeSantis and his flying monkeys said, 'If she continues to work there, do not try to do business with us.'"

In July of 2020, the *New York Times* reported that DeSantis had asked his top fundraiser, Heather Barker, to tell his growing donor network to refrain from raising money for the Republican National Committee. This move was a reaction to the fact that the Trump campaign had recently brought Wiles back into the fold after her fervent disagreement with DeSantis, whose falling-out with her and ensuing rivalry had since become the stuff of Florida political legend.

The decision to hinder fundraising for Republicans' biggest election-year event was seen as small-minded even by some DeSantis allies, but to the governor, this was of no consequence: his seething hatred for Wiles was the operative emotion of the moment, even overcoming any desire he had to help Trump. Rumors circulated that huge donors were among those who had received the call to refrain from financing the event, including Ken Griffin, a hedge-fund billionaire and major Republican donor who has given $10 million to DeSantis over the years, and Florida Power & Light, a major political donor in its own right. (Both denied they were asked not to contribute.)

"That was what happened," said a Trump campaign adviser directly involved in RNC planning. "Some of that we do think went back to the Susie stuff, but others were openly wondering even then if this guy wanted Trump to win or if he wanted the next cycle to open up early for him. The lack of cooperation [from DeSantis] was very real."

The 2020 election cycle in general accelerated feelings in Trump World that DeSantis was "not on the team" and that he did little to boost the reelection ambitions of a president who viewed him as important only when useful. One may even compare Trump's attitude at the time to that of Sid Phillips, the antagonist of *Toy Story,* who enjoys torturing and destroying playthings only to cast them aside once they've served their purpose. For Trump, the governor of Florida was just that: a plaything he could use when it suited him, to be thrown aside when he was done.

The idea that DeSantis was not "all in" for Trump in 2020 was established early. On the eve of Trump's formal reelection launch, in June of 2019, DeSantis told reporters that he "probably won't be that involved...I've got a job to do, so I'm going to be focusing on that."

The tone DeSantis set was immediately noticed by the Trump campaign: Trump's team never shook the idea that DeSantis did not do enough to help someone who, they felt, had handed him his political career.

"There was a belief he could have and should have done more. It was a feeling specifically about DeSantis," said a top 2020 campaign adviser. "There were elected officials on TV a lot for us. Trump did so much for him, and he never returned the favor. There was a notable absence of him on places like Fox News, and Trump noticed."

It further distilled the now open sense of disloyalty and lack of gratitude felt both within Trump's orbit and by the president himself, who, aides say, was beginning to change his perception of DeSantis from someone he would occasionally have differences with but could generally control to someone who paid no heed to the president's political ambitions.

"[Trump] understands that Ron is operating for Ron and not the team," said a longtime Trump adviser. "Donald Trump wants loyalty, both to him, but equally as important, to the MAGA movement. Ron is not on the team. He is on the Ron-and-Casey team; that's the only team he has."

Toward the end of the 2020 election cycle, the discontent between the two men, which had largely been concealed behind unattributed quotations and scenes of palace intrigue, began to bubble up publicly. During a rally in Ocala, Florida, just weeks before election day, Trump offered a not-so-veiled threat to the first-term governor in the event that he lost his reelection bid in Florida.

"Hey Ron, are we gonna win the state, please?" Trump said to crowd cheers as he pointed at DeSantis, who was seen on camera nervously smiling in the crowd. "You know, if we don't win, I'm blaming the governor. I'll fire him somehow."

That type of overt provocation, though, did remain relatively rare over the following few years. Trump not only won Florida but also tripled his margin in the state. That win insulated DeSantis from direct criticism from Trump. It also shielded him from pressure to support Trump's unfounded claims of a rigged 2020 vote and demands to audit the state's elections, which even Republicans acknowledge are among the smoothest in the country. DeSantis took advantage of the slight leeway he'd been given, refraining to back (or deny) Trump's allegations of a stolen election. As Trump became increasingly preoccupied with rehashing the 2020 results and untangling his various legal battles, DeSantis took further advantage, using the momentum he had built with national conservatives throughout his term to push through the GOP-led legislature a series of hallmark culture-war bills that further endeared him to the base, including initiatives to crack down on big tech "censorship" and ban critical race theory, the study of systemic racism in American institutions. Republicans across the nation started dubbing him America's Governor and bringing MAKE AMERICA FLORIDA gear to rallies across the country, including those where Trump was the speaker—a sign of the political war that was to come.

In contrast to his controversial purge of the Republican Party of Florida and the beginnings of what would become an all-out war with Donald Trump, DeSantis used a surprisingly softer touch as he began to cobble together a policy portfolio—one that, at times, Democrats liked more than Republicans did.

Democrats had just come off a bruising campaign against DeSantis that had been cutthroat from the beginning. There were no polite campaign ads in which DeSantis and Gillum introduced themselves to general-election voters without acknowledgment of the other: from the beginning, DeSantis relentlessly painted Gillum as a far-left extremist and hammered him for public corruption in Tallahassee during his time as mayor, while Gillum built a campaign around DeSantis's race-related comments, including the infamous "monkey it up" comment. The nastiness of the whole affair, coupled with DeSantis's support from Trump, led Democrats to expect a bruising partisan slog over policy.

So it was to many people's astonishment when DeSantis's first budget included a huge per-student educational funding increase, a proposal to increase environmental spending by $1 billion, and a plan to take no money from Florida's affordable housing trust fund, which for years had been depleted by lawmakers to plug holes in other areas of the budget.

"Today I released my budget proposal for fiscal year 2019–2020 which not only satisfies a statutory requirement, it affords an opportunity to share a *Bold Vision for a Brighter Future* with my colleagues in the Legislature," DeSantis said in a February 2019 statement releasing the spending plan. "My $91.3 billion budget proposal is aspirational yet attainable and recommends $335 million in tax cuts for Floridians. How we spend reflects how we serve and the people of Florida should be served by leaders who spend with fiscal restraint while addressing the pressing issues facing our state."

That statement underscores the extent to which DeSantis evolved during the years leading up to his presidential run. By 2023, public messaging out of his office consisted of culture war–infused rhetorical bombs dropped on his political foes. The DeSantis running for president would never use dry, hollow language such as "statutory requirement" to roll out his proposed budget. He would never call his priorities "aspirational." And perhaps most notably, he would never refer to members of the legislature as his "colleagues." In fact, DeSantis would go on to dominate the Republican legislature more than any governor in recent memory: he doesn't view its members as colleagues any more than a cat views a mouse it's tossed in the air as a colleague.

Along with making spending requests that seemed inconsistent with the extremist candidate Florida had come to know, DeSantis made other moves early in his administration that sparked annoyance from the right and uneasy approval from the left. One such move was selecting a Democrat, former state representative Jared Moskowitz, as his emergency management chief. He made a more shocking move shortly after being sworn into office: he pardoned the Groveland Four, a group of four young Black men wrongly convicted of raping a white girl in 1949. One of the men, Ernest Thomas, had been gunned down during a manhunt. Two others, Samuel Shepherd and Walter Irvin, had received the death penalty but were shot by the sheriff while being transported to prison; Shepherd eventually died from his wounds. Both Irvin and the fourth man, Charles Greenlee, ended up sentenced to life in prison. The incident sparked violent backlash against Black residents near and around the city of Groveland, in Lake County.

The pardon technically came from both DeSantis and the Florida Cabinet, a three-member panel made up of the state's attorney general, CFO, and agriculture commissioner that is independent from the executive branch. Despite its on-paper autonomy, however, in practice, any governor can push through, or stall, issues before the cabinet. For much of Rick Scott's time in office, for example, there had been a vocal push to get him to pardon the Groveland Four, and while the GOP-dominated Florida House issued a posthumous apology to the four in 2017, action was never taken. So when a pardon did come—and partially from DeSantis, no less—it was seen by

Democrats as a hopeful signal that DeSantis the governor might not be as extreme as DeSantis the candidate.

As DeSantis's first few months as governor passed with surprisingly little fanfare, shell-shocked Democrats were unsure how to digest a tenure mostly punctuated by policy wins they had long sought.

"I am encouraged to see the governor's commitment to priorities Democrats have long embraced, especially the cleanup of our water and increased funding for public education," said state senator Audrey Gibson of Jacksonville, at the time the top senate Democrat.

Conversely, DeSantis's first budget annoyed Republican leadership, including the Speaker of the Florida House, Jose Oliva, a South Florida politician whose reputation was that of a fiscal hawk. To him, DeSantis's plan to increase the state budget by $2 billion did not fit the conservative framework.

"The Constitution requires a balanced budget, but we have an additional responsibility to respect Florida's taxpayers by spending each dollar wisely," Oliva said in a statement. "To meet this goal, the House will craft a budget that reduces per capita spending."

But during DeSantis's first year or so in office, this was the tenor of his administration: he had become a moderate. The man who had introduced himself on the campaign trail as a Trump-endorsed flamethrower had built a moderate policy platform.

This was a metamorphosis that, it turns out, was wholly deliberate: the transformation had been meticulously plotted by the likes of Gaetz, Wiles, and Strum in order to create a popular, digestible, reasonable governor whom today's Ron DeSantis likely would not recognize. It seems like the setup to a counterintuitive one-liner: What do you get when you put Trump supporters in a room and tell them to remake Florida? A moderate Republican governor.

But that's exactly what happened. DeSantis's first two legislative sessions in Florida were devoid of the exclusive focus on the culture war–infused politics that have since brought him to the national dance. And the plan worked. DeSantis's early public approval ratings hovered at nearly 70 percent, and he was able to cobble together an early, if uneasy, truce with Democrats, who were surprised that the man who had vilified everything about their beliefs now appeared to be partially on their side.

"We made specific policy choices to try and expand his base dramatically," Gaetz said of the seeming about-face in a 2021 interview. "It was all very intentional."

And indeed, in the early days of DeSantis's administration, as top aides eagerly awaited Morning Consult's national governor approval ratings—a list generally led by former Massachusetts Republican Charlie Baker—DeSantis was always in the top tier.

"We would joke about trying to be the most popular because one guy, Charlie Baker, was always in first place," said one former top aide. "At that time our public polling was near 70 percent, which is crazy. I believe [instead that] we were firmly around 55 percent approval."

Others, though, were not wholly convinced.

"It was a strange way to start, but I'm not sure I ever believed it, not after how [DeSantis's] campaign was run," Evan Jenne, a Democrat who served in the Florida House for more than a decade, said of DeSantis's moderate turn during his early days in office.

He added, "I came to just see it as brilliant, tactically. Brilliant for someone trying to run for president."

As DeSantis was developing his uneasy truce with Democrats, he was also trying to walk the political tightrope of giving a public safe haven to Trump.

House Democrats were ramping up their efforts to make him just the third US president to be impeached after it was revealed that he had used a diplomatic phone call as a pretext to pressure the Ukrainian president, Volodymyr Zelensky, to dig up dirt on Joe Biden, who at the time had not yet announced his presidential run. The impeachment push was mainly led by Democrats, but a growing number of Republicans—nearly one-third of the party, based on public polling in the fall of 2019—were in favor of at least an impeachment inquiry.

To create this place of solace, DeSantis turned to one place: the Villages.

"President Donald Trump is leaving Washington for the first time since House Democrats ramped up their impeachment inquiry and he's heading straight into the warm embrace of a Republican stronghold," is how veteran Florida Associated Press reporter Brendan Farrington framed the visit in an October 2019 story. "Trump is due to visit The Villages, the sprawling retirement hub about an hour north of Orlando that is a must-stop for GOP candidates."

Leading the charge to shield Trump from his political foes was DeSantis, who picked up where he left off in Congress and became a vocal attack dog targeting impeachment supporters, breaking away from the bipartisan line he had been walking in Florida. This time, though, DeSantis also wanted to kill two birds with one stone: have the back of his political mentor and raise some campaign cash.

To thread that needle, he established something he called the Presidential Protection Fund. An email to supporters explained that the fund would be used to "protect" Trump.

"As governor of Florida, I want the president to know that we have his back in this fight 100 percent, so today I'm issuing the Presidential Protection Fund to fight back against this disgusting attempt to overturn a legitimate U.S. election," the message read.

But the announcement also conveniently included a call-to-action button urging readers to contribute to the Republican Party of Florida. DeSantis by that time controlled the state GOP, which became the vehicle through which he financed much of the Republican voter registration efforts that ultimately helped the GOP wrest the registration advantage from Democrats and fuel his near twenty-point reelection win.

Florida had spurned Trump's attempts to meddle in the 2016 elections, but then Trump turned to the state—this time led by DeSantis—for a political lifeline as the Russia investigations heated up and his potential reelection was starting to peek over the horizon. When he accepted DeSantis's invitation to hold a rally in the Villages in late 2019, he found a governor ready to, once again, serve as his defender in chief, highlighting the fact that despite their overall mercurial history they had at one point been publicly very close and were willing to use their respective positions to help each other. Though the alliance was largely strategic, particularly on Trump's end, it was one he was happy to maintain with federal cash and all the assistance Florida could ask for—that is, as long as it continued to benefit him.

"It is widely accepted that DeSantis's only real emergence on the national radar was his defense of Trump on the Russia hoax, especially when he had a spot on the judiciary committee," said a Trump adviser. "DeSantis's credentials also impressed Trump, who likes Ivy League guys. One thing led to another, and Trump eventually saw him as a loyal defender of him and his agenda.

"Trump was just thinking, 'We are boys, and we should take care of each other.'"

CHAPTER SIX

LOOKS CAN BE DECEIVING

Nearly four years to the day after President Donald Trump announced his first, long-shot bid for the White House, the Manhattan billionaire, now president of the United States, strolled onto a stage in Orlando's Amway Center in front of an audience of adoring fans. Trump was itching for a fight, and under the sea of red MAKE AMERICA GREAT AGAIN hats were the soldiers of his partisan army: men and women ready to serve on the front lines of the culture war that Trump hoped would win him a second term.

For Trump, who would be impeached for the first time a few months later, the venue of his June 2019 reelection rollout was just as important as the message.

"I'm thrilled to be back in my second home. That's what it is, my second home," Trump, who has since become a Florida resident, bellowed to the crowd of twenty thousand, all of whom were hanging on his every word—and all of whom represented votes he most certainly needed. "In some cases, I think I could say it's my first home, if you want to know the truth. It's the great state of Florida," Trump finished, to the audience's roaring approval.

Trump had won the state in 2016, but back then, the narcotic-like effect of his MAGA messaging had not yet reached full strength. Back then, too, Ron DeSantis had been a mere congressman. Now he was the state's governor and a powerful ally of the president who had helped win him that office—a president who had millions of Republican voters fawning over his every word. Trump could have been forgiven for thinking that he had DeSantis in his back pocket.

But looks can be deceiving. Trump's standing in Florida in 2019 wasn't as solid as it may have seemed to his audience. Indeed, the Orlando event wasn't just a starting line for Trump's reelection campaign; it was also a signal that one of the most important relationships in modern American politics was quietly unraveling.

By the time of his Orlando event in June of 2019, Trump was growing increasingly skeptical of the Floridian monster he'd helped create.

Trump and DeSantis had long played the part of best political pals. DeSantis could not step out on Trump without risking the former president's turning on him, a retaliation that, for most of their relationship, would have kneecapped his political aspirations. Trump, for his part, was happy to have what he saw as a staunch political foot soldier in an important state.

But even at the relationship's best, Trump had never totally respected DeSantis. He saw him as a political creature he'd created with his thumbs and an iPhone rather than as an equal—the way he viewed Rick Scott, whom he admired for his wealth and success in business.

Scott, who had preceded DeSantis as Florida's governor, had built a billion-dollar net worth as cofounder and CEO of Columbia Hospital Corporation, which then merged with Hospital Corporation of America to form Columbia/HCA, a hospital chain that on his watch was fined nearly $2 billion as the result of the largest-ever Medicare fraud settlement. This forced Scott out in 1999 but helped him build the wealth that would later nourish his career as a two-term governor and US senator. He was paid a nearly $10 million settlement and left the company with ten million shares of stock worth $350 million, something that Democrats tried and failed to use as a political weapon against him. Since then, Scott has deployed his deep personal wealth to steamroll Democrats in three statewide Florida campaigns.

For example, amid the legislative fights that surrounded passage of the Affordable Care Act, Rick Scott concocted a scheme that underscores his mind-boggling level of wealth. Over lunch at the Four Seasons in Miami, the future Florida governor told Republican pollster Tony Fabrizio, who would go on to help run Scott's 2010 gubernatorial campaign, that he was so opposed to a public option being included in the Obamacare legislation that if such an option were approved, he would create his own hospitals on cruise ships. Scott's plan would be to buy ships, park them off the coast, and essentially set up his own hospital system, unregulated by the federal government.

"It was something," Fabrizio said during a 2022 interview. "He told me he really wanted to do something to stop this and told me that if Obama really goes through with it, he could go buy a few cruise-ship hospitals, keep them offshore, and he would make an even bigger fortune. He told me he would shuttle people back and forth with helicopters."

It's that level of wealth that put Scott in a different category from DeSantis in the mind of Trump.

"He treats Rick Scott differently, as a peer. Because he is a billionaire," said a longtime Trump aide. "You're not just some politician who makes $100,000 a year; you are a successful businessman who has made it in life. You started from a doughnut shop. I don't want to say he disrespects DeSantis; he just sees Scott on the same level [as him]."

But in 2019, on the surface, Trump and DeSantis were solid political allies. As DeSantis grew into a national political force, the perception of the two was that of father and son: Trump was the movement-making political anomaly who had put his uniquely powerful brand behind an obscure Florida congressman, and DeSantis was his grateful beneficiary and benefactor. During his first two years as governor, DeSantis's administration greatly benefited from both the perception and reality of being an ally with the president. Federal aid quickly rained down on the natural disaster–prone state, and very few DeSantis requests for federal cash were ignored. In return, DeSantis, for the most part, did what he could to help the president, at least at first. When Trump hyped hydroxychloroquine as an early COVID-19 cure in spite of medical experts' protests, DeSantis gobbled up one million doses for the state of Florida, few of which were used because state hospitals did not want them. However, it signaled that DeSantis was with Trump, willing to follow the president's lead in what had become a bizarre bit of deadly pandemic political theater.

But tension was never far away. Despite the relationship's rosy veneer, Trump harbored a long-held unease toward DeSantis that stretched back to fights over Hurricane Maria and the infamous

"Build the Wall" ad in 2018. And it was during the heated reelection battle that Trump's team began to see DeSantis as a cravenly ambitious politician using Florida—and Trump—as the launchpad for a national political career. Also, during the 2020 election cycle, while DeSantis raised $15 million for Trump's reelection and refrained from negative comments about the president, aides noticed a considerable change in the tone of the relationship.

The Republican Party's most powerful politician and his Mini-Me were on an inevitable march toward a very open, very hostile clash.

In late 2019, after Trump announced his reelection campaign at the event in Orlando, he and DeSantis remained publicly in each other's good graces. Behind the scenes, though, there was growing resentment among the people in DeSantis's orbit over the fact that Trump was by far the bigger star, even in DeSantis's own state.

During a meeting of top DeSantis administration officials in June of 2019, six months after DeSantis took office and during the window in which the two men still appeared close, a clear message was relayed: we are seeing too much of Trump.

Shane Strum, then DeSantis's chief of staff, was going over details for an event coming up in the Villages. At the time, the massive retirement community comprised a huge swath of Trump World, and previous DeSantis events in the region reflected that: the front row, often within camera range, was packed with the red MAKE AMERICA GREAT AGAIN hats that were the calling card of Trump, who at that time remained the unquestioned leader of the Republican Party. But the MAGA red had caught DeSantis's eye, and he was not pleased.

"I was just going through some notes the other day, just cleaning stuff up, and I found one that read, 'Shane Strum: Anyone in MAGA gear or MAGA hats in the back of the room. No one near the front. Last Villages rally looked like a fucking Trump rally, so fix that,'" said a former DeSantis administration official during a November 2022 interview.

It was clear to this person that Strum was not going rogue with a request to disrespect people wearing Trump gear but rather executing the orders of DeSantis. While DeSantis had yet to be on explicitly bad terms with Trump, he still had a massive ego that required tending to.

"I stumbled on that note and recall at that time just thinking things were changing a bit," the person added. "I knew that if Shane was talking like that in staff meetings and making that explicit of direction, he was not doing so without approval."

And so it was that even when things seemed friendly, there was a simmering tension, even an understanding, from Trump and DeSantis that one day their trajectories would clash. After all, the prospect of a 2024 return to the White House for Trump, or an ascent to it for DeSantis, was enticing, to put it mildly. Power is a hell of a drug, and both men craved it far more than they cared about maintaining their friendship, or what passed for it. All the while, Trump seemed to be unable to help himself: his annoyance with DeSantis, and what he saw as his lack of gratitude, often seeped out into the open.

"No one gave President Trump a real chance in 2016, when he was just one of sixteen or seventeen or eighteen onstage during the primary. It was him with his own work ethic, intuition, and instincts. He did it on his own," said a longtime Trump adviser. "What many people like Ron DeSantis got after 2016 was the Trump endorsement shortcut.

"I mean, DeSantis was calling the White House and trying to get into Mar-a-Lago to try and get President Trump's support instead of working harder or smarter like President Trump did," the person added. "President Trump wanted candidates to prove their own value, and I don't think DeSantis ever did."

But somehow, despite the tension, the veil of friendship stayed in place, and the two continued to have it both ways through the end of 2019. DeSantis defended Trump against Democratic-led investigations, and the two worked in lockstep during DeSantis's first few years in office. Meanwhile, the governor was still able to cash in on his relationship with Trump to secure big-time federal perks for Florida. That included resources on issues ranging from hurricane relief to Everglades restoration funding to health-care reforms. Early in the DeSantis administration, no task was too big, and very few requests—if any—were turned down.

"We were told to ask for grants and other types of money because they were so friendly and receptive to us," said a former DeSantis administration staffer. "I remember being told we should ask the federal government for anything we wanted because we were getting it, or thought we could get it."

Early in his administration, DeSantis was not only eager to rely on his relationship with Trump to get behind-the-scenes help, he also wanted to openly tout it as a means of showcasing his ability to be an effective governor. In the wake of 2018's Hurricane Michael, a monster storm that devastated the Florida Panhandle, DeSantis used his first State of the State address to amplify the Trump administration's help in recovering from the storm.

"I've already traveled to Washington, DC, and secured a historic commitment from the Trump administration to provide assistance to the communities that Michael battered," the newly elected governor said during the March 2019 speech.

The Trump administration did grant a 100 percent federal cost share reimbursement for debris removal and emergency protective measures, a move that ultimately pushed federal assistance in response to the storm to more than $1 billion. But this was not the "historic" level of help DeSantis made it out to be: the Trump administration had previously extended 100 percent reimbursement to Puerto Rico for sixty days, longer than the forty-five given to Florida, in the wake of Hurricane Maria and had done the same for the Virgin Islands after Hurricane Irma.

Nonetheless, the reimbursement remained a huge early administration win for the then new governor and painted a rosy picture of two politicians who were as close as can be. "Before any of the rivalry and the political fighting focused on 2024, there was a friendship there," said a DeSantis adviser. "[DeSantis] thought the president's personality was funny. I've been in the room with them. They use swear words and kind of just talk like normal guys. The governor always seemed excited around Trump in person."

And so, for a time, things were relatively—if tentatively—peaceful in the Trump-DeSantis arena.

But 2020 was just around the corner, and soon, one thing would be made all too clear: the quiet had just been the eye of a much larger, far deadlier storm.

PART II

A GIFT FROM WUHAN

CHAPTER SEVEN

PANDEMICS AND PRESIDENTS

January 5, 2020, was not a normal day for the Florida surgeon general, Scott Rivkees.

The DeSantis-appointed head of the Florida Department of Health was in his office when a troubling email came in from the US Centers for Disease Control and Prevention. There had been forty-four cases of a mysterious respiratory illness that looked like pneumonia in a place called Wuhan, the most populous city in central China.

When Rivkees had been tapped as the DeSantis administration's first top health official, he was a practicing pediatric endocrinologist and a former professor of pediatrics at the University of Florida College of Medicine. His Florida Senate confirmation, in 2019, was anything but rosy, though, delayed by the uncovering of a 2014 sexual harassment investigation undertaken by the University of Florida, during which Rivkees acknowledged that he had made inappropriate comments to a group of veterinary medicine students. He was ultimately confirmed by the senate, but the bumpy start turned out to be a mere preamble to a tumultuous two years in office, during which he would publicly butt heads with DeSantis as the pandemic progressed.

At the beginning of January in 2020, however, the virus was in its early days, and trouble seemed worlds away. Still, as cases crept closer to American shores and disturbingly cryptic messages from the CDC continued to arrive, state health-care officials began to understand the gravity of what they might be facing. By the second half of January, the CDC—in the person of Nancy Messonnier, then the director of the National Center for Immunization and Respiratory Diseases, and her team—was making regular phone calls to states. Florida, meanwhile, was preparing to mobilize medical teams and holding conversations about hospitals' pandemic plans with a focus on boosting the number of open beds and increasing intensive-care-unit capacity by upwards of 20 percent. Elsewhere, state officials focused on boosting infrastructure to ensure that the state could respond to the unfolding emergency as nimbly as possible.

"It was a 24-7 operation at that point, and sometimes [it] felt like we were flying blind," said a former Florida Department of Health official.

Meanwhile, DeSantis had started convening his agency heads and top health-care officials in his office's conference room for daily meetings, discussing what appeared to be the inevitable march of a global pandemic. Their focus was assessing how much personal protective equipment the state had on hand and how much the federal government could help; at that point, there was a "trust but verify" approach regarding the Trump administration's promises of pandemic-focused aid.

While Florida is relatively experienced in tackling one-off natural disasters, the systems in place were ill equipped to manage sustained emergencies such as a global pandemic. In 2004, the Emergency Status System, or the ESS, had been developed to allow statewide emergency-related data to be entered into a centralized database. Under normal circumstances, officials enter data regarding supplies needed in the short term, as in the wake of a hurricane; however, with the advent of COVID-19, the system needed to be retrofitted—and quickly—to report data points such as hospital capacity and quantities of PPE needed across the state.

Early in the pandemic, the retooled ESS reporting system became the lifeblood of the state's response. However, amid continual requests for data, there was no sense of how to disseminate it as quickly as was needed or how to do so in a digestible, regulated manner. The system was akin to a high-stakes game of Whac-A-Mole as officials haphazardly scurried from emergency to emergency. All the while, the shoddiness of the retrofitting meant that hospitals were not fully reporting the information they had: thousands of emails sent from a handful of state agencies underscored the early, dramatic push officials had to make to get health-care facilities to report the most basic of data points.

Jackson Health System, a Miami-based health system that is one of Florida's largest, was one of the biggest early culprits.

"Hospitals don't report regularly," Tom Wallace, the state's deputy secretary for health care finance and data, said in an email to several state officials concerned about reporting lapses. "JMH [Jackson Health System] is the top offender, please see reporting below, skipping entire days, and reporting hospitalizations in the morning and then 0 later in the day. They have underreported nearly 500 hospitalizations alone."

Though Florida was lucky to have the ESS in place, it was clear from the outset that health-care workers and officials were going to need data faster and in ways that were more understandable than ESS could provide. To rectify the situation, the DeSantis administration quietly moved a company doing data work for Florida's Agency for Health Care Administration from that agency's headquarters to the governor's executive suite, in downtown Tallahassee. This unprecedented move was done quietly.

The company that received the promotion was Knowli Data Science, a research and analytics firm based outside Tallahassee and focused on "improving the health and well-being of the public with actionable data science insights." The firm had long had a contract with the AHCA to produce data-driven reports on preventable diseases and other similar issues. Now, though, it and its chief operating officer, Matthew Cooper, had essentially received a call to the big leagues: the DeSantis administration craved presentable data that could be used to craft a coherent response strategy—and attack critics and political foes.

"Hopefully the Secretary [of the Agency for Health Care Administration] can get the information she needs out of this," Cooper emailed to a collection of AHCA officials in mid-April of 2020. "There's a lot to look at but we'll boil it down…looking forward to your feedback."

This was the frenetic pace the administration adopted through late January and into much of February, a period of time when Florida had not yet reported its first case of COVID. That happened on March 1, 2020, when the Florida Department of Health announced two positive cases, one a twenty-nine-year-old Tampa-area woman who had traveled to Italy—one of the world's first hot spots—and the other a sixty-three-year-old man from Manatee County who had contracted the virus after encountering an infected person from another state.

But even before these cases were made public, the bipartisan facade DeSantis's team had worked so hard to maintain was beginning to crack under pressure. On February 28, 2020, DeSantis held a press conference to explain why his administration, despite several requests, had not released data related to the number of Floridians who had been tested, the number of Floridians who were isolating because of having had close contact with an infected person, and which regions of the state were most vulnerable. DeSantis told reporters that he wanted to release all the data but that surgeon general Scott Rivkees had advised him of "regulation[s] and [a] statute" that didn't allow him to publicize the numbers. Considering that every state in the country, including Florida, would eventually release such figures, this was a clear misreading of state law, one Democrats were eager to point out—marking the first Floridian partisan clash in a pandemic era that would go on to be defined by interparty ire.

"This is a new interpretation, and an incorrect interpretation, of our state statute, the one that deals with public information," said then Florida senator José Javier Rodriguez, a Miami Democrat and attorney.

As the bipartisan honeymoon slowly came to an end, DeSantis met in Palm Beach County with Vice President Mike Pence, who days earlier had been tapped by Trump to lead the White House Coronavirus Task Force. The press conference accompanying that meeting was full of acknowledgment that the nation would be ready if a spread occurred, but a mere day before Florida would announce its first two cases, the instinct was still to downplay the seriousness of the situation.

"I want to conclude by saying to the people of Florida that, according to our health experts, the threat of coronavirus spreading in the United States is low," Pence said. "But people of this country can rest assured we are ready."

By the end of March, Florida had recorded 6,741 positive cases and eighty-five deaths.

The month had been marked by a rapid succession of DeSantis administration actions as the reality took hold.

On March 1, 2020, DeSantis signed the state's first emergency declaration. Eight days later, he expanded the order by making it easier for the state to buy emergency supplies, allowing out-of-state health-care workers to work in Florida, and approving the construction of field hospitals. On March 13, he ordered his administration's top workforce agency to conduct an assessment to gauge how the pandemic was affecting state businesses. On March 14, he banned most visitors to state nursing homes and assisted living facilities. On March 20, he banned all on-site consumption of food and alcohol at restaurants in what was his initial flirtation with economic lockdowns that were briefer in Florida than in other states but definitely did occur. On March 24, three weeks after the Pence press conference, he asked Trump to declare Florida a "major federal disaster area," a request that was approved one day later. And on March 28, he set up motorist checkpoints on Interstates 10 and 95 and required travelers from Connecticut, Louisiana, New Jersey, and New York to isolate for fourteen days when arriving in Florida.

The series of steps to try to mitigate the spread, however, was not enough to drown out the growing chorus of criticism from his mostly Democratic opponents who thought economic shutdowns and more stringent mitigation measures, which were already popping up in other states, were what was needed. Those critics for the first time included then presumptive 2020 Democratic presidential candidate Joe Biden.

"In this moment of growing uncertainty and anxiety, Floridians want—and deserve—to hear from the public health officials leading the charge," Biden said in late March of 2020. "To get through this, we need our leaders to listen to the public health experts and their guidance."

Finally, on April 1, DeSantis did something that to this day he says is his only pandemic-era regret: he issued a statewide stay-at-home order, an edict that would only last for roughly a month, a limited time compared to most other states.

The directive, which DeSantis branded Safer at Home rather than Stay at Home, a phrase avoided by some conservative politicians at the time, came after Democrats and public health experts had pushed the governor for weeks to close the state down as cases and deaths continued to creep up. DeSantis had defied those pleas while some local governments issued their own stay-at-home orders—that is, until Trump, under pressure, extended social-distancing guidelines through at least the end of the month.

"At this point, even though I think there's a lot of places in Florida that have very low infection rates, it makes sense to make this move now," DeSantis said at the time. "I did consult with folks in the White House. I did speak to the president."

In this statement, as in his other pronouncements at the time, DeSantis was not shy about his motivation or about who helped get him to finally shut down the state. As the pandemic era started to take shape, Trump often served as DeSantis's guiding light.

Little could the then president know where this light would lead his former pupil.

Nestled into bright yellow chairs in the Oval Office, flanked by the nation's top science advisers, Trump and DeSantis sat side by side on April 28, 2020, looking very much like two old friends. It was early in the pandemic, but the river of public opinion was already flowing away from DeSantis, who had yet to fully assume the contrarian, knife-wielding persona that makes him a standout, even by MAGA standards of conduct.

DeSantis was ready to give a levelheaded defense of his state's pandemic response, and Trump was happy to use the biggest bully pulpit in the world to amplify his mentee's pandemic gospel. The governor was at the White House to talk about Florida's "senior first" strategy, implemented the day before, which aimed an intense early focus at nursing homes—a move that ended up being almost universally lauded—and to extol the virtues of reopening Florida's economy. DeSantis, his administration records show, had in fact started plotting his path back to reopening almost as soon as he'd issued his early April lockdown orders. Despite evidence to the contrary, he has maintained that he largely avoided COVID-19 lockdowns, perhaps in an effort to hold on to support from a conservative political base that quickly saw them as government overreach. In reality, nearly everything in Florida had shut down for some time, but DeSantis can wear the mantle of the governor who was quickest to reopen his state.

"We are with the governor of Florida, Ron DeSantis, who has done a spectacular job in Florida," Trump said to open the meeting. "He enjoys very high popularity."

In his address that day, the Ivy League–educated governor, who had not yet removed himself from Trump's political shadow, flashed the sort of intellect Trump has never possessed. DeSantis's grasp of Florida's response to the pandemic and the direction he thought the nation should head was encyclopedia-like, even sharper when juxtaposed against the sometimes bumbling responses from Trump, who at times seemed insecure in his answers to the assembled reporters. His discomfort prompted him to turn to his favorite crutch: trashing the media.

As if guided by a grumpy brand of muscle memory, Trump targeted a Yahoo! News journalist whose question was framed around the idea that South Korea was doing more testing than the United States, a contention that the White House coronavirus response coordinator, Deborah Birx, explained was incorrect, much to the delight of Trump.

"Are you going to apologize, Yahoo?" Trump said, interrupting the back-and-forth. "That's why no one knows who you are, including me."

"Just check it again," Birx told the reporter, very politely.

"You should get your facts right," Trump continued, getting it out of his system. "Your facts are wrong."

DeSantis, too, at times griped about the criticism he was receiving, which was just a fraction of what he would face later, when the pandemic raged through the state once more, taking nearly ninety thousand lives with it, numbers that horrified public health experts. For now, though, the fact that Florida had reopened sooner but did not fare significantly worse than other states in some metrics offered an exquisite line of attack for DeSantis when going after critics who said he should have instituted harsher lockdowns.

At that point, the Trump White House's pandemic playbook was largely the one DeSantis read from. And so, in the face of a chorus of warnings from the public health community, DeSantis flashed his trademark stubbornness and did not shut down the state's economy—that is, until Trump signaled that it was okay to do so. When DeSantis finally issued a lockdown order on April 2, 2020, he said, "When you see the president up there and his demeanor the last couple of days, that's not necessarily how he always is." DeSantis was not just waiting for signals from Trump before acting; he was also directly pointing to the president's anxiety about COVID—noticeable for the first time—as his motivation for finally instituting safety measures. In other words, he remained Trump's devotee.

From the start, though, there were some state-level decisions DeSantis leaned into that were creations of his own administration. During the Oval Office meeting, he was quick to point out his team's efforts to screen staff in all the state's long-term care facilities, suspend nursing home visitation, require the use of PPE, and send in "strike teams" to test both symptomatic and asymptomatic nursing home residents.

"Our nursing home population [is] obviously very vulnerable in the state of Florida," DeSantis said.

The statement was far truer than he'd let on.

In many ways, the Oval Office meeting on April 28 was emblematic of Florida's split-screen pandemic response. DeSantis presented his quasipolitical response to the pandemic as a perfect balancing act: he could keep the state's economy alive while protecting Florida's huge elderly population. But that very day, as DeSantis was cashing in on his status as Trump's favorite governor, the state's top health-care administrators were battling an outbreak in a South Florida nursing home.

"As per our conversation this morning, Fair Havens tested about 250 residents on Saturday…This morning we started receiving the results," read an April 28 email from Amina Dubuisson, a vice president at Ventura Services, which operated the facility. "Currently, the facility has about 90 residents [who have] tested positive. We are moving all positive residents up on the second floor where we are cohorting the positive cases."

At that point, much like other states, Florida was concerned about the possibility of COVID-positive seniors returning from hospitals to long-term care facilities and fueling the virus's spread among a vulnerable population.

"We are experiencing confusion between hospitals and long-term care residential providers regarding testing of asymptomatic residents prior to discharge back to the assisted living facility," Mary Mayhew, secretary of the Florida Agency for Health Care Administration, said in an email to Scott Rivkees, the Florida surgeon general, on April 27, 2020, one day before DeSantis visited the Oval Office and the news about Fair Havens broke. "There are hospitals that are refusing to test asymptomatic residents prior to discharge. Can you give some thought to whether we want to be more proactive in recommending that testing?"

The state's health-care officials quickly sprang into action. The AHCA, which regulates state long-term care facilities, put together an emergency rule requiring COVID-19 testing before any patient is discharged to a long-term care facility such as a nursing home or assisted living residence.

"I need to know what authority we have to make an emergency rule that would require hospitals to test," wrote Mayhew in an urgent email to her top staff. "I also need to be advancing an emergency rule to require all staff to be tested. Please get back to me about this as soon as possible."

The agency did indeed have the legal authority to issue such an emergency rule, and ten hours later, its general counsel, Stefan Grow, had a draft written and on Mayhew's desk.

The rule was quickly enforced, and the administration eventually constructed an early pandemic response that focused on seniors and performed much better in protecting society's most vulnerable citizens than the measures enacted in many other states. But DeSantis's Oval Office victory lap came with little acknowledgment that the outbreak was very real in his state and that health-care officials were working nearly around the clock to mitigate the pandemic horrors that were routinely left out of his public remarks.

DeSantis also seemed happy to bury another inconvenient detail: he had been privileged with special assistance from the highest echelons of the White House's COVID response team.

One day back in March of 2020, the phone rang in the governor's suite, and on the other end of the line was Jared Kushner, the president's son-in-law, with an offer: What do you need?

Kushner had just been elevated to serve as the Trump administration's point person on pandemic response. He had quietly taken over a private sector–led task force designed to gather desperately needed PPE, and he used his newfound sway, including his oversight of the Federal Emergency Management Agency, to make sure that DeSantis in particular had what he needed.

"No doubt Florida's [pandemic] response benefited from its relationship with the Trump administration, and that was generally done between Kushner and the governor and then, by extension, the president," said a former DeSantis administration health-care official. "We were definitely awarded things like additional PPE. At every point, Florida was unquestionably afforded additional leniency on reporting or requests for resources.

"There was a weekend in late March where we had to get the inventory status of every major hospital in the state. Kushner had just taken over FEMA and wanted to know the numbers by Monday or Tuesday. It happened fast," added the official. "He said, 'Get us your numbers; we want to make sure Florida gets what it needs.' I did not get the sense other states were getting that kind of call."

A second former administration official confirmed that "Kushner was directly helpful a number of times" and that the requests were vetted by staff but ultimately left up to DeSantis to respond to directly.

"The governor would go straight to the president on these things," the former staffer said. "It was definitely unique to have that direct line to Jared, and it was helpful in those early stages to have him say we would get whatever we needed."

Kushner and DeSantis talked on a regular basis through much of 2020, and this high-level assistance almost surely helped Florida avoid the same catastrophic results as other populous states. Indeed, DeSantis would come out of the early stages of the pandemic looking much better than Kushner: in May, the *Washington Post* reported that a whistleblower complaint filed with the House Oversight Committee had alleged that the Kushner-led pandemic response effort was a bumbling failure that often relied on political allies and at times duplicated and complicated existing federal efforts to secure personal protective equipment and other supplies, including ventilators.

The political stock of yet another Trump had plummeted.

DeSantis, meanwhile, was riding high.

CHAPTER EIGHT

"WE'VE GOT TO STOP WITH THIS COVID THEATER"

F lorida's response to the pandemic might be one of history's greatest political Rorschach tests. For Democrats and public health experts, it was a politically infused exercise in irresponsibility and overstep because, compared to other governors, DeSantis did very little to implement lockdowns, promote the use of masks, and encourage people to get the COVID-19 vaccine. Further, he used his authority under a long-running emergency order to crack down on any local government that even tried to institute pandemic mitigation efforts and later used his sway over the Republican state legislature to make public health–related mandates virtually impossible to impose. But what Democrats saw as reckless, life-threatening policies designed to drum up support from the right, conservatives saw as DeSantis creating an oasis of liberty far removed from the "lockdown states" using the pandemic as cover for authoritarianism.

The influence of Florida's pandemic response, and how it would reshape political discourse across the country, can't be overstated. For Democrats and late night talk show hosts, Florida was the butt of jokes and the target of horrified disdain. For Republicans, it was the answer to the only question that really mattered: Which is the freest state in the nation? The pandemic, too, marked the moment in which DeSantis morphed from a mere Trump-endorsed governor to a larger-than-life political figure with a burgeoning cultlike following that would cheer as he upended long-standing cultural and political norms.

Democrats demonized DeSantis's decision to reopen the state's economy ahead of most other states and his push to reopen state schools, which is now widely regarded as the right economic move. He did so over the warnings of public health experts, but the decisions proved widely popular, helping people resume somewhat normal lives, keeping businesses open, and helping Florida's economy roar back to life. Conversely, the strategy left nearly ninety thousand people dead, relied on input from dubiously qualified scientists seen as extreme outliers by their peers, and created a culture in which it was acceptable to call local pro-mitigation officials "petty tyrants," an ironic title considering DeSantis's wielding of his own emergency powers to ban them from instituting any substantial health mandates.

Neither side got everything right, but only one side is willing to admit its shortcomings.

"I think I have to acknowledge that mistakes were made and things were not what people thought they were at times," said Jill Roberts, an associate professor at the University of South Florida's College of Public Health. "Lots of people were trying to predict the future, and in some cases they were wrong."

Among those mistakes, Roberts says, was the CDC's statement

that masks were not a necessary part of COVID-19 mitigation. The agency quickly pivoted and strongly recommended masks through the height of the pandemic, but the initial advice, which came as early as February of 2020, became fuel for many conservatives critical of government institutions and their pandemic response.

"In some cases they were wrong, which opened everyone up to criticism, even if some of it was bad faith," Roberts said. "We do need to be humble and say where we got things wrong and why. That's how science works."

People's perceptions of the pandemic response in Florida often comes down to their opinion of DeSantis. His biggest critics are reluctant to give him praise even when it might be deserved because he does not open himself to it: he has created an environment of hostility that leaves no room for compromise. DeSantis is intrinsically incapable of not being in attack mode, a brash arrogance that does not give his detractors an opportunity to be contrite or acknowledge when he is right. On the contrary, he does not apologize and never admits to wrongdoing, instead taking every opportunity to point out others' mistakes—even when they don't exist.

Nowhere was that dynamic on fuller display than during a March 2022 press conference near Tampa. The event itself was about an education bill that was controversial in its own right, but DeSantis immediately took attention off the business at hand when he walked onto the scene and started scolding a handful of mask-wearing kids standing behind him at the event, presumably to create the proper press conference aesthetic.

"You do not have to wear those masks. I mean, please, take them off," DeSantis said, directly confronting the schoolchildren in an audibly annoyed tone. "Honestly, it's not doing anything. And we've got to stop with this COVID theater."

Later that night, Dawn Marshall, the mother of one of the students dressed down by DeSantis, was interviewed on local television and slammed the governor, framing what he did as antithetical to the parental choice philosophy he publicly espouses.

"He pretty much said take off your mask, it's stupid. Take off your mask, your parents don't matter," she told Tampa's CBS affiliate. "Even though I'm telling you parents matter and he's telling my minor child to take off his mask. He's putting us at risk. Oh yeah, I was upset. Very upset."

Under a traditional set of political circumstances, the script for what comes next would be easy to follow. The politician, of course, must apologize and walk back his comments not only because they are inappropriate but also because an angry mother on TV unleashing a torrent of criticism is simply bad optics. In the new reality created by DeSantis, however, the proper reaction—as it always is—is to double down. His then press secretary, Christina Pushaw, a DeSantis-hired social media troll who helped build him an intense extremist following, took to Twitter to make fun of the mother. DeSantis's political committee sent out an email blast raising money off the angst of a mother who thought her governor had overstepped his bounds.

"Predictably, the leftist propagandists in our media had a meltdown and called me a 'bully' for allowing children to breathe fresh air," the email read, ignoring the fact that some of the students said they had no problem wearing the masks.

This was who Ron DeSantis had become. His pandemic-driven heel turn—from a governor who wanted everyone to like him to one of the most polarizing people in modern American politics—was complete.

And it was only just the beginning.

April of 2020 represented a bit of a tonal shift in Florida's pandemic-era political battle. DeSantis started the month by shutting his state down, which was what many Democrats had pushed for, but he was quickly eager to reopen. It was then that Florida's national notoriety for thumbing its nose at COVID-19 really began to develop.

DeSantis's critics, the list of whom was growing by the day, began to view the state as the epicenter of irresponsible public health and the governor's pandemic response as an extension of the state's quirky-at-best reputation. Once again, a "Florida gonna Florida" sentiment began to permeate the country, and left-leaning television shows were eager to mock a Republican governor who was becoming an easy target. They seized the opportunity when DeSantis offered churches and religious institutions an exemption from his newly issued Safer at Home order.

"Even when DeSantis finally did something right this week, he still managed to fuck it up," John Oliver said during an April 5, 2020, episode of HBO's *Last Week Tonight*. "You're not protected from coronavirus just because you're in church."

Late Show host Stephen Colbert also took shots at DeSantis in early April for acting only on cues from Trump, waiting to shut down the state until after the president had begun to express concern about COVID.

"It wasn't the data or the scientists; it was Trump's demeanor," Colbert said. "How does that work? Is he the coronavirus groundhog? Legend says if Punxsutawney Trump folds his arms and frowns, six more weeks of quarantine."

As is often the case for DeSantis, conservative media came rushing to the rescue.

Because DeSantis increasingly signaled that his instinct was to reopen Florida ahead of most other states, conservatives held him up as a governor who had "gotten it right." He was the guy who would put your liberty above all else, they said.

"How did you do this?" asked Sean Hannity, expressing his admiration for DeSantis in an April 23 interview televised on Fox News.

He then handed the microphone to the governor, who proceeded to beam his administration's talking points into the homes of millions of conservatives across the country.

"You're right, Sean. People were predicting us to be worse than New York—like another Italy, they said this week," DeSantis said. "One of the newspapers in Florida said we would have 460,000 people hospitalized. The actual number is two thousand."

DeSantis would often criticize news outlets for reporting projections made by COVID-tracking organizations, implying that they had plucked numbers out of thin air to make him look bad rather than that they had reported scientific caseload projections (which, in his defense, often ended up being wrong).

The Hannity interview came at the same time as DeSantis's push to reopen the state after a few weeks of lockdown. In mid-April, the governor convened the Re-Open Florida Task Force, a twenty-two-person executive committee supported by a series of industry-specific subcommittees comprising hospital, business, and tourism officials. The group was given just a few days to craft a plan to reopen the state. The Florida Cabinet's two Republicans—the state CFO, Jimmy Patronis, and the state attorney general, Ashley Moody—were on the executive committee, while the cabinet's lone Democrat, the agriculture commissioner and failed 2022 gubernatorial candidate Nikki Fried, was left off. It was a nod to the increasingly partisan feel that had taken hold as DeSantis settled into the pandemic.

The quick pace of the task force's work, coupled with the fact that it was led in large part by DeSantis allies unlikely to deviate from his instructions, offered the distinct feel that the entire exercise was simply an attempt to create the impression of a deliberate process when, in reality, none existed.

The timeline that follows only lent credence to that perception.

On April 27, DeSantis's then deputy general counsel emailed a "draft work product" of the final task force recommendations to state health-care officials. She directed them to reach out to Chris Spencer, the governor's policy director, if they had any questions. The draft document, which included edits and notes from DeSantis's then deputy chief of staff, Anna DeCerchio, was thirty-eight pages long and packed with background information, a message from the governor, and comparison data. It was clear that the document had been worked on for some time. The draft was sent just two days after the task force wrapped up its duties, which included a wave of public-facing meetings—sometimes as many as four a day—over the period of a single week.

Put differently, the governor's office wanted to create the perception that the report, which was forty-four pages long in its final form, was created in a remarkably short period of time.

That perception, however, was not the reality. As the task force and its subgroups held public meetings to "seek input," DeSantis's budget office and state agencies had long begun internally drafting the recommendations that would ultimately comprise the final report, absent any consideration of what was happening during the public meetings. Each state agency and DeSantis's main budget office wrote its own recommendations, but ultimately DeSantis had the final say over what to include.

"There were these public calls with people appointed and different policy task forces that allowed for lots of public comment by different 'experts of industry,'" said a DeSantis staffer on the task force, "and meanwhile all agencies and the [budget office] were frantically writing their own reports to be consolidated and embedded into a master report. We spent days aggressively drafting it and saw a final product on a Sunday or Monday, and then it was published."

Those involved at the time acknowledge in retrospect that the best response was probably not to try to incorporate formal recommendations made by ramshackle panels that could not keep up with the rapidly evolving situation on the ground.

"Candidly, the response was so dynamic that I'm not sure COVID lent itself to some blue-ribbon task force," one staffer said.

The staffer added that it would be nearly impossible for the task force to chart a credible path forward to reopening the state, regardless of the time frame, because it did not have access to key public health data; only administration officials did.

"No matter who comprised the task force, the recommendations were going to be written by [the governor's office] in shaping the 'DeSantis response,'" the staffer explained. "I mean, there were a lot of well-intentioned folks and legislators on these committees, but they didn't have [enough] access to the real-time data and information to credibly chart a response."

The final report, whoever was behind it, ultimately laid out a three-phase approach. Phase 1, which DeSantis openly said was modeled after Trump administration recommendations, allowed retail stores and restaurants to operate at 25 percent of capacity and allowed restaurants to seat people outdoors if they maintained six-foot social distancing guidelines. Phase 2, which hit a few weeks later, allowed for additional restaurant patronage and the reopening of gyms, schools, and bars with diminished occupancy. Phase 3, which was not initiated until September, essentially fully reopened most of the state.

DeSantis released his "Safe. Smart. Step-by-Step." reopening plan on April 29, just one day after his Oval Office visit and subsequent national press conference, in which he was seated next to Trump.

"He is going to be opening up larger portions and ultimately pretty quickly because he has great numbers," Trump said during the meeting.

DeSantis, when asked about his reopening plans, insisted he would rely on his task force, even though the final recommendations had already been written and circulated by his office. He said he would "review" the proposal that day, less than twenty-four hours before releasing his plan.

"I created a task force, and I have all kinds of folks, some of the great health systems; we have great docs, business folks, elected officials, they have submitted a report to me," DeSantis said during the April 28 meeting with Trump. "I am going to be reviewing it today. We will announce tomorrow about the next step forward for Florida."

As infection numbers rose and waves of national criticism came crashing onto Florida's shores, the DeSantis administration was struggling to frame its pandemic response as better than that of other states—states that were getting much better press.

Enter "the slides."

This was a data presentation that quickly became a huge focus of the administration's pandemic response. Data is, of course, a key ingredient of any strategy, but these slides in particular were deliberately weaponized to juxtapose Florida's response against that of Democratic-led states. The governor's office relied on Knowli, the team of outside data scientists, to capture as much data about the virus and its impact on the state's health-care infrastructure as possible—but crucially, it was up to senior staff members and political appointees to shape that data in a way that made Florida look good.

"[We need figures on] hospitals and deaths per 100,000 for Acela corridor states (DC, Maryland, NJ, PA, NY, CT, MA)," read an email from Adrian Lukis, the governor's former deputy chief of staff, to several health-care officials.

Lukis used a term that would later become commonplace for DeSantis in many of his public briefings and remarks: "the Acela corridor," referring to the Amtrak express train service that runs through the Northeast and is used by the nation's political elite as they shuttle back and forth from Washington, DC, to places along the Eastern Seaboard, including New York City. Politicians use "Acela corridor" as a sort of shorthand when they need to make it seem as though they are of the people, not of the ruling class. In short, in the political lexicon, the Acela-corridor class is them, not us.

As the pandemic progressed, the term quickly seeped into DeSantis's regular talking points, especially when he tried to distinguish Florida from other states. What is particularly notable is the use of "Acela corridor"— generally seen as a disparaging term—in official state emails in addition to public-facing messaging, presenting a unique snapshot into the mindset of the administration at that time.

Lukis, at the direction of the chief of staff, Shane Strum, was charged with a wide range of pandemic-related duties for the administration. At the very top of that list was messaging and a persistent need to make sure Florida looked better than Democratic states. This would ensure that DeSantis had plenty of ammunition with which to hammer media and health-care professionals if they implied that Florida was doing poorly.

In an April 22 email to a handful of state health-care officials, Lukis made it clear that he needed a "rush" mockup of slides that compared hospitalizations and deaths in Duval County, which includes the city of Jacksonville and a coastal slice of northeastern Florida, to those in "New York, New Jersey, Connecticut, Massachusetts, Pennsylvania, Maryland, and Washington, D.C." His request came one day before DeSantis was set to hold a press conference, in part to defend Jacksonville after a decision to reopen its beaches on a restricted basis. The decision was met with immediate pushback from public health officials and DeSantis critics across the country and prompted the hashtag #FloridaMoron to trend nationally on Twitter.

"I was really disappointed to see a lot of folks in the Acela corridor taking potshots at Jacksonville a few days ago," DeSantis said during the press conference. "You can criticize who you want to, but if you are going to criticize someone on the COVID-19 response, you should probably check the facts before you do it."

DeSantis said that he went over a series of slides created by his team the night before, comparing Jacksonville to areas in Democratic-leaning states, and the numbers were favorable, showing that Duval County had just 6.9 people per 100,000 hospitalized, which was better than most of the Acela-corridor comparison figures.

"For those who try to say you are morons," DeSantis said, referring to the viral hashtag, "I would take you over the people who are criticizing you any day of the week."

Many times over the following months, information from state data vendors was repurposed into slideshow presentations comparing Florida to Democratic-leaning states. Each time the request came from Lukis, likely carrying out orders given to him by Strum or others higher on the governor's ladder. In the heat of a once-in-a-lifetime global pandemic, it makes sense to have digestible data, and it makes sense for any governor to want that data to present the best picture possible of the state's response. However, notably, the governor's office rarely, if ever, wanted to compare itself to Republican-led states: it was always only interested in making its case against blue states and hammering its point home slide after slide after slide.

The slide strategy was not reserved for state-level press conferences that got little attention outside of Florida.

"Why don't I let you make your case?" Hannity said during DeSantis's April 23 appearance on Fox News, just one day after he had defended the Jacksonville "morons." "And we will put these slides back on the screen."

Sure enough, the slides went up, and DeSantis went over them, as he had many times before, making the same "Acela corridor" points.

While having data at the disposal of public health officials is indispensable, especially during a pandemic, there was a sense even among top administration officials at the time that the slides veered outside the contours of good governance and were used as tools for overt political maneuvering as the partisan intensity around the pandemic grew. Many DeSantis administration officials, both current and former, will defend Florida's pandemic response and believe the state got a raw deal from a media-coverage and public perception standpoint, but there remains an admission that there was a part of the response that was inextricably linked to politics.

"What I would say was borderline political is when we were putting slides together for press conferences," said a former administration health-care official. "The governor was very interested in the slides and how they were presented. He had a clear outlook on what he wanted and which states we wanted to compare and contrast with. That came from the top, no question."

There was a sort of bunker mentality that formed among the core group of top staffers tasked with pandemic response, especially since other governors were getting more positive coverage—specifically, the now former New York governor Andrew Cuomo, whose daily COVID-19 press conferences got national coverage on CNN. Headline after headline praised his administration's response: the *Wall Street Journal* screamed, IN CORONAVIRUS RESPONSE, ANDREW CUOMO WINS OVER PAST CRITICS. POLITICO said Cuomo was having a "reputational renaissance." The *New York Times* said he was "best suited" to handle the pandemic. And true to form, the *New York Post* wrote a story about women finding Cuomo attractive. The most egregious example of journalistic malpractice, though, was when CNN allowed Cuomo's brother, Chris, host of the network's prime-time show *Cuomo Prime Time,* to interview the governor about New York's pandemic response, an interview that felt like a nauseating bit of self-congratulation that strained even the loosest interpretations of journalistic integrity.

The praise became so overwhelming that some media-industry trade publications began to question the ethics of it all.

"Most importantly, the same question must be asked of Cuomo that journalists are rightly demanding of Trump: Why weren't you more prepared? New York is a global city," writer Ross Barkan pointed out in the *Columbia Journalism Review* in March of 2020. "Coronavirus was ravaging China in January and was likely to reach the five boroughs. Why wasn't the state of New York ready to enact harsher policies—closing down schools, businesses, and major gathering places—when the first COVID-19 case appeared on March 1?"

It was against that early pandemic backdrop that DeSantis's team was operating. They took a drastically different approach from Cuomo's—and were getting crushed for those decisions, something that did not go unnoticed.

Cuomo "was getting universal praise as America's Governor, and we were getting destroyed, and we just did not have our messaging right," said a former top administration official of the role the slides played. "We were trying to figure it out, but the bottom line is that we needed to get a clear message out, and that of course is going to have some political elements. You can't take politics out of politics."

Cuomo's fall from grace would be swift. There were fifteen thousand deaths in the state's nursing homes during the pandemic, and a big reason for that was a health department directive requiring nursing homes to readmit patients who had tested positive for COVID-19. That disastrous policy permanently tarnished Cuomo's pandemic legacy, a dynamic exacerbated by the fact that he later tried to hide data in order to cover up the policy decision. Cuomo, who would later resign after several credible sexual harassment allegations surfaced, failed to shore up his state's nursing home population, a fact that was held up in stark contrast to DeSantis's pandemic focus on state nursing homes and its huge elderly population. That effort in Florida included early staff screenings, a massive deployment of N-95 masks, and the use of Florida National Guard–led strike teams to flood troubled facilities with tests. Later, DeSantis turned his focus to preserving the initial wave of COVID-19 vaccines for seniors, defying CDC guidelines that said they should go to frontline workers, whom DeSantis and his health-care team said were younger and less vulnerable than senior citizens.

The push for real-time data became so intense that the administration set up a data war room in the governor's suite. The assembled team was a collective of data scientists from Knowli, the firm that had been quietly transferred to just outside the governor's office to churn out data that would guide the administration's response and help defend it from what it saw as political attacks.

"It's been kind of fun, to be honest," Matthew Cooper, Knowli's chief operating officer, who was among the officials leading the data war room, said in a May 2020 email. "Although I would like to get down to the beach or just go get a beer at a bar like a human being, but why, that time will come again, right? Numbers look good again, btw."

Knowli, an outside vendor whose staff was given state email addresses, was kind of a secret operation running in the background to help animate the state's response. Few knew it was there, and its presence remains something that was never publicly discussed during the pandemic.

"How did you know about that?" said a former top administration health care official when I asked about Knowli's move to the governor's office.

The data itself, though, was not always easy to come by for those outside state government.

Not only did DeSantis not release testing and hot-spot data early in the pandemic, his team also kept confidential the reams of COVID research being churned out that, under almost any reading of Florida's generally broad open records laws, should have been publicly available. Several reports I obtained from 2020, including those outlining case counts, surge capacity, COVID-19 patients admitted to the hospital from long-term care facilities, and hospital bed capacity, among many other things, all came with a clear disclaimer noting, "Data included in this dashboard series are confidential and not for public use." This disclaimer, essentially stating that the information was exempt from state public records laws, came with no explanation, only the insistence that the data should not be released publicly.

As it turns out, the state was able to block the release of those reports by broadly interpreting a Department of Health statute that allowed epidemiological research to be exempt from open records laws.

In March of 2020, as the pandemic was just getting started, South Florida's *Sun-Sentinel* asked for a list of nineteen long-term care facilities that the Agency for Health Care Administration secretary, Mary Mayhew, said had suspected or confirmed cases of COVID-19. The Fort Lauderdale–based newspaper was simply asking for the names and locations of the facilities but was told by the agency that the information could not be released, citing, in part, an exemption for "epidemiological investigation notes," a term that became key to the state's public records strategy through much of the pandemic and that gives the state surgeon general some flexibility over what to release and what to keep confidential.

The newspaper argued in court that it was asking for a simple list, which under the state's broad open records laws should be public.

"Thus, to be clear, the Sun-Sentinel is requesting a simple list of the names and locations of the 19 facilities Ms. Mayhew *publicly* announced were impacted by COVID-19," read an email sent in March 2020 from attorney Daniela Abratt, who was representing the newspaper. "Because she announced there were 19 (as of last week), the list of names is clearly in AHCA's possession and control."

During the height of the pandemic, the *Sun-Sentinel*'s lawsuit was among several filed by the media challenging the administration's interpretation of state open records laws and its unwillingness to release basic COVID-related data. Several media organizations, including Florida's First Amendment Foundation, also joined a September 2021 lawsuit filed by Florida state representative Carlos Guillermo Smith, an Orlando Democrat, alleging that the state's denial of public records requests was at odds with state law. His lawsuit came as the state decided to stop publicly reporting daily data, instead moving to weekly data dumps. Requests for daily information after that switch were repeatedly denied.

In January of 2022, Judge John Cooper, who has regularly been a thorn in the side of DeSantis and legislative Republicans, sided with Smith and the media organizations, stating that the DeSantis administration's top health-care agency did not have the authority to block requests for daily COVID-19 information.

"Only the Legislature can create statutory exemptions from disclosure under the Public Records Act," Cooper wrote. "It is well established that a court may not create or expand a statutory exemption from disclosure. It follows that an agency may not redefine a statutory exemption from disclosure through an administrative rule."

As of July 2023, that decision is on appeal, but to some administration health-care officials, it was not a surprise. There was a sense among rank-and-file staff members in health-care agencies that the DeSantis administration was invoking an exemption to state open records laws that were far more expansive than originally intended.

"With respect to the press, there was no doubt at times a vacuum of information," an administration official said when asked about Cooper's ruling. "We had the benefit of real-time information. There were reporters and others asking legitimate questions and challenging assumptions, and naturally the administration was pushing back and in many cases had information to push back that the public did not have.

"I think the epidemiological exception was used very liberally," the official added. "There were times when it was used for public records that could have been made available, but those were the decisions [that the administration] leadership made at the time."

The Florida surgeon general, Scott Rivkees, the DeSantis appointee who may have been the first Floridian to receive word of the Wuhan outbreak, eventually defied the administration's party line on COVID messaging and as a result disappeared—kind of literally.

Rivkees held a much more mainstream view of medicine and pandemic response than the governor did, which increasingly had him in disagreement with what he and other public health experts thought was DeSantis's laissez-faire approach. This, ultimately, led to a public clash with DeSantis.

During a COVID-19 press conference in April of 2020, as the administration was starting to view the disease through a political lens, the focus was very obviously shifting to downplaying the seriousness of the virus in an effort to reopen the economy as quickly as possible. Rivkees, who had been a pediatric endocrinologist and tenured professor at Yale before joining the DeSantis administration, apparently hadn't gotten the memo.

During the meeting, held in the Florida Cabinet room, located in the basement of the state's capitol, Rivkees offered a dose of reality that at that time was almost directly at odds with DeSantis's carefully crafted message.

"We don't have a vaccine at the present time, so our mitigation measure is the social distancing six feet away from each other," Rivkees said during the meeting. "As long as we are going to have COVID in the environment, and it is a tough virus, we are going to have to practice these measures so that we are all protected."

He told the room full of reporters during the meeting, which also included DeSantis and Mary Mayhew, that measures like the ones he described would have to be in place for "probably a year, if not longer."

Shortly after his comment, Helen Aguirre Ferré, who was communications director at the time, emerged from the back of the room. She tapped Rivkees on the shoulder in the middle of the meeting, whispered something in his ear, and abruptly whisked him out of the room.

The optics of the moment were clear: Rivkees had either gone off script or had refused to abide by the script. Either way, he was not playing along with the administration's edicts at a time when loyalty and obedience were valued above all else.

The hook was seen around Florida's political world. The heavy-handedness of a political foot soldier yanking a health-care expert from a high-profile meeting after he had clearly gone rogue was widely mocked, viewed as the overt injection of politics into pandemic decision-making.

But fear not: Ferré had an explanation. Rivkees was pulled from the meeting, she said, because of a scheduling conflict. In a statement that even in the moment felt tenuous at best, Ferré said that Rivkees had been pulled into a meeting with Adrian Lukis, the deputy chief of staff who oversaw the governor's office health-care experts. Her assertion was that the state's top health-care official had somehow been double-booked and thus needed to attend a separate meeting—at the same time as a planned statewide press conference.

To no one's surprise, there was no double-booking. Rivkees's disloyalty to the administration's narrative, and the administration's heavy-handed response, served as an important marker of the ways in which the DeSantis administration was transforming in the moment.

Rivkees did end up meeting with Lukis in a conference room, but it was not a meeting that had been planned, only an "awkward" exchange; everyone knew why he was there. And it had nothing to do with a double-booking.

"That was Helen being Helen," said a former administration official. "It was a normal government press conference, [and] it was clear it was going in a way that was not totally on message, so that was just her sloppy, overly aggressive way of ending it." This was only an early example of what has become one of the DeSantis administration's bedrock principles: Believe us, not what your eyes are telling you.

Rivkees was never really heard from publicly again. The longtime pediatrician and respected academic continued to serve in the administration, but never again was he featured in a press conference or in a public event at which the governor addressed the pandemic. He would go on to be openly critical of DeSantis's pandemic response.

"Some people suggest that severe COVID-19, which means cases needing hospitalization or resulting in death, only affects children who have underlying medical conditions," Rivkees would write in a March 2022 op-ed in *Time*. "This is wrong."

The surgeon general's punishment was noticed by state and national reporters.

"Dr. Scott Rivkees has largely avoided public messaging after he suggested at an April news conference that social distancing practices could be necessary for another year," CNN journalists wrote in December of 2020.

Ferré's pulling Rivkees from a public meeting got everyone's attention and signaled a new sort of operating norm for the administration. Had it happened today, it would still evoke outrage, no doubt, but anyone who has watched DeSantis evolve would see it as nothing new, just something in line with the politician he has become.

At that time, though, despite his growing hawkishness, it was not yet the norm. The incident was one of the first signals of the transformation that turned DeSantis into a national icon for conservative voters—a status that would soon rile Trump and serve as the grist for the early stages of their national rivalry.

CHAPTER NINE

THE KNIVES COME OUT

I n May of 2020, just two months after COVID had shut down most of the United States, photographers captured one of the most iconic images of DeSantis taken during the pandemic.

The occasion was a press conference with Mike Pence, who was in Orlando to tour a long-term care facility and talk about Florida's pandemic response. But the event was hijacked by DeSantis, who began ranting about Rebekah Jones, a thirty-year-old Florida Department of Health data manager turned congressional candidate. Jones had made a massive splash when she alleged that the DeSantis administration was manipulating COVID-19 data, an accusation DeSantis swiftly pushed back on. She was later viewed, even by most Democrats, as someone who had grossly overstated her claims and was subsequently exiled to the fringes of Florida politics. She would make appearances at Florida Democratic Party conventions, forcing elected leaders there to try to politely avoid her, and ran for Congress in 2022 against Matt Gaetz in a super-conservative district she had no chance of winning. She lost badly and thereafter assumed her place as a footnote in Florida's political history.

The Jones rant, with Pence standing quietly by his side, would soon be seen as classic DeSantis behavior. He blasted Jones, the media, the scientific community, and the COVID forecasting models that many relied on, along with anyone else who had happened to annoy him that day. In his defense, he had been peppered by many claims that Florida would become the next COVID-ridden Italy or New York City, among other predictions, most of which did not come true. However, DeSantis greeted these arguably reasonable assertions with unvarnished anger and hatred for anyone who dared have a viewpoint that was not his own.

"Hell, we're eight weeks from that and it has not happened," DeSantis said as he threw his arms down and puffed his chest out in a way that gets you punched in the face in a bar.

From there the mold was set. DeSantis would continue to respond to the pandemic in a way Democrats and many public health experts thought was overtly political and that Republicans thought was revolutionary and liberty-preserving.

His administration denies that its response in 2020 was tethered to the Trump and White House public announcements, but it was hard not to spot the similarities. In April, Florida ordered nearly one million doses of hydroxychloroquine, the drug Trump had just referred to as a "game changer." Trump had started to heavily push the drug, a move that caught many in the medical community by surprise. Hydroxychloroquine is most often used to treat malaria and autoimmune diseases such as rheumatoid arthritis and lupus but was never found to be particularly beneficial for COVID-19. Trump jumped on the hydroxychloroquine bandwagon after a few small studies early in the pandemic showed some benefit, but later, larger studies showed the opposite and indicated that it could cause heart issues for some patients.

But like many Trump-hyped things at that time, it spun off a wave of defenders in the conservative ecosystem willing to tout something they had never heard of and attack its detractors, which in this case was the mainstream medical community. In Florida, DeSantis was among those to snap up tons of doses, but none of the hospitals in his state wanted any; in June of 2020, my POLITICO colleague Andrew Atterbury and I reported that months after the purchase, the state was still sitting on nearly all of them because hospitals and medical professionals did not believe in the drug's effectiveness.

At that point, DeSantis was making decisions based on suggestions from Trump and national physicians ideologically aligned with him rather than on guidelines from his own medical advisers, including the then sidelined surgeon general, Scott Rivkees.

"We recognize a lot of this was political. That will happen when you have Trump talking about things like hydroxychloroquine, which itself actually started as a tweet from Elon Musk," said a former member of the DeSantis administration's health-care team. "One thing that we have seen is that when people are in desperate situations, they will do very unusual things and blindly follow very unusual advice. I think you saw a lot of that."

There was also a distinct sense among those in his inner circle that DeSantis followed Trump down the unproved-medicine rabbit hole because he thought it was good politics—and it had the added benefit of letting him stick it to the experts he increasingly loathed. For many, though, it was hard to fathom the idea that someone who had excelled academically his entire life could so seamlessly drape himself in the rhetoric of those who ignore modern science in order to accumulate money and fame. And indeed, despite having a world-class education, to this day DeSantis regularly disparages the scientific community and institutions of higher learning. He has discovered over the years that in order to tap into the powerful currents of political populism, it is beneficial to ignore his own background and lean into the skepticism that increasingly drives the Republican base. And while DeSantis may indeed have some ingrained distrust of the expert class he so eagerly derides, he is also aware that it is good politics in the age of the new GOP.

There were always unspoken acknowledgments, though, that in his view, none of the underlying ideas were serious. In an early April press conference in Tallahassee in which he first addressed hydroxychloroquine—an event that included testimonials from a doctor and patient praising the drug as a COVID-19 fighter—DeSantis signaled that some of his pandemic-rhetoric persona was purely theatrical. As the press conference was wrapping up, DeSantis was preparing to leave the room when he looked directly over at Scott Rivkees and, according to the surgeon general's former staffers, gave him a "wink and a smile"—an uncharacteristic move for a typically stern governor and a clear signal to Rivkees, they thought, that the governor was not truly in support of the drug he just touted.

"He looked over, and it was very clear, there was a wink from DeSantis," recalled a former Rivkees staffer. "That was interpreted—by [Rivkees], at least—that this was more for show than science, or whatever. DeSantis knew what he was doing was mere politics."

The politics of the moment extended far beyond administrative action and meetings shenanigans. At the time, DeSantis's emergency order remained in place, giving him sweeping authority, including the right to outsource work tied to the state's effort to fight COVID-19 without going through the state's normal procurement process. And he did. Hundreds of millions of dollars' worth of taxpayer-funded no-bid contracts were given out during the pandemic, a move that looked innocuous at first: no doubt such quick agreements were needed in the face of a once-in-a-lifetime pandemic. Some of the biggest no-bid contracts, records would later reveal, went to companies that would later help DeSantis build a massive war chest ahead of his 2022 midterm reelection bid.

One such company was Nomi Health, a Utah-based startup endorsed on its website by Pence and other politicians that in 2021 landed more than $50 million in state contracts, mostly for COVID-19 testing. Thereafter, it gave $100,000 to a DeSantis-controlled political committee that served as the Florida GOP's main fundraising arm.

Nomi Health was not alone in this; millions of dollars in contributions flowed in to the DeSantis administration from other vendors who landed no-bid contracts, but the administration has repeatedly denied any connection between the campaign cash and the contracts. According to a DeSantis spokesperson, "Political donations did not factor into decisions in any way."

Perhaps no one issue underscores DeSantis's evolution from a believer in mainstream pandemic science to a leading skeptic of it than the advent of the COVID-19 vaccines, a quickly developed medical marvel that was almost universally praised—including by DeSantis—before it became the focus of the political wars that have come to define the pandemic.

By December of 2020, Florida was starting to receive regular shipments of the vaccine, and DeSantis was the public face of the distribution plan as his administration took the lead in coordinating the efforts. The first wave was sent to hospitals and health-care facilities for the benefit of frontline health-care workers, and by week three of the program, in late December of 2020, DeSantis had returned his attention to the populations most vulnerable to the virus, especially the elderly, on whom much of his response had been focused. He quickly, however, got in trouble: in January of 2021, he faced allegations that vaccine sites were being set up in wealthy, predominantly white zip codes, allowing the rich, and sometimes politically powerful, earlier access to them than otherwise would have been possible.

The vaccination site that got the most attention was Lakewood Ranch, a very white, very wealthy, very Republican community lying partially in Manatee County developed by DeSantis's campaign supporters. Text messages obtained by the *Bradenton Herald* showed that the site was organized by people who wanted to give a political boost to DeSantis.

"Gov said he might show up. Should try to see if that would help him get exposure here," texted Rex Jensen, the developer of Lakewood Ranch.

"Excellent point," responded the Republican Manatee County commissioner, Vanessa Baugh. "After all, '22 is right around the corner."

The publication of text messages showing that organizers at the site had DeSantis's political fortunes in mind didn't embarrass the increasingly combative governor. Instead, he used it to fuel his rapidly escalating war with the media, which had the audacity to report the issue.

To save face, DeSantis turned to Fox News, his go-to port in a storm. As negative news about the pop-up vaccine sites in wealthy communities swirled, DeSantis went live on *Fox & Friends* to watch as health-care workers vaccinated a World War II veteran. It was touted as Florida showing off its "house call" program for seniors who could not go to vaccine sites, but it resembled a political event, complete with fawning coverage and unchallenging questions.

It was around then that DeSantis's politically focused approach to the pandemic went from implicit to overt.

In the spring of 2021, DeSantis hired Christina Pushaw as his press secretary.

Pushaw, a former adviser to the president of the independent republic of Georgia, remade the position of communications director There has always been tension between the press and the communications staff of most any administration, but Pushaw's entrance onto the scene in Florida made that tension a featured element. She would publicly opine that she did not like the press. She boasted that it was part of her role to actively make it harder for "legacy media"—her term for anyone who does not write glowing one-sided stories about DeSantis—to do its job. She amplified and helped create a web of far-right pop-up media organizations that gave DeSantis fawning coverage and blasted his critics and the press. Coincidentally, these outlets generally focused their reporting on whatever grievance, real or imagined, Pushaw happened to be concerned with that day on Twitter, her main vehicle for injecting a new brand of toxicity into Florida's political ecosystem.

Pushaw's swift and foundation-rattling arrival occurred after she spent time actively lobbying for the job. In March of 2021, she wrote an email to DeSantis's administration saying that she was a big fan of the governor and wanted a job in his communications office because of the "pervasive...false narratives" she saw in the press—specifically, its early coverage of Rebekah Jones, the former Department of Health employee who claimed the DeSantis administration was cooking COVID-19 numbers. Pushaw's previous post as a media adviser to former Georgian president Mikheil Saakashvili, in addition to her intense, almost 24-7 brand of communications, led some in Florida politics to openly speculate about who Pushaw was and what she wanted with Florida politics.

Because of her previous work, under the Foreign Agents Registration Act, Pushaw was forced in June of 2022 to register as a foreign agent, a designation given to someone who serves as a representative of, or under the order of, a foreign government or entity. The designation delighted her critics and spun off a wave of headlines. DeSantis doubled down in his support for Pushaw, who by that time had huge sway with him; he raved about her cutthroat style. Pushaw, in turn, got a series of right-wing news outlets to critique the mainstream media for writing stories about the press secretary of the governor of Florida now being registered as a foreign agent, a move that deliberately ignored the inherent newsworthiness of the situation.

Pushaw's bellicose style made her the perfect mouthpiece for what would become the DeSantis administration's full embrace of COVID-19 conspiracy theories, an attitude that captured the attention of conservatives across the country, encouraging them to crown DeSantis the de facto leader of their movement.

Around this time, DeSantis welcomed into his inner circle the scientists and doctors behind the October 2020 Great Barrington Declaration, a controversial document embraced by conservatives arguing that everyone but the most vulnerable should go about their day-to-day lives unburdened by the pandemic around them. Governments, the theory goes, should take few steps other than protecting the most vulnerable, and economic lockdowns do far more harm than good. The declaration, which was publicly supported by the Trump administration, was opposed by more than a dozen public health groups, including the American Public Health

Association. Each organization signed an open letter in October of 2020 saying that the declaration would "sacrifice lives." The declaration was signed by Dr. Jay Bhattacharya of Stanford University, Dr. Sunetra Gupta of the University of Oxford, and Dr. Martin Kulldorff of Harvard University.

This collection of scientists, along with Dr. Scott Atlas, also of Stanford University, became key to DeSantis's pandemic messaging and were regular guests at taxpayer-funded roundtables hosted by the governor. Their first appearance on the Florida scene was in the spring of 2021 at one such roundtable held in the Florida capitol. DeSantis moderated the event, lobbing softball questions designed to move the conversation in the direction it was always intended: giving his positions scientific legitimacy. The meeting highlighted the biggest pandemic wedge issues of the day: masks were bad, lockdowns did more harm than good, and mainstream public health experts and the media had it all wrong.

"How would you rate, from a scientific perspective, how the media has performed during this, in terms of providing the information with context and perspective?" DeSantis asked at one point. "Are they trying to be more fantastical and hysterical in the coverage?"

The pointed question was, of course, what the entire event was really about. Kulldorff was happy to take the bait.

"The media has some kind of herd thinking that's taking place," he said. "Those scientists that go against the media have been assaulted by the media in a variety of ways. Many scientists don't wish to speak up because they don't want to go through all the nonsense."

Jill Roberts of the University of South Florida's College of Public Health said that the emergence of such doctors and scientists who veered so wildly from the scientific community's consensus included those who were well credentialed in their fields but knew nothing about public health in addition to those who were simply trying to take advantage of the situation for publicity or financial gain.

"Some of them know very well what they are doing. They are basically grifters," she said. "They can make a lot of money on documentaries and through speaking fees. They will do things like take one example—like a single adverse effect from the vaccine—and amplify it over and over again while totally ignoring all the positives, like the fact it drastically reduced deaths and hospitalization rates."

Finally, in a hard pivot from his early stance, DeSantis began openly flirting with the antivaccination community. While he never stated his opposition to the vaccine outright, he did everything he could to platform those who had. He amplified the voices of medical professionals who were antivax, and he started to disparagingly refer to the vaccine as "the jab"—even though he'd gleefully attended events where it had been administered to elderly Floridians on live television. He also convened the Florida legislature in the fall of 2021 for a special session that forbade businesses from imposing vaccine mandates unless they allowed for worker exemptions.

It was roughly one year into the pandemic, and his stance was clear, even if he hadn't explicitly stated it: DeSantis had sidelined his own administration's health-care professionals in favor of fringe scientists who blindly affirmed his own hands-off pandemic instincts. He had transformed his communications operation into an extension of his political team, gleefully ready to attack critics at all hours of the day. And through threat of punishment, he had hampered local officials' ability to implement mask mandates, economic lockdowns, and other preventive initiatives. This enraged Democrats and delighted Republicans—which was the point.

But the cherry on top for DeSantis critics was the hiring of Joseph Ladapo as the state's surgeon general, in September of 2021.

Ladapo was the perfect vehicle for DeSantis's messaging as a whole, parroting the governor's stance on pandemic response and, later, on politically charged health policies surrounding gender-affirming care for trans youth. The Harvard-trained physician and former tenured professor at UCLA's David Geffen School of Medicine started openly bucking much of the medical community's recommendations. In April of 2020, early in the pandemic and as DeSantis was ordering lockdowns in Florida, Ladapo had written a *Wall Street Journal* article titled "Lockdowns Won't Stop the Spread," arguing that "stopping the coronavirus and protecting the economy are one and the same, but is too late to do either." DeSantis would go on to build his own pandemic philosophy on this exact sentiment. It was as if the two men were made for each other, much to the chagrin of public health experts.

Ladapo's hire and DeSantis's turn against the COVID-19 vaccine are particularly interesting when juxtaposed against Trump's own position on the vaccine. DeSantis and Trump at that point had not really started publicly feuding yet, but DeSantis's read on the Republican political base at that moment was that he should adopt a public persona in general opposition to "the jab."

Trump, meanwhile, has never really adopted antivaccine rhetoric. He has long tried to take credit for the vaccine, touting Operation Warp Speed, the name his administration gave to the process by which it was quickly developed. The vaccine marks a key point where DeSantis and Trump deviate on pandemic policy, one that would help define their rivalry when it exploded into public view.

As the politics of 2024 started to take shape, Trump did not often talk about his role in helping create the vaccine, but he never backed away from it, either. DeSantis supporters, meanwhile, did everything they could to tie Trump to a vaccine they thought would be a political loser for him nearly three years after it first became available.

"We can never allow 'Warp Speed' to trump informed consent in this country ever again," DeSantis told the Florida Family Policy Council in a May 2023 speech.

Even before he officially began his job with the state, Ladapo proved why he aligned so well with one of the nation's best-known antivaccine health-care administrations. During the background check that preceded his tenure in Florida, Ladapo's former supervisor at UCLA told the Florida Department of Law Enforcement that Ladapo had become a pariah in the school's medical department.

"The situation created stress and acrimony among his coworkers and supervisors during the last year and a half of his employment," the unnamed supervisor told investigators.

Ladapo told my POLITICO colleague Arek Sarkissian in a February 2022 interview that he thought those critics were mounting personal attacks.

"It's OK to disagree, and I've had no problem with disagreement, but what has been really disappointing is how disagreement has become a ticket or a passport to activate personal attacks," Ladapo said. "It's just sad, it's not scientific and it's disheartening."

Ladapo quickly morphed into another in a long line of DeSantis administration pandemic-era lightning rods, eventually becoming one of the highest-profile voices against "the jab." He even went so far as to recommend that healthy children *not* get the COVID-19 vaccine. His guidance led Florida to become the only state in the country to ignore US Centers for Disease Control and Prevention guidelines on the matter. The move was widely criticized by others in the medical community.

But as the pandemic fights morphed into political hand-to-hand combat, not only did Ladapo double down, DeSantis's defense of his administration's top doctor also intensified. Their critics, whose stances were intentionally misconstrued, were publicly censured as the administration began to lead a crusade to frame medical consensus as an attempt to limit free speech, claiming they were "defending freedom of speech for health care workers."

"As a health sciences researcher and physician, I have personally witnessed accomplished scientists receive threats due to their unorthodox positions," Ladapo said during a DeSantis-called press conference focused on "free speech" in January of 2023. "However, many of these positions have proven to be correct, as we've all seen over the past few years. All medical professionals should be encouraged to engage in scientific discourse without fearing for their livelihoods or their careers. So many things continue to evolve, and this is just one reason why it's not sensible to try and restrain freedom of speech from our physicians."

These were the events DeSantis routinely used to elevate fringe voices that disagreed with medical consensus. At that same event was Panama City dermatologist Jon Ward, someone with no public health experience who has become a go-to mouthpiece for DeSantis, particularly when he needs someone with a medical background to bolster his administration's positions. Ward has long been controversial in Florida's medical community and is a pariah in the Florida Medical Association, the state's largest medical group. Ward, too, is vehemently opposed to the vaccine, even stating in 2021 that parents should "train" kids to lie about their vaccine status to "game the system" so they could avoid having to quarantine. Ward later said he felt "regret" for the statement—but not others in which he called for former National Institute of Allergy and Infectious Diseases director Anthony Fauci to "face a firing squad."

"For Fauci, given what we know about the gain-of-function research in Wuhan and for him knowingly collaborating with international scientists to publish a paper [stating there was] no way that COVID was manmade," said Ward in September of 2022, "I think Fauci should face a firing squad myself."

DeSantis's willingness to openly associate with someone who gleefully called for the execution of one of the nation's public health officials was an indication of where Florida stood at that moment. A governor embracing such fringe elements was no longer a fringe part of the state's politics; rather, it had become a core feature of them.

CHAPTER TEN

THE GREAT CONSERVATIVE HOPE

B y the time DeSantis's pandemic strategy had become political catnip for conservatives across the country, his ascent through the national Republican ecosystem was well underway. As his profile skyrocketed, he wasn't just in high demand by the conservative media and the talking-heads circuit; he was also someone whose presence they fought to have.

Fox News in particular had a sort of internal turf war going on among hosts jockeying to get DeSantis on their programs. They would show off their ratings to try to persuade the governor to appear on their shows and quietly disparage other hosts for the sake of gaining leverage with DeSantis's office. They also gave DeSantis and his team extensive editorial control, doing whatever it took to secure the high ratings that came with his presence on their programs.

"[How about] Monday? He made time for Tucker last night," said a December 2020 email from Karrah Kaplan, a Fox News booker, to

Meredith Beatrice, DeSantis's press secretary at the time. "I'd appreciate the opportunity and thank you!"

Kaplan's message was a desperate attempt to use a recent DeSantis appearance on *Tucker Carlson Tonight* to book him on a show hosted by Martha MacCallum. At the time, as DeSantis was becoming a conservative political celebrity, such *Lord of the Flies*-esque internal fights to get DeSantis on the network were common.

"We can make any day of the week work, we just ask that you please not make us follow another show on the Fox News channel for the interview," read an email to Meredith Beatrice, this one from Andrew Murray, a *Fox & Friends* producer, on March 21.

DeSantis and Fox News have always had a close relationship, but headed into 2021, their roles had shifted.

Early on in his political career, DeSantis needed the influential conservative network in order to get on Trump's radar, a relationship he managed with expert precision. Once DeSantis proved himself a loyal soldier, his team, along with the White House, would regularly push Fox News to get DeSantis on its airwaves. "The White House was booking him on the Russia stuff. They were calling and saying, 'We want DeSantis on all the time,'" said a former campaign staffer. Without the Fox News coverage Trump had helped DeSantis secure, the governor's race could have looked very different—and DeSantis, perhaps, would not be preparing for a 2024 presidential bid.

But as time went on, DeSantis began to outshine Fox News, whose producers quickly learned to beg for the pleasure of his presence. The relationship remained beneficial to DeSantis, who got softball questions and a national conservative audience. But despite the symbiotic nature of the relationship, Fox News soon needed DeSantis more than he needed the network. Emailed requests from Fox News staffers for interviews came with fawning praise of the governor, messages that played to his considerable ego in an effort to get past DeSantis's gatekeepers.

"Trey is hosting next week and he would love to have the Governor join us," Kaplan emailed in March of 2021, referencing former Republican congressman Trey Gowdy, who was serving as a guest host. "He wants to talk about his visionary leadership in Florida and all that he is doing now that's really paving the way for the future of the GOP. We can talk about how he is cracking down on China, Big Tech, Covid, among other things!"

Playing to the idea that DeSantis was Trump's heir apparent became a regular part of the pitch. At the time, DeSantis was still publicly downplaying the idea that he was considering a run for president, even as advisers and those close to him openly gabbed with reporters about the idea to make sure his name remained in the national conversation. And so, despite DeSantis's then reticence, the writing was on the wall—and Fox News could read a political room. Trump had lost his reelection bid and was quickly turning his focus to overturning the vote, a messy endeavor that had begun to fatigue non-MAGA Republicans and influential donors. The network was in the process of handing the keys over to DeSantis, whom it saw as the heir apparent. For years, Trump had been the unquestioned king of Fox News, but as DeSantis got his footing in the pandemic-era Republican Party, the Rupert Murdoch–run network began to focus on DeSantis much more than on the ex-president, in the process ignoring Trump or, even worse for the former president, allowing groups to run negative ads about him on its airwaves.

"What good is it if Fox News speaks well of me when they continually allow horrible and untruthful anti-Trump commercials to be run—and plenty of them?" said an irate Trump in an October

2021 statement. "In the good old days, that would never have happened and today it happens all the time."

It was the kind of thing that never would have happened when Trump was in office but had become commonplace. Trump retaliated by trying to get his followers to watch even more extreme far-right networks, such as OAN and Newsmax.

For the time being, Fox News was DeSantis's network. It not only begged him to appear, it was also happy to be spoon-fed his talking points and to blast them out to its national audience.

"Haven't heard from Katie with research yet, but wanted to check in as we would really love to get the Governor on with Brian [Kilmeade]," wrote Kaplan, the Fox News booker, in a January email. "We see him as the future of the party and an example of leadership on coronavirus."

The comment about "research" was a reference to DeSantis's talking points, or whichever hot-button issue the governor wanted to discuss that day. Fox producers were waiting for direction from Katie Strickland, a DeSantis staffer, for while the network was, on paper, an independent media outlet, behind the scenes DeSantis ran the show. Getting talking points from his office had become a normal part of the booking process; Fox News hosts would use the administration's guidelines to tailor questions to the messages DeSantis's office wanted to highlight that day.

DeSantis's team seemed to understand the power it had over Fox News, and they took advantage of it, making sure that his appearances stayed on topic and did not stray from his desired messaging. This was on full display in April of 2021, as Fox News host Laura Ingraham was planning her "Red State Trailblazers" town hall, which was to be held in Orlando with DeSantis and four other Republican governors—Greg Abbott of Texas, Tate

Reeves of Mississippi, Kim Reynolds of Iowa, and Pete Ricketts of Nebraska.

As the event approached, DeSantis's office was unhappy; they disliked that he was sharing the stage with four other Republican governors and that the network was trying to change the list of potential questions late in the planning process.

"We are concerned about having so many additional topics added last minute that deviate from the original scope of the theme agreed to for the show," wrote Meredith Beatrice to Jessica Curry, a Fox News producer. "When we first engaged with Laura, the topic was 'liberty versus lockdown' and now the topics appear to be [a] moving target with no cohesive theme...we don't appreciate having these unrelated topics added so last minute when we have been in discussion for weeks.

"With this many topics, and 5 governors, I'm not sure we will be able to feature the wonderful stories and guests that we worked so hard to provide at Laura's request," continued the email, which was sent one day before the April 30 event. "It seems like a wasted opportunity."

Tommy Firth, one of the network's senior executive producers, quickly responded in an apologetic tone, assuring DeSantis's office that the show would not go off script and specifically promising not to mention climate change, a topic that had been in the news because Hawaii had just issued the first ever climate-related state of emergency.

"Just so everyone is clear—we are not dedicating a segment to climate change," he wrote. "Hawaii just announced today they are the first state to declare a climate emergency. A question MIGHT come up in the first block about how this is representative of how blue states will use the pandemic afterglow to exert restrictive measures on their citizens and those who visit. In keeping with the theme of liberty."

The roundtable went off without a hitch. Each DeSantis concern was taken care of, and Ingraham got to host a widely watched round-table—a proverbial win-win on the conservative media scoreboard.

This came as a handful of Murdoch-owned media powers, including Fox News, the *Wall Street Journal*, and the *New York Post*, turned from heaping praise on Trump to heaping praise on DeSantis. Afterward, Fox News gave DeSantis unfettered access to its airwaves while Trump all but disappeared. The *Post* ran a front-page picture of DeSantis and his family with the headline DEFUTURE the morning after the 2022 midterms. Conversely, when Trump announced his reelection bid, the only attention the *Post* gave him was delivered via the words FLORIDA MAN MAKES ANNOUNCEMENT, at the bottom of the front page. The story ran on page 26.

DeSantis and Fox News's love affair held strong throughout his rise to national relevance. But when DeSantis's presidential bid started to falter, in mid-2023, Fox News turned on him, too, and started to give him the Trump treatment. He got less airtime, and when he was on he was asked noticeably tougher questions, a change that was clearly read as the Murdoch empire souring on the Republican politician it helped create. In 2022, though, DeSantis remained Fox News royalty.

At the time the network was turning on Trump and showering DeSantis with praise, the change in tone from News Corp–owned properties was the subject of much speculation, most of which centered on the theory that Murdoch had grown tired of Trump. The change, though, coincided with the March 2021 hire of Nicholas Trutanich, who is now News Corp's executive vice president of litigation and chief ethics and compliance officer. Prior to his coming on board at News Corp, Trutanich was a Trump-appointed US attorney from Nevada as well as chief of staff to Adam Laxalt, the former Nevada attorney general, who is also an unsuccessful Senate candidate and one of DeSantis's oldest friends. DeSantis, who has a social circle that could fit in the back seat of a Mini Cooper, is not a man of many chums—but he has long been close with Trutanich and Laxalt, the latter of whom was his roommate when the two were coming up together in the navy and for whom he held a rally and fundraiser during the 2022 midterm cycle.

DeSantis, Laxalt, and Trutanich, then, are close far beyond their political alliance.

"Let me draw an A-to-B connection for you," said a veteran Republican consultant familiar with the DeSantis-Laxalt-Trutanich relationship. "The three are very close and go back a long time. It's kind of like a little secret society."

Over the years, the three have had regular dinners together at which they dive into the wonky nuances of the Federalist Papers and discuss the legal philosophies of US Supreme Court justices.

"It's boring as fuck," said the GOP consultant, who has attended one of the dinners. "They talk about what Clarence Thomas meant in his written dissent and stuff like that. I feel like the stupid little brother."

They described DeSantis as Laxalt's "lifeline" following his failed Senate campaign. Laxalt, for his part, went on to play a leading role in a pro-DeSantis super PAC called Never Back Down, which pledged to spend more than $200 million to get DeSantis elected governor.

DeSantis's rise, aided by Fox News, offered Florida a much more prominent spot on the national stage, an elevation that has made it the most important state in the modern conservative moment.

"Florida is leading the charge," said the longtime consultant. "They are the model for the Republican Party and its governors. All other governors are envious and jealous of what DeSantis is doing.

It is DeSantis and everyone else, and you can see it by the fact that everyone is moving there."

To put it in context, when Barack Obama won the state in 2012, there were 700,000 more registered Democrats than Republicans, a lead that only took Republicans roughly a decade to overtake. It indicates a yearslong reddening of the state, a process expedited by DeSantis's getting a national platform.

"He speaks fluent [Republican] base," the consultant added. "Like, Rick Scott was a good, conservative governor, but he was like Mr. Burns from *The Simpsons*. DeSantis is just different, and it has Florida on top of the party."

DeSantis's fluency in "base" has long been part of his political DNA. It was the bedrock on which he started building his political ascent, first at Tea Party rallies, then as an überconservative cofounder of the Freedom Caucus in Congress, and then as the Trump-backed governor who largely kept his state open during the height of the COVID-19 pandemic. The defining feature of his political career, and in many ways his adult life, has been his innate ability to speak to the Republican Party's far right.

As DeSantis's star continued to rise, though, an increasing number of former staffers and advisers felt burned by the governor and started thinking he was getting too much credit. The idea that DeSantis single-handedly made Florida a conservative paradise, they quietly griped, was complete fiction. While none could deny that DeSantis had played a role, Florida, they pointed out, has had a long line of Republican leaders who built the Florida GOP into what it is today, brick by brick. This is a line that goes back to the state's former governor Jeb Bush, who during his eight-year tenure had DeSantis-like levels of power and influence as he worked to institute conservative policies such as the nation's first education reforms focused on school choice and prioritizing annual standardized test scores, which laid the groundwork for similar reforms nationally.

"Florida didn't turn red because of you, motherfucker. It was twenty years of hard work," said one longtime Florida Republican consultant. "It started with Jeb and continued with Rick Scott, who himself raised $1 million for voter registration programs.

"It has been frustrating to see the narrative that has formed around DeSantis on this stuff," the consultant added. "This was a long process that began before anyone knew who he was."

The conference area of the Rosen Shingle Creek was packed with conservatives from across the country.

It was February of 2022, and they were gathering for the Conservative Political Action Conference, or CPAC, which has made Florida a common right-wing stop in recent years. The hotel was filled with conservative media outlets and stars of the far-right movement, including Matt Gaetz, Kari Lake, and Marjorie Taylor Greene, who were milling around with adoring grassroots activists. Panel discussions such as "Lock Downs and Mandates: Now You Understand Why We Have a Second Amendment" dotted an agenda that catered to the increasingly violent instincts of a Republican base that felt its way of life was slipping away—in part because groups like CPAC told them it was.

Any snapshot of CPAC's 2022 Orlando event would have given the impression that it was Trump's Republican base to lose, but scattered throughout were signs of insurgency. These included numerous MAKE AMERICA FLORIDA hats and T-shirts, which became popular as DeSantis's star rose during the pandemic and—though you couldn't tell from a glance—voters on the cusp of casting aside their Trump allegiance for the governor heralded him as a bright light in an era of supposedly decreasing freedoms.

"I just moved here from California six months ago, and Governor DeSantis is a big reason why I did it," said Liem Bui, who was among the people sporting DeSantis swag at the packed CPAC event. "About forty years ago, I escaped Vietnam looking for freedom. He has created a heaven on earth for freedom. It's why I escaped California for here."

Trump was the scheduled keynote speaker and easily won the event's 2024 straw poll, pulling in 59 percent of the vote compared to DeSantis's second-place 28 percent. But at times it felt like the governor, not the ex-president, was the main draw. Because Trump had secured the keynote spot, though, this didn't draw his ire in the moment, but there was a realization among some people that the reaction to DeSantis at the event was one to keep an eye on: although DeSantis had been given a daytime speaking slot (not exactly prime time), he'd still drawn one of the biggest audiences and given one of the most applause-filled speeches of the weekend.

"CPAC, let me welcome you to the freest state in these United States," DeSantis said to massive cheers as he opened his twenty-minute speech.

The speech itself wasn't particularly polished, stringing together DeSantis's go-to talking points as if for a greatest hits album, but the robotic recitation didn't much matter. Those in attendance ate up every word, responding energetically each time DeSantis transitioned from one red-meat issue to the next. There were pandemic-era favorites such as the "biomedical security state" and an insistence that Florida had resisted a transformation into some "Faucian dystopia," but the overarching theme was that the state was on the vanguard of a culture war—and DeSantis needed faithful soldiers to help with the fight.

"We need people all over the country to be willing to put on that full armor of God to stand firm against the left...I can tell you this:

in Florida, we will be standing our ground. We will be holding that line. We are not going to back down," DeSantis said, using a phrase that quickly became one of his go-tos when giving speeches to conservative audiences.

The phrase is a political twist on a line from the Bible: "Put on the whole armor of God, that ye may be able to stand against the wiles of the devil" (Eph. 6:11). In DeSantis's version, you may have noticed that "devil" is replaced with "the left." It's subtle, I know. In a September 2022 article written for the *Miami Herald*, Ana Ceballos pointed out DeSantis's repeated use of the phrase, arguing that the governor was increasingly using rhetoric that appealed to Christian nationalists. In response, his office fell back on its old standby: rather than pushing back on the claim, they criticized the outlet for reporting it at all.

"I think, at best, DeSantis is playing with fire," Brian Kaylor, a Baptist minister who studies the relationship between politics and religion, told the *Herald*. "If asked, I'm sure he would tell you he is not telling people to literally go and fight. But this rhetoric in this political climate is dangerous."

DeSantis has used an often unsubtle flirtation with white nationalist rhetoric to become a poster boy for those who see an authoritarian instinct creeping into modern politics. And what's notable is not just what he says; it's what he does not say. When neo-Nazi rallies have taken place in Florida—as they have several times during his tenure—the normally out-front DeSantis has sat idly by and let partisan warriors not just wage the war for him but also blast anyone who dares to think that the leader of a state should condemn any Floridian—even if the Floridians in question happen to promote white supremacist beliefs.

There were those who saw in DeSantis's increasing use of language that energized white nationalists echoes—intended or unintended—of Trump's now infamous speech at the 2017 Unite the Right rally in Charlottesville, Virginia. The event was staged by groups who opposed Charlottesville's decision to take down a statue of Confederate general Robert E. Lee and was marked by riots between those groups and counterprotesters. The violence left one woman dead.

In the wake of those clashes, Trump said there were "very fine people on both sides," something that immediately became controversial because event organizers included neo-Nazis who were seen on video marching and chanting things like "Jews will not replace us."

Trump the next day insisted that he handled the comments "perfectly" and said they were directed at people there to protest the statue's removal, not the neo-Nazis.

As DeSantis established a larger political presence, the rhetoric he employed was increasingly compared to some of the most controversial comments of the Trump era, which were often seen as white nationalist dog whistles.

"He has autocratic tendencies," Ruth Ben-Ghiat, a New York University professor who studies authoritarian figures, told my then POLITICO colleague Michael Kruse in 2022. "He has absorbed the lessons of what you need to get ahead in the GOP today. And that is to be a forceful bully, even to high school students. The way he carries himself and speaks has gotten much more aggressive."

Ben-Ghiat has regularly sparred with the DeSantis press secretary, Christina Pushaw, on Twitter and has become an increasingly vocal critic of the governor, whom she sees as following the authoritarian-type path blazed by Trump.

In 2022, she wrote, "Ron DeSantis is turning Florida into his own mini-autocracy." She cited examples such as DeSantis's attempt to overturn antigerrymandering language in the state constitution and his championing of the so-called Stop WOKE Act, which expanded Florida's antidiscrimination laws by forbidding teachers and companies from disseminating material that could cause students to "feel guilt" based on their race or sex. DeSantis said that allowing such teaching in the classroom or in workforce training amounts to "state-sanctioned racism." A federal judge called the new law, which as late as the spring of 2023 was on hold amid ongoing legal fights, "positively dystopian."

Ben-Ghiat also mentioned, as other critics have, an elections investigations office that DeSantis pushed lawmakers to create during Florida's 2022 legislative session. The office, he said, showed that Florida was serious about voter fraud. The first public action it took was arresting twenty people, mostly Black, for voting illegally. All twenty had served prison sentences for felony convictions that made them ineligible to vote. In each case, however, when they registered to vote, their paperwork was approved by county and state elections officials. As a result, they were sent official voter identification cards, a clear signal that they *could* vote even though the previous felony conviction should have meant they were ineligible. They were detained by law enforcement in the fall of 2022. By the end of the first year, the DeSantis administration claimed to have referred more than a thousand cases of individuals who allegedly voted illegally in 2020 or 2022, but most never faced charges.

To put it another way, people were arrested for voting after the DeSantis administration told them they could.

"Why would you let me vote if I wasn't able to vote?" asked one such person, according to police body-cam footage obtained by the *Tampa Bay Times*.

"I am not sure, buddy," an arresting officer responded.

The first three people arrested had the charges against them dropped after judges determined that Florida's statewide prosecutor did not have jurisdiction over their cases. DeSantis doubled down. In a special legislative session held in January of 2023, he persuaded lawmakers to pass legislation granting the statewide prosecutor jurisdiction in cases of election law. After the reworked law passed, those arrested started agreeing to plea deals.

DeSantis's clear rise had come at a moment in time when Trump was largely on the sidelines. Throughout the summer of 2022, Trump received little more than his baseline level of attention from the political press, including coverage of a July 2022 speech at the America First Policy Institute's first annual summit, given just blocks away from the site of the January 6 insurrection. The speech featured traditional Trump fare, including his inaccurate claims that he had won the 2020 election, but it also projected signals that he was likely going to be a presidential candidate again in 2024.

The sleepy Trump news cycles came to an end, however, in early August of 2022, when the FBI executed a search warrant on Mar-a-Lago, his postpresidency residence. The search was tied to an investigation into whether Trump had taken classified documents with him when leaving the White House. Trump would later be indicted on thirty-seven charges alleging that he had in fact taken documents he should have left at the White House. Pictures released as part of that indictment showed boxes of the documents in question stashed in the Florida resort, including one particularly infamous photograph showing several in a bathroom.

I think very few things can put a finer point on the personal style of Donald J. Trump than a chandelier in a bathroom.

The raid reset the moment. For Republicans across the country, it was a clear signal that their fears of the federal government weaponizing the justice system were based in reality. In response, Trump got a bump in the polls, and there was current of intensity sent through Republican voters, even those who may have been starting to lean toward DeSantis. The idea that a Democratic administration was targeting a top Republican political foe was horrifying—and unifying. In the moment, it was unacceptable to do anything but support Trump and blast the feds, and DeSantis knew it.

"These agencies have been weaponized to be used against people that the government doesn't like," DeSantis said in August of 2022, referencing the raid.

In an ironic twist, the comments were made during a rally for Arizona Republican gubernatorial candidate Kari Lake, who would later push forward a series of election conspiracy theories when she lost her race and became one of Trump's biggest 2024 allies. She would go on to serve as Trump's political attack dog, a role that included trashing DeSantis.

At one point she falsely tweeted that George Soros, the Democratic megadonor hated by the political right, was backing DeSantis for president. The claim, on its face, was absurd.

THE KISS OF DEATH—FLORIDA GOVERNOR RON DESANTIS ENDORSED BY GEORGE SOROS read the headline of an article Lake shared on Twitter.

This occurred fewer than six months after DeSantis appeared on a stage in Arizona trying to help make her the state's governor—and it was a clear example of the fast-changing dynamics of the Republican Party as allies of Trump and DeSantis positioned themselves ahead of their incoming collision.

CHAPTER ELEVEN

STORMING THE MOUSE HOUSE

O n a stage in the Villages in June of 2022, Ron DeSantis was glowing with pride.

He was set to announce his veto of a record $3.1 billion budget, passed months earlier by the Republican-dominated legislature. DeSantis had the culture-war lane to himself at that moment, and there could be no better way to display his fiscally conservative chops than by decimating a state budget drawn by his own party's legislative leadership.

No one escaped the wrath. The Republican state senate president, Wilton Simpson, lost nearly $1 billion of top priorities socked away in the spending plan. The Republican senate budget chief, Kelli Stargel, lost $50 million, originally set aside for a new courthouse in her district. A $1 billion fund proposed by house Republican leadership to deal with rising inflation was not spared, either. (In a bit of fun with acronyms, Republican leaders in the state house of representatives had originally proposed calling it the Budgeting for Inflation that Drives Elevated Needs fund, or BIDEN fund. When pressed on this point by reporters, supporters assured them it was a coincidence.)

Despite the fact that DeSantis was preparing to rip their priorities to shreds, legislative leaders were standing by his side, grinning from ear to ear, ready to clap at all the applause lines and offer public assurances that there was no bad blood. When DeSantis went so far as to openly point out that he was shooting down the budgeting priorities of the state's top lawmakers, all they did was laugh along. At one point Stargel even said, in a voice loud enough to hear on the broadcast, that they weren't mad. She was in the process of running for a congressional seat ultimately won by Republican representative Laurel Lee, the DeSantis administration's former top elections official, and didn't want to turn the governor's ire against her.

The event oozed humiliation. The most powerful lawmakers in the state, people who in past iterations of Florida political history would not have kowtowed before the governor, were now doing so with glee.

The dynamic was noticed by Florida's political world.

"Stargel is gonna have to stand there and watch her precious courthouse get whacked," texted one veteran lobbyist as the press conference was ongoing.

"He will take down $1 billion in Wilton priorities alone," the lobbyist also noted.

"Thank you for portraying legislative leadership as bootlickers in your story," texted another veteran Republican observer of Florida politics. "As a former proud legislative staffer, who prides himself on the co-equal branch, it's sad to witness."

The display underscored a political dynamic that had debuted under DeSantis: a Republican-dominated legislature needed to completely cave in to the governor in order for his national rise to occur as planned. Most of the Florida legislature, including its leadership, were not MAGA-type Republicans. Instead, they represented a pre-Trump era defined by a fondness for blue blazers and boat shoes and held an allegiance to the chamber of commerce. Most, of course, will say all the right things and support whomever they need to in order to stay on the good side of the new breed of conservatives, but their political DNA is not infused with the culture wars that DeSantis and his supporters obsess over.

"As soon as he became the tip of the spear on lockdown policies, he was quickly jolted into the national spotlight. COVID made him a household name even when Trump was in office; it was the launching pad," said a DeSantis adviser. "But taking on issues like immigration, education, culture-war fights, and stuff like gender identity sent him into orbit."

That does not happen, at least as smoothly as it did, without Republicans being terrified of crossing DeSantis. He won his 2018 election by less than a half a point in a race that went to a recount, but he has governed as if he has an overwhelming mandate, more than any governor in recent Florida history.

After winning by just 32,000 votes out of 8.2 million cast, DeSantis pushed through a platform of right-wing reforms that rewired many of the state's key institutions. He horrified Democrats, but the change also served as the foundation for his national rise and what would eventually become an inevitable falling-out with Trump.

In two short years, Ron DeSantis remade Florida in his beefy, brawling image.

Among the most controversial of these efforts was a crackdown on protests in the wake of the riots that came after George Floyd's death—a legislative counterrevolution that was so contentious that the United Nations said the bill "unduly restricts the right to peacefully assemble." (DeSantis later bragged about the UN's comment.) The legislation was very notably filed on January 6, 2021—months after DeSantis publicly floated the idea—as supporters of Trump stormed the US Capitol in an effort to block certification of the 2020 election. The filing of the bill itself was not expected and did not occur until 7:40 p.m., hours after coverage of the January 6 riots had blanketed the airwaves. It was an attempt to file the bill undercover and avoid criticism that the entire idea was motivated by the Floyd protests across the country. DeSantis and his team argued that they were filing the bill on the day Trump supporters stormed the Capitol as a way to show they would not tolerate any violent rioting, an argument Democrats were not buying.

"He announced the legislation last summer," former Democratic Florida state representative Omari Hardy said at the time. "It's ridiculous to say that this is a response to the events of today. It is a response to the protests of the summer."

DeSantis himself has had an evolution of opinion on the January 6 riots. When they first happened, he said they were "totally unacceptable" and that "those folks need to be held accountable." Two years later, as the issue morphed into a partisan one, DeSantis said the riots allowed the media "to create narratives that are negative about people that supported Donald Trump" and pushed back on anyone labeling it an "insurrection." It's an issue that Trump and DeSantis, despite their volatile relationship, have never really disagreed on. DeSantis has not spoken much about the January 6 riots since their occurrence, but his later stated positions on them were not as strong as Trump's in that he has never argued that the 2020 election was stolen. However, he has also never acknowledged that the storming of the nation's Capitol in an attempt to block the certification of an election was as dire a moment in American history as most now see it to be.

DeSantis, like many other Republicans, has adopted a simple strategy for dealing with questions about January 6: sidestep them.

When asked about the issue in June of 2023 at a New Hampshire campaign stop, he simply said Republicans would not win if they were "relitigating things that happened two, three years ago."

This hands-off approach is particularly notable for DeSantis, considering that Florida was home to more people arrested on charges related to January 6 than any other state.

DeSantis has also championed election reforms that cracked down on voting by mail, limited the use of the ballot drop boxes that emerged during the pandemic, and established the statewide election investigations office that led to the arrest of the twenty mostly Black former felons who voted in 2020.

He also created a program that offered teachers bonuses to take a civics training program coordinated by his administration that attendees said tried to instill a distorted view of history, one that downplayed the role of slavery and took aim at the separation of church and state. The presentation, reported the *Miami Herald*'s Ana Ceballos and Sommer Brugal in 2022, included slides that said "less than 4% of enslaved people in the Western hemisphere were in colonial America" and argued that the nation's slaveholding founders "did not defend the institution [of slavery]" even though they did, in fact, participate in it.

"It was very skewed," Barbara Segal, a twelfth-grade government teacher at Fort Lauderdale High School, told the newspaper at the time. "There was a very strong Christian fundamentalist way toward analyzing different quotes and different documents. That was concerning."

Finally, DeSantis also took it upon himself to slaughter some of Florida's longest-running political sacred cows, most prominently one of the state's largest employers and most consequential political donors: Disney.

For years, the Walt Disney Company has helped fund Florida's GOP majorities. The company is a classic example of a transactional political donor: in California, Democrats run the state, so Disney predominantly gives to Democratic politicians; in Florida, the GOP runs the show, so it is the beneficiary of the company's political largesse. And so when DeSantis took office, the company's executives surely could not have imagined that they would find themselves in a drawn-out public feud with the state's most important Republican politician.

But that's exactly what happened.

The entertainment giant started to feel DeSantis's wrath after issuing a statement opposing the Don't Say Gay bill. That bill, which aimed to ban the discussion of gender identity and sexual orientation in classrooms up to the third grade, was filed in January of 2022 and was initially pushed by the Florida House without DeSantis's direct involvement. Even before the legislation was making national headlines, Disney knew the bill could put the company in the problematic position of being at odds with Republican lawmakers.

"From the very start, even before there was a real awareness of the bill, we knew it could put us in the culture-war crosshairs, which is not a place we wanted to be," said a Disney executive.

Disney's team huddled with its massive contract lobbying team, a meeting that included major Florida firms such as the Southern Group; GrayRobinson; and Metz, Husband & Daughton. Their aim was to sketch out a strategy that would allow them to both quietly defeat the bill and stay out of the toxic waters of a national culture war. Out of a desire for secrecy, the efforts initially began in the Florida Senate, whose rules do not require that entities publicly disclose the specific bills they are lobbying for or against—not so in the Florida House, where entities must disclose such actions online.

"The world would know Disney was engaging on this bill if we were working the house, and we didn't want that," the Disney executive said. "In the senate, we could stay a bit more off the radar."

The Florida House passed the bill on February 24, 2021, a moment when the issue became exceptionally real for Disney, which to that point thought it might have a chance to kill the bill. When the house passed the measure, it began to gain national attention. In response, the company crafted an amendment that was ultimately sponsored by state senator Jeff Brandes, a St. Petersburg Republican who was among the most experienced lawmakers in the legislature but who had fallen out of favor with his own party's leadership. The amendment would have replaced the phrase "sexual orientation or gender identity" with "human sexuality or sexual activity," an effort to dull the politically explosive nature of the bill while maintaining supporters' desired policy outcome.

In response, the Florida Department of Education, which is part of the DeSantis administration, spent a weekend in late February of 2022 crafting talking points against the amendment, which was ultimately voted down.

At that point, Disney knew it had no shot at killing the bill, but it still had a decision to make: whether to go down swinging and make things tough on everyone or be team players.

The company's lobbying team set up a call between DeSantis and then Disney CEO Bob Chapek, who floated the idea of drawing up a signing statement, something generally used by presidents at the time of a bill signing. The statement allows presidents to comment on a bill, addressing areas of the legislation they may disagree with or find controversial.

"We were just trying to do whatever we could to get out of a bad situation," the Disney executive said.

By that time, conservative media outlets were fully engaged. It was an effort that centered on branding Disney as a "groomer," a term frequently used by right-wing extremists to describe political opponents and members of the LGBTQ community, painting them as sexual abusers of children. (An August 2022 report from the Human Rights Campaign found that a relatively small number of Twitter users with huge followings, including Christina Pushaw, DeSantis's controversial press secretary, were amplifying the term.)

Disney, which has long been one of Florida's most politically powerful companies, announced in early March that it would be suspending political contributions. The move shook the state's political world. Weeks later, DeSantis signed the Don't Say Gay bill into law, which prompted Disney to issue a now infamous statement vowing to fight for its repeal.

"It was not a strategic decision," said one member of the Disney team. "It was shortsighted, with no exit strategy. No recognition of the unique dynamics in Florida. No acknowledgment that some Republicans had been quietly helping us and many Democrats were openly helping us."

Disney sat out the 2022 midterms in Florida, and some of the company's biggest allies lost their reelection bids, in many cases to DeSantis-endorsed challengers.

"All of this has absolutely had a [detrimental effect] on our company, and I think it will for the foreseeable future," the Disney executive said.

Without notice, on opening day of an April 2022 special legislative session, DeSantis announced he was pressuring the Florida legislature to strip Disney of its ability to self-govern many key business operations outside of state or local government oversight. He didn't shy away from the fact that adding an assault on Disney to an already controversial redistricting special session was political retribution for Disney's opposing the Don't Say Gay legislation.

"Disney thought they ruled Florida. They even tried to attack me to advance their woke agenda," DeSantis wrote in a fundraising pitch one day after the announcement. "Now, parents see Disney for what it is. And now is the time to put the power back in the hands of Floridians and out of the pockets of woke executives."

Supporters of Disney said the decision could shift the burden of the company's nearly $1 billion in debt onto taxpayers in the two-county region near Disney World. Disney's public perception is that of an entertainment empire, but behind the scenes, its Orlando operation is largely run by a special governing district and its board of directors. That district, over its decades of existence, has built up debt after paying for things such as maintenance and transportation projects, and the idea that this debt could be shifted to area taxpayers was the cause for concern. DeSantis insisted this would not happen, but for an entire year he did not offer a solution, instead blasting anyone who asked the very reasonable question, "How is the debt load going to be handled?"

In the end, the legislature created a DeSantis-appointed board to oversee operations. This would be a sword of Damocles hanging over Disney executives. Although the reforms were not as dire as they had feared, having DeSantis appointees with real authority over the company ensured that Disney would not step out of line again.

More than any other issue, perhaps, the strong-arming of Disney underscored the fact that the Republican Florida legislature had simply become an extension of DeSantis's office. Most lawmakers, especially Republicans, had gotten some form of political support from Disney, which for years had been untouchable by Florida politicians. But when DeSantis told legislators to attack, they attacked. Disney got steamrolled, and Republican lawmakers who previously loved Disney were the ones doing the steamrolling.

Not all Republicans agreed with the decision to take on an entertainment icon and one of Florida's biggest employers, including national politicians who themselves were eyeing a 2024 White House bid.

Though DeSantis won the initial stage of his fight with Disney, the issue would prove to be a political weight around his neck in the months to come.

Many of DeSantis's most controversial reforms, including the election law changes, the Disney proposal, and most of the education reform bills, faced subsequent and in some cases ongoing legal challenges. But getting sued was not a bad thing for DeSantis, who would use the opportunity to fundraise off his opponents' angst and hammer "activist judges" when his policy priorities were overturned in court. No matter the outcome, DeSantis had created an environment where simply picking the fight meant you'd won.

"However despicable, risible, or just merely irritating you may find him, the guy is no dummy. DeSantis knows exactly what he's doing, and he understands that no matter the outcome of each case challenging the culture war laws he has championed, the governor has a way to emerge a winner—at least among the most hardcore of his GOP base," wrote Liz Mair, a longtime Republican communications strategist who has carved out a reputation as an anti-Trump columnist and media personality. "If DeSantis and Republicans somehow prevail, and these laws are deemed constitutional by courts, DeSantis will be the culture war gladiator who delivered victories for his adoring crowd.

"If, however, courts nix the laws or force Florida back to the drawing board, the governor is more than capable of turning that to his advantage, too," she continued, largely hitting the nail on the head.

The dizzying array of conservative-inspired reforms that began to take hold at the start of the pandemic was initiated under the banner of "freedom." Each controversial reform was supposedly adding to Florida's reservoir of freedom as though it were some measurable commodity, all while those in the LGBTQ community, Black voters, and others in marginalized communities said they did not feel part of this bounty of "freedom." DeSantis dubbed his realm the Free State of Florida, while others viewed the term as a bit of Orwellian doublespeak.

"Parents, teachers, doctors, business and faith leaders, and countless others in communities across the country are increasingly standing up and uniting to speak out against these vicious efforts to marginalize LGBTQ+ students," Joni Madison, then interim president of the Human Rights Campaign, said in the summer of 2022.

"Shameful efforts to replicate DeSantis' 'Don't Say Gay or Trans' law in other states are being pursued by extremist legislators trying to rile up a small but radical base, who foolishly believe peddling hate against children will win them support at the ballot box come November," she added.

That sort of commentary from DeSantis's political foes began to really pick up as his 2022 reelection effort came into view. DeSantis was challenged in the general election by Democrat Charlie Crist, the former Republican governor, who put up very little fight. DeSantis at that point was a hated figure among Democrats across the country, but national Democratic organizations had little interest in spending heavily in an effort to knock him out of the governorship before he could run for national office. They made the calculation that DeSantis was going to win no matter what, so they spent their money elsewhere.

While DeSantis was despised by Democrats who could not stop him, he was completing his takeover of every element of the state's political machinery as he laid the blueprint for his reelection and a White House bid he hadn't yet announced but that most saw as inevitable. And this was a takeover that he would pursue no matter who stood in his way—even if they were fellow Republicans.

Republicans have dominated Florida politics since the mid-1990s but have not avoided regular circular firing squads and at times open clashes. This was most obviously on display when former governor Rick Scott got into a massive fight with former Florida House Speaker Richard Corcoran over taxpayer-funded incentives for corporate recruitment and tourism marketing. The open feud was fierce and led to Scott's running thirty-second campaign-style ads in the districts of Republicans who opposed him.

"The politicians in Tallahassee don't get it," said the ad's narrator. "They don't understand how jobs are created. If the politicians in Tallahassee say they don't want to market our state and we lose tourists, then we are going to lose jobs."

A Republican governor running ads in the backyard of Republican lawmakers over a fairly obscure policy fight seemed wild, even at the time. Now, though, the concept of a Republican openly disagreeing with DeSantis is almost unthinkable.

"He has built so much political capital with his national presence, whether he runs for president or not. He can deploy that capital to help other governors or senators get elected, but also it helps him at home," said a DeSantis adviser. "It's a huge benefit that comes with being him."

CHAPTER TWELVE

"JUST KIND OF SAD AND WEIRD"

L evel 8 is a bar perched on the roof of Hotel Duval, in downtown Tallahassee. It's a swanky-looking place, at least by Tallahassee standards, frequented by business travelers and the area's political class.

But on January 6, 2022, exactly one year after the Capitol riots, it was the most "based" place in town.

That night, Christina Pushaw was playing host to some of the biggest names in the conservative influencer sphere. The group included YouTubers, Twitter personalities, and others who rose to stardom in the insular world inhabited by conservative social media stars, including Dave Rubin, Lisa Boothe, Karol Markowicz, Benny Johnson, Dave Reaboi, Josh Hammer, and others. Pushaw, a member of this circle, was key to getting DeSantis into the group's good graces.

These heavily followed social media personalities had slowly started to center their entire identities on being DeSantis supporters.

This was a chronically online group of people who, paradoxically, branded their political foes as "snowflakes" without the realization that their own professional existence is based on stoking a sense of victimhood among their followers. To help hype DeSantis, they'd morphed into online attack dogs, persistently going after anyone who questioned or criticized the governor and citing reasons why his policies made Florida an oasis for conservatives everywhere. It was a strategy born of the Trump era, one that eventually took the vitriol far beyond even the former president's level of disdain for traditional media.

This spike in aggression was a precursor to the very public war between Trump and DeSantis that was rapidly approaching: even though most right-wingers had supported Trump when he was in office, they would quickly transition into becoming some of DeSantis's most vocal supporters, placing themselves on the front lines of the Twitter war that would break out once the Trump-DeSantis rivalry spilled out into the open. The group would clash with Trump supporters in ceaseless nitpicky battles over things such as rally-crowd sizes—engaging in the sort of personal attacks on each other that are more likely to turn off average voters than persuade them to support their candidates of choice.

At the Level 8 bar, throughout the night, the group posted pictures to chronicle its first in-person interactions in DeSantis Land. The evening began with dinner at the governor's mansion with DeSantis himself, an affair colored by the type of social awkwardness you would expect from an assemblage of people less accustomed to normal human interaction than social media fights.

"It was weird," said one person who saw the group on its Level 8 field trip to the real world. "Was literally just a bunch of people taking selfies and screaming [about] how 'biased' people are as they sat in the corner away from everyone else."

Another person who was there that night was even harsher. "I'm not really sure what these dorks are doing, or if they think they're cool," said the longtime Republican lobbyist. "But it was just kind of sad and weird."

Sneering observations from Tallahassee's political class aside, the group did prove to be a huge asset for DeSantis as he quickly shot through the ranks of the national party and started to approach the Trump-level type of support among the base, eventually stoking the ire of the former president.

Most members of the group tweeted endlessly about each of DeSantis's policy and political decisions, characterizing them as revelatory bits of strategic thinking that should be followed blindly by the Republican Party. In return for their unwavering loyalty, the group would be thrown empty-calorie "exclusives" on social media before the content was sent far and wide to the rest of the public. They were also granted access to DeSantis events that were off-limits to members of the traditional media—whom, at that point, DeSantis was no longer talking to.

Though most people likely don't know who the members of this group are, they have huge sway with the millions of very online Republicans who were not politically engaged until Trump welcomed them into the party. These Republicans not only follow members of this social media army, they also consider their content the political compass by which they orient their ideologies. By mid- to late 2022, this compass increasingly pointed to DeSantis and Florida and away from Trump.

The group has even taken it a step further: most members have, in fact, picked up their lives in other parts of the country and moved to Florida, making the state not just their political North Star but also the center of their self-professed identities. A subset of the influencers invited to dinner with DeSantis have said they consider themselves a "Florida recruiting committee." One of them, Dave Reaboi, who indeed moved to Florida, wrote a column for *Newsweek* in January of 2022 anointing the state the head of the nation's conservative movement.

"Even as many blue state conservatives (and especially Californians) decamp to Texas, with both Trump and DeSantis in Florida, there can be no denying the gravitational pull the Sunshine State now has for the American Right," he wrote. "There is a sense here that this place is the future, especially as GOP voter registration has now overtaken Democratic voter registration for the first time in the state's history."

Because of the efforts of this rabid following, DeSantis's reach has been expanded, and the state that serves as his throne has been transformed from a place that was on the conservative radar because of pandemic policy to a land that many on the far right want to call home. None of that likely would have happened—certainly not to the extent it has—without Christina Pushaw.

Pushaw's hire, in the spring of 2021, had been a seminal moment in DeSantis's transition and completely changed how public-sector communications operated in the Republican political ecosystem. She was openly antimedia, extending far beyond what in the past had been a natural tension between the press and communications staffers. She was in perpetual attack mode; even the smallest perceived slight against DeSantis was greeted with a personal condemnation. With each online offensive she mounted—offensives that DeSantis himself could not launch—her power within the administration grew. At the beginning of his tenure in Tallahassee, DeSantis hated it when staff made news; that all changed as Pushaw's reputation as the far right's favorite press secretary grew. A slew of conspicuous profiles from both traditional and conservative media outlets followed.

She did initially avoid anything perceived as anti-Trump, a tight-rope everyone in DeSantis Land had to walk before his rivalry with the former president broke out publicly and it became clear he would challenge Trump for the 2024 Republican nomination. But eventually, Pushaw and her followers would also take the lead in attacking Trump and waging endless social media wars with his online supporters, most of whom were basically mirror images of the DeSantis troll army—only with a different boss to promote.

But before that social media DeSantis-Trump influencer clash, the DeSantis stans had to meet their new obsession, a moment that came during the January 2022 night in Tallahassee. The collection of Florida-centric influencers descending on the state's capital city is a good example of what the communications landscape looks like post-Pushaw. As I wrote for POLITICO in January of 2022, DeSantis was courting these social media types at the same time as his stock rose within the Republican Party—which turned out to be a shrewd decision in his burgeoning shadow war with Trump.

"Many conservative media stars, most of whom have long been some of Trump's most vocal supporters, have been hyping DeSantis in recent months for the governor's rejection of Covid-related mandates and constant hammering of President Joe Biden," I wrote at the time. "But the support has increased in intensity in recent weeks, a spike easily noticeable on social media and podcasts throughout the social media ecosystem."

The story wasn't particularly negative, and in a past political era, it may even have been well received by politicians eager to drum up publicity. But in the chaos-filled world of Christina Pushaw, the story was a clear slight, and it required a response. In this case, she and her online supporters concocted the idea that I wrote the story because I had not been invited to the dinner at the governor's mansion.

To be clear, I find few things on earth as distasteful as the idea of sitting through a dinner trying to make small talk with people who openly profess to hate me. The notion that I had written the article because I felt slighted by my lack of an invitation was absurd—but as is often the case these days, the absurdity is the point. Stoking outrage, no matter how detached from reality the message might be, is the endgame. It's often very effective at blowing someone up, boosting his or her social media following, and generally creating a mentally exhausting world of nonstop insults and toxicity.

"BREAKING: Politico gossip columnist's feelings are hurt, because he was not and will not be invited to dinner at the Governor's Mansion," Pushaw tweeted shortly after my story was published.

I politely responded that it had been "meat loaf night" at my house, which I would not have missed for the world. That did not seem to dissuade the army of Pushaw trolls from filling my timeline for a day or so, making fun of me for not being invited to the dinner. Months later, and a long time after I had stopped thinking about the dinner, the tweet, or the meat loaf, Pushaw drummed up the same attack, implying I was still hurt by an event that had, in fact, not crossed my mind for months.

"Matt is still mad that he wasn't invited to the Governor's Mansion for dinner that one time and nobody who was at the dinner would return his creepy texts," Pushaw tweeted in May of 2022. "Neither Politico nor Florida politics has inside sources in @GovRonDeSantis office so they resort to trolling like this."

Pushaw's decision to reengage with me over the mansion dinner was in response to a tweet I had sent that had nothing to do with that event. I had drawn attention to a story written by then *Florida Politics* reporter Scott Powers about Pushaw's implying on Twitter that a neo-Nazi rally featuring DeSantis Country flags outside Disney

World was not just fake but also a creation of Daniel Uhlfelder, a Jewish attorney and then Democratic candidate for attorney general.

Her tweet drew attention to a story about Nazis that was not great for her or her boss—a frequent unintended consequence of the actions of extremist influencers. In leveling her unfounded accusation, she'd given much more air to a story that painted DeSantis in a bad light, giving his opponents an opportunity to frame him as someone who does not denounce Nazis.

As it happens, Pushaw eventually flew too close to the sun.

In August of 2022, she took to Twitter to hype a press conference set to take place the following day, promising it would prompt the "liberal media meltdown of the year." This press conference turned out to be about DeSantis's suspension of Hillsborough County state attorney Andrew Warren, whose offense was pledging not to enforce the state's new fifteen-week abortion ban and who would eventually sue DeSantis over the move.

Additional records and testimony as part of that lawsuit show that DeSantis was not pleased with Pushaw's tweet. Turns out he didn't want his team hyping the suspension of a two-time elected prosecutor as if it were a monster truck rally. The private attorney representing DeSantis, George Levesque, told the court that Pushaw had been taken to the "proverbial woodshed" over the tweet. DeSantis's communications director, Taryn Fenske, also testified that DeSantis was "very stern" with Pushaw over her actions. Just over a week after the initial tweet, Pushaw had resigned and was assigned to the position of rapid response director on DeSantis's reelection campaign.

Pushaw, though, never really lost her clout in the DeSantis orbit at that time. Her prioritization of "owning the libs" above all else made her a star with conservatives. Post-MAGA Republicans now see Republicans of a past era who still engage with the media in any nonhostile fashion as traitors of sorts for continuing to engage with an institution they view as the enemy.

"Nation's most based comms director, @ChristinaPushaw, lays out the path forward: cut off the mainstream press and treat them as the enemy they are," tweeted Matthew J. Peterson, a fellow at the Claremont Institute, a conservative think tank that believes there is a civil war brewing over the cultural future of the country. "They need access for credibility. Remove it. Only grant access to whoever covers fairly. Raise up new media figures/ecosystem."

His tweets came as Pushaw spoke at the National Conservatism Conference, which in August of 2022 was held in Miami. "Second main @ChristinaPushaw point: If you're explaining, you're losing. When mainstream media makes bad faith attacks, don't defend yourself—attack them."

Despite her title change, Pushaw was at that point never ousted from her role as chief attack dog. Her legacy lived on: DeSantis's communications strategy throughout his 2022 reelection campaign was often Pushaw-esque, consisting of attacks on members of the media and other supposed enemies as much as attacks on his true opponents—Charlie Crist and the rest of the Democrats on the ballot.

Following Pushaw into DeSantis's world is to encounter a web of startup conservative media sites best known for publishing flattering puff pieces about the governor under the guise of being the true "fair" press. They also use their websites to attack opponents of DeSantis, whom they dub the legacy media, an apparently derogatory term they apply to established mainstream organizations.

Leading the charge in this new wave of far-right press is the *Florida Standard,* an online news platform whose editor in chief, Will Witt, says he dropped out of the University of Colorado at Boulder after "personally experiencing the left's relentless indoctrination." He rose through the right-wing media ranks as a video producer at PragerU, an advocacy group cofounded by conservative radio host Dennis Prager.

The second mainstay of the post-Pushaw media is *Florida's Voice,* a self-proclaimed digital news network led by Brendon Leslie, a political commentator who admitted to breaching the Capitol on January 6 and who once interviewed DeSantis while wearing a shirt bearing the insignia of the Three Percenters, a far-right antigovernment group that disbanded after the Capitol insurrection. He later told the *Huffington Post* that he was unaware the logo was connected to the group.

"The shirt is really cool and badass and I don't care what you or any liberal journalist think," he said.

Both the *Florida Standard* and *Florida's Voice* have similar origin stories centered on the supposedly "liberal activist" traditional media and the need to step forward with the "truth." No one exactly knows who funds either organization, but there is a tacit acknowledgment that they were initially bankrolled by Republican donors, fully supportive of DeSantis, who wanted to create an alternative to what they saw as unfair treatment by Florida political media outlets.

Specifically, they wanted to defend DeSantis against *Florida Politics,* a St. Petersburg–based website that has become the biggest political media outlet in Florida. The site employs dozens of reporters throughout the state, often those recently laid off by traditional media outlets, but its publisher, Peter Schorsch, has espoused very public anti-DeSantis positions. He takes to social media to offer opinions that increasingly align with those of the Democrats. A former Republican political direct-mail vendor, Schorsch notes he has likely done more to get Republicans elected in Florida than Pushaw ever has; in recent years, though, he has exhibited a progressive-leaning public persona and has since been involved in numerous online spats with Pushaw.

There had long been talk within DeSantis's camp about a need for a corrective to Schorsch. It's into that void that the *Florida Standard* and *Florida's Voice* have stepped.

"Peter Schorsch is a smart guy, and he has worked tirelessly to build a very powerful platform," said Florida Republican lobbyist Slater Bayliss, a longtime DeSantis supporter. "He has detractors, and some feel he has weaponized his enterprise. To borrow from the old adage about not getting into fights with people who buy ink by the barrel, the majority of Adams Street has found ways to get along with Peter."

For years, truces such as these have been a default setting in media-government relations. Schorsch had often faced criticism for some elements of his enterprise perceived as pay-to-play, but as traditional media pulled resources out of the Florida capitol, he filled in the gaps, gaining influence in the process. DeSantis's world, however, was anything but amenable to the approaches that have long defined politics in the Sunshine State. There quickly became an overwhelming sense among Florida political observers that supporters of the governor were bankrolling far-right DeSantis cheerleaders as a sort of antidote to *Florida Politics*.

"Some in the governor's orbit do not see *Florida Politics* as news; they see it as a gossip instrument run by a gangster that leans left and extorts those in Tallahassee in the process," said a veteran Florida Republican consultant. "The prevailing theory is that the financial backing of the *Florida Standard* [comes from] interests who have problems with Peter and *Florida Politics* and are looking to curry favor with the DeSantis administration."

Schorsch said that he was told directly from lobbying firms close to DeSantis's office that the governor was actively trying to undercut *Florida Politics'* advertising revenue.

"I was made aware by several lobbying firms who advertised on *Florida Politics* that the Governor's Office was purposefully and specifically attempting to undercut our operations by urging them to cease advertising with us and instead spend that money on *Florida Standard*," Schorsch told me. "Governor's Office staff also worked with the *Standard* to develop content that mimicked some of the insider-y content we provide, such as the top lobbyist rankings."

There are few clearer examples of this dynamic than an August 2022 interview with Witt, editor in chief of the *Florida Standard*, conducted just weeks after the outlet's website launched. The interview, which was held in the governor's office, focused on DeSantis's "battles with leftist media" and "woke capital," and Witt asked DeSantis why he would not go on *The View* "and other leftist talk shows."

Witt also turned out to be quite the augur. Among his first questions to DeSantis was, "Why is the blueprint for Florida so successful?" The framing aligned perfectly with the title of DeSantis's second book, *The Courage to be Free: Florida's Blueprint for America's Revival,* which was released in February of 2023. The book debuted at number 1 on the *New York Times* hardcover nonfiction bestseller list and was promoted with a national book tour that resembled a series of political rallies, only further intensifying the already fervent speculation that DeSantis was running for president. (The book appeared on the *Times* bestseller list with a dagger sign next to it, a mark the paper puts alongside books for which "some bookstores report receiving bulk orders." Political authors' campaign funds and even the RNC have been known to place the bulk purchases that can get conservative authors' books onto the bestseller list.) DeSantis's massive book sales would go on to enrage Trump, who was insecure about DeSantis's potentially selling more books than he did. He took to Truth Social to call reports of massive sales "FAKE NEWS" and accused DeSantis of orchestrating bulk buys, which he did but which is common practice among politicians who write books.

The Witt interview that previewed the title of the DeSantis book was filled with fawning comments and softball questions, at one point professing that the people knew DeSantis was "working for them." In his lead-up to the next question, he went on to say, "Something that I think is important is that in terms of the office you hold as governor of the state, you're not afraid to use that office to get things done for the citizens of the state of Florida."

Each groveling line was more debasing than the next for someone who calls himself a journalist. Later in the interview, in the perfect cherry on top of the irony sundae, DeSantis noted that he was disdainful of traditional media outlets because they were "dedicated to partisan narratives."

By early 2023, Witt would be a regular keynote speaker at Republican Party events across the country.

Florida is on the leading edge of what longtime Republican adman turned Never Trumper Rick Wilson calls "the Republican hamster wheel."

Wilson is a cofounder of the Lincoln Project, the group that is notoriously anti-Trump. It has expanded its reach and now goes after other Republicans it sees as following in Trump's footsteps, including DeSantis. Wilson, notably, helped create early versions of the "hermetically sealed" Republican media ecosystem—something he now says he regrets.

"The Republican hamster wheel is this: you say something cruel, conspiratorial, or crazy. And instead of being punished for it politically, Fox News says, 'Come on *Tucker* tonight. Come on Sean or Laura or *Fox & Friends* and tell us how the libs are canceling you,'" Wilson said, naming a handful of prominent network hosts and shows.

"DeSantis has gotten very adept at using the system that rewards anger or craziness," he continued. "He would go on *Tucker* and say, 'The libs are trying to cancel me for saying we should eat live babies.' Then he sends an email to raise money that says, 'Did you see me on *Tucker*? I defended our right...to eat live babies.'

"Rinse, repeat. That's the Republican hamster wheel," he added.

Some conservative Republicans have been critical of this new functionally sealed media bubble. This reflects the opinion held by some on the right that their candidates should have center-right media coverage that keeps them in line and philosophically pure. If politicians are not pushing for further abortion restrictions, for example, there should be a press that calls them out on that, the theory holds.

"That is what has annoyed me. We need honest conservative journalism," said former Florida representative Anthony Sabatini, one of the first Florida Republicans to openly support Trump over DeSantis. "When you're not holding anyone's feet to the fire, I think you're contributing to the problem. Honest criticism could make our positions stronger."

For many reporters, the rapid shift in tone and strategy largely popularized by Pushaw was a shock to the system because the temperature was never turned down.

Trump popularized the term *fake news* and had a notorious rivalry with the press, but DeSantis built on that toxicity and took it to a new level. The natural layer of tension that often exists between media and communications handlers has always been there, but for the most part, past administrations and campaigns kept it to a point of natural civility: we could yell at each other on the phone, then go get a beer after work. But as it became clear that the new reality was one of genuine dislike rather than professional tension, the onslaught of daily attacks became mere background noise for many: although being under constant attack for simply doing your job isn't fun, the DeSantis team's insistence on swinging at every pitch and bringing unhinged fury to every encounter has, paradoxically, made it all that much easier to ignore. If you know you are going to get tossed into a troll tornado no matter what you report, there is little reason to get defensive or excited when it happens. Ultimately, the constant noise had a dulling effect on people in my line of work.

Few have been better at highlighting this shift in communications strategy than Mac Stipanovich, a longtime Republican consultant and lobbyist who in a past life was chief of staff to former Republican Florida governor Bob Martinez. He was among the first wave of Republicans to become Never Trump and has now become a vocal critic of DeSantis, whom he not so affectionately refers to as Tater; to continue the theme, he refers to DeSantis's communications staffers as Tater Tots.

When Pushaw was sent to DeSantis's reelection campaign, in August of 2022, Stipanovich wrote a goodbye letter of sorts in

Florida Politics. In it, he framed Pushaw's move from press secretary in the governor's office to rapid response director on the campaign as a demotion. And on paper, it certainly seemed that way, but even as she was sent to the campaign world, she still was held in exceptionally high regard by Ron and Casey DeSantis, which was all that really mattered. This was beside Stipanovich's point, however; the purpose of the letter, after all, was to get under Pushaw's skin. And in that regard, Mac, whose nickname is Mac the Knife, was successful.

"Pushaw tried (wo)manfully to put the best face on a bad business, tweeting, 'now the gloves are off,' as if she is now free to call Nancy Pelosi a communist, Joe Biden senile, public school teachers groomers, and the FBI the Cheka (Bolshevik secret police), all of which—and more and worse—she said while working in the Governor's Office," he wrote.

He continued, "There were no gloves. In fact, it was her rapid, rabid, abusive, and unprofessional responses that made her the darling of right-wing media, or at least that very online niche of right-wing media of which normal people are blissfully unaware. And that success was her undoing.

"She got too big for her britches, too full of herself, and down to earth she plummeted, like Icarus, who also flew too close to the sun," he concluded.

DeSantis has long needed help on the communications side to make palatable his standard demeanor—one that can best be described as perpetually visibly annoyed—and to gloss over his inability to forge true bonds with most people. It's been an interesting defining feature for him as he has become a national-level politician, a status that generally requires the gift of gab or, at the very least, some measure of charm. By contrast, DeSantis's style of communication is blunt and direct, and he struggles to soften his tone when the moment calls for a light touch or simple empathy.

"His ego is off the charts, and I think that can get in the way of him being able to connect," said a former administration staffer.

Whether that would be a deal-breaker for voters outside Florida, only time would tell.

PART III

FLAME WAR

CHAPTER THIRTEEN

IT ALL FALLS APART

A head of the all-out Trump-versus-DeSantis battle, there remained an odd bit of asymmetrical warfare. Throughout DeSantis's 2022 reelection, which was never really in doubt, Trump took shots at the Florida governor, giving crystal-clear signals that DeSantis was no longer his favorite political son. But DeSantis, in a move that would soon become all too familiar, refused to really punch back.

DeSantis went on to steamroll Democratic opponent Charlie Crist by nearly twenty percentage points, a result that shocked the political world. Throughout that race, there was a clear sense that DeSantis had bigger aspirations, and that was not lost on Trump and his team, who, while not yet in full attack mode, were closely watching DeSantis put his stamp of dominance on Florida and continue to cement himself as the governor most beloved by conservatives across the country.

The Trump-DeSantis fight was not yet exactly a headline-grabbing daily occurrence, but it was certainly not in a cease-fire. In fact, the monster win for DeSantis during the 2022 midterms only expedited what was to come.

DeSantis had become a star among the national Republican base. Much of that was a reaction to his policies rather than a consequence of the active fueling of presidential speculation on the part of his close-knit political operation—except for the occasional out-of-state fundraiser that got national media coverage. The sideline sitting ended as the 2022 midterms heated up and DeSantis, unburdened by any concern that he could lose his reelection bid to Crist, held rallies across the country for party-backed gubernatorial and US Senate candidates in key states.

In August, he led rallies for Arizona Senate candidate Blake Masters, Arizona gubernatorial candidate Kari Lake, Pennsylvania gubernatorial candidate Doug Mastriano, and Ohio Senate candidate J. D. Vance. In September, he traveled to Wisconsin to rally for the GOP gubernatorial nominee, Tim Michels, a trip that also brought him to Lambeau Field for a Green Bay Packers–Chicago Bears game I also happened to attend. (I tweeted a picture of myself welcoming DeSantis to Lambeau, but in a stunning show of reticence, the governor's team did not reach out to me.) Then in October, DeSantis held a rally for New York Republican gubernatorial candidate Lee Zeldin, a trip that underscored the dual nature of his budding national efforts: he, of course, wanted each candidate he was stumping for to win (none did), but it was also an effort to build a national network that he hoped would be with him in the future, even if that landed him in a prolonged battle with Trump, who had also endorsed and rallied for most of the same candidates.

The October trip in particular underscored this dynamic. Before leaving, DeSantis quietly huddled with the then New York State Republican Committee chairman, Nick Langworthy, on the tarmac. Langworthy was a longtime Trump devotee, and he had been endorsed by the former president in his successful 2022 midterm bid for Congress. To this day, Langworthy has never backed down from his public support of Trump, even as he signaled that he was meeting with DeSantis.

"Those are the sort of things [DeSantis] is doing to start building a broader network," said a DeSantis adviser. "Not sure there are others really doing it to the same degree."

Because most frontline Republican candidates lost in the 2022 midterm red wave that never materialized (except, of course, in Florida), questions emerged about the influence of Trump's endorsement and if it could still be considered the political gold it once was. DeSantis backed all the same candidates, after all, and Democrats tried to tether him to losses in an effort to spin their own inability to defeat him. Their half-hearted postprimary battle cry largely echoed an MSNBC column that proudly proclaimed, "DeSantis Won, but DeSantis-ism Lost."

But try as the Democrats might, DeSantis was largely unaffected: most of the stink stuck to Trump, and the perception emerged that his rallies for major Republican candidates actually weighed down their tickets. It left his team on defense, trying to distance Trump from the carnage. They were quick to point out, for example, that not only did Trump raise $350 million nationally for key Republican races, he'd also given to campaigns directly, and DeSantis, while he had held rallies and helped raise money, had given none of his own.

"It's a fucking fact that Donald Trump thought we were going to get clobbered in the midterms post *Roe v. Wade,* and no pollster could tell him different," said a Trump adviser heavily involved in the 2022 midterms. "[But] he does not regret getting involved, and I would say this: Where the fuck was Ron? He just followed Trump to a couple of states and sat on $60 million. He was also one-quarter of [the Republican Governors Association's] expenditures when he didn't need a dime of help and we were getting wiped out in a lot of governor's races."

At this point, the angst felt by Trump and his team was very real; DeSantis was being painted by national conservatives, including those who formally supported him, as the great GOP savior, while Trump was seen as a meddling former president who had tanked key Republican Senate campaigns. It was also the moment when Trump's view of DeSantis evolved from annoyance to open hostility. The first time it was put on a huge public stage was during a Trump rally in Pennsylvania just before election day.

"There it is, Trump at 71 [percent]," Trump said during a late election-cycle rally in Pennsylvania while standing in front of a screen showing 2024 primary projections. "Ron DeSanctimonious at 10 percent. Mike Pence at 7; oh, Mike Pence [is] doing better than I thought."

As designed, the new Trump nickname and biggest overt attack to date immediately lit social media and the political news cycle on fire as people began to assume that open warfare—at least in one direction—was about to break out. The following day, Trump was set to hold a rally near Miami for Marco Rubio, so the expectation was high that Trump would stroll onstage in DeSantis's home state and trash his onetime political protégé. As it turned out, however, the ex-president took a break from flamethrowing for at least one day. He did so for an odd reason: he was following the counsel of his legendary "dirty trickster," Roger Stone.

Trump wanted to hammer DeSantis, even as staff and top advisers told him it was a bad idea, especially in Florida. The planning of the event itself had already stoked Trump-DeSantis intrigue because the governor was not invited, a perceived snub that spun off its own version of rivalry stories, especially because DeSantis had decided to hold his own set of competing rallies on the same day. The Trump camp did not technically say DeSantis could not come, but they hadn't invited him, either. Alex Latcham, who served as White House deputy political director during Trump's time in office and who currently works for his campaign, called Helen Aguirre Ferré, who was by then executive director of the Florida GOP, to invite all statewide elected officials to the event.

"He did not say Marco; he did not say Rick; he did not say Ron. He said, 'Every statewide elected official,'" recalled a Trump adviser familiar with the planning. "I mean, we did not issue him a personal invitation like we did with Rick and Marco, but he was not *not* invited."

As Trump's speaking slot approached, his advisers urged him not to take the stage and hit DeSantis for a second night in a row; some of Florida's biggest-name Republicans were in attendance and set to speak, and it would have put them in an awkward position. If they took the stage against the backdrop of what felt like an anti-DeSantis rally, it would have made things much more difficult between them and their home-state governor, who at that point was well known for having a vindictive streak. This group included Joe Gruters, state senator and chairman of the statewide Republican Party—who had picked Trump's rally over those held by DeSantis—and Rick Scott, who had also long favored Trump over DeSantis.

Gruters and DeSantis have a notoriously icy relationship, and the senator has long been a huge Trump ally. As chairman of the Republican Party of Sarasota County, Gruters gave Trump two "statesman of the year" awards and cochaired Trump's 2016 Florida campaign. Gruters was such a backer of Trump that, in 2015, he'd swallowed his pride to defend Trump in television interviews in the wake of his controversial comments about Arizona senator John McCain. ("He's not a war hero," Trump had said, to boos from the audience. "He was a war hero because he was captured. I like people who weren't captured.")

Gruters had not wanted to defend the comment because he considered it disrespectful to veterans. Corey Lewandowski, then Trump's campaign manager, was unhappy with the decision and asked Joe a simple question: "Are you on the team or not?"

Gruters did the interview.

Gruters's allegiance to Trump over DeSantis is well known, but Trump's staff thought picking a fight with DeSantis onstage would overshadow the others at the event, including Marco Rubio and Rick Scott. They worried that if the president continued picking fights, they, too, would be pulled into the battle.

The advisers, though, had not yet convinced Trump of this. They tried negotiating with him and asked what they could do, and finally Trump said, "Find me someone with the balls to convince me not to do it."

They turned to Roger Stone, the veteran political dirty trickster and longtime close adviser to Trump, who was in attendance at the event.

"He sought a lot of counsel about whether or not to attack Ron that night, and for a while it felt like it was a fifty-fifty proposition," said a Trump adviser. "We sent some folks out to find Roger, and they did. What he told President Trump was that 'now is not the time,' and he listened."

The idea of Stone talking any politician, much less Trump, out of a political knife fight might seem surprising considering that he is among history's most pugilistic political advisers—and considering his infamous hatred of DeSantis. But on that night, Stone represented the voice of reason.

"At the end of the day, [Stone] loves President Trump more than he hates Ron DeSantis," the adviser said.

Stone's role as the voice of reason in Trump's ear would not last. I had a chance to see his calming influence evaporate firsthand while I was sitting in a corner of the bustling Caffe Europa in downtown Fort Lauderdale. As I walked in, Stone was sitting by himself, scrolling through his phone. He was dressed in a perfectly tailored suit adorned with a matching pocket square. He was overdressed for the venue, but I would expect nothing less.

I had flown down from Tallahassee to meet with the veteran of many political wars just after the 2022 midterms, which DeSantis won in dominating fashion—fueling the narrative that the Republican Party had moved on from Trump, someone for whom Stone had served as a close adviser. The two had a longtime association, one that made headlines in late 2020 when Trump issued a presidential pardon on Stone's behalf. Stone had been sentenced to forty months in prison for lying to Congress and threatening a witness during special counsel Robert Mueller's investigation into Russian interference in the 2016 election. (Stone called the charges "bullshit" and insisted that the whole thing was a Democrat-orchestrated setup.)

Stone had long been an anti-DeSantis voice in the party, even before DeSantis's rivalry with Trump had bubbled to the surface. During the 2018 gubernatorial primary, Stone's self-described protégé, Everett Wilkinson, a conservative activist, ran a dark-money group that spent more than $700,000 on ads hammering DeSantis over his association with Kent Stermon, the defense contractor whose company had lobbied Congress and was among DeSantis's biggest donors—and whose condo DeSantis was renting.

The Stone-connected attack ads called DeSantis a "swamp creature" and tried to paint him as a political insider, a label contrary to the narrative he ran on. It's unclear who precisely funded the ads, but one of Stone's biggest clients is U.S. Sugar, a political powerhouse that has long feuded with DeSantis and whose positions have long been backed by Wilkinson. DeSantis's campaign also blamed the sugar industry for the ads.

Stone continued to take shots at DeSantis long after the 2018 race ended. In October of 2022, he piled on to Trump World's growing narrative about DeSantis, saying that rushing into a challenge of Trump in 2024 "would be the most stunning act of ingratitude and treachery in the history of American politics."

Through the years, Stone remained a close Trump adviser. Besides talking Trump out of attacking DeSantis at the Miami rally, he was also among the people Trump called after news broke that he had dined with Nick Fuentes, a white nationalist and Holocaust denier and longtime friend of Kanye West. At the dinner, things got heated after Ye said he was considering running for president and that Trump should be his running mate, something that angered the former president, NBC News reported at the time.

Trump said after the dinner that he did not know who Fuentes was. The damage, however, had been done, and waves of Republicans denounced Fuentes and the dinner, which took place just days ahead of Thanksgiving in 2022.

"He called me after the Kanye thing, and I asked him, 'Why did you meet with this guy?'" Stone recalled. "Trump said, 'He is very popular with the Blacks. When he supported me, he helped me a lot with the Blacks.'"

"Did you know he is talking about running for president?" Stone asked on the call.

"I didn't know that," Trump responded.

Trump told Stone that Ye had never been to Mar-a-Lago, and when they'd finally arranged to meet, Ye had shown up with Fuentes and asked if he could join.

"What am I going to say—no?" Trump said to Stone.

Stone has long been an unquestioned Trump foot soldier and would do anything to help him, but there also exists a distinct strand of DeSantis hatred that is a part of his DNA and has nothing to do with his advisee.

Over pizza and chicken Parmesan at the downtown Fort Lauderdale eatery, Stone told me that he had already been thinking about how to best frame messaging against DeSantis if he ran for president—a venture the governor has since officially announced.

"Ron, why do you want to shift billions of dollars to Ukraine when we are not sealing our own southern border?" said Stone, at that point growing animated and flashing his well-known underbite as he previewed potential attack lines against DeSantis.

Ukraine had become a foreign policy litmus test for America First Trump supporters, who opposed the Biden administration's sending billions of dollars to the war-torn nation. DeSantis had condemned the invasion but at that point had only spoken about it a handful of times, blaming Putin's aggression on Biden's "weakness." Nonetheless, Stone thought using the issue was the approach Trump should take as the battle for the heart of the Republican base started to take shape.

"Why are you trying to get us into World War III?" Stone asked, continuing his pseudorehearsal. "You are with all these guys who want to ship billions to Ukraine. We have hungry and homeless veterans on the street."

It was a snapshot of what the next logical progression would be in the fight for the heart of the Republican Party. In the aftermath of the 2022 midterms, the fast-approaching 2024 Republican primary was largely seen as a two-person race, and for good reason: Trump remained a commanding presence in the party and still had a stranglehold on a large percentage of the Republican base, some of whom, it seems, would not abandon Trump under any circumstances.

Undeniably, however, there was a sort of "Trump fatigue" settling in over large swaths of the party. For many, Trump had consistently introduced so much chaos and distraction—not the least of which were his endless legal fights and the pall of the January 6 investigation—that many were ready to move on. As the fight came into national view, DeSantis was framed as a sort of Trump lite: some Republicans hoped he would usher in many of the policies lauded by Trump supporters while being less of a quasi-authoritarian figure. And despite Floridian Democrats' attempts to counter this digestible framing of DeSantis, the narrative began to take hold.

Trump, of course, received a shot of momentum in August of 2022 after the FBI's infamous search for classified documents at Mar-a-Lago. This wave of support brought those growing tired of Trump back into his corner, including potential 2024 rivals such as the Virginia governor, Glenn Youngkin; the South Dakota governor, Kristi Noem; and, momentarily, DeSantis himself.

"I had gotten calls from people last night that were getting kind of tired of Trump, not so much [that] they wanted to move on from him but more that they were sick of the drama," Shiree Verdone, cochair of both Trump's Arizona campaigns, told me at the time. "Well, that's over. Just talking to people now, they are irate, and they are ready to support Trump."

As jockeying for Republican support began ahead of the 2024 presidential election cycle, some self-inflicted wounds hindered Trump's search for early momentum. Many Republicans were initially turned off by the former president's attacks on other prominent

Republicans, including DeSantis and Youngkin, who faced his own direct criticism from Trump in November of 2022.

"I mean, I just think some of the conversations he has had since the election kind of concern some people, you know?" said Steve Scheffler, a veteran Iowa Republican organizer and a member of the Republican National Committee, referring to the attacks Trump launched on fellow elected Republicans, including DeSantis.

In gauging how Republicans in the early primary states view a potential Trump matchup with DeSantis, Scheffler also said that Trump's preoccupation with overturning the 2020 election has hurt him with all but his most intense supporters. He points out that the issue has not played well in his state, whose caucus is the first 2024 primary contest.

"I'll be real honest with you: some of our leading people here in Iowa, like [Governor] Kim Reynolds and Chuck Grassley, got the Trump endorsement, but they did not spend any real time talking about a perceived or real stolen election," Scheffler said. "They centered their message on their accomplishments and what they wanted to do. And when you look across the country more broadly, a lot of Republicans who were successful did not spend a lot of time talking about [a potentially stolen election].

"Conservative Republican activists understand there were some shenanigans that went on, [but] whether it was enough to change an election, I don't know for sure," he added. "But when you exclusively talk about that, I think a lot of people that you need in the middle become kind of wary and turned off."

Trump not only refused to shy away from the topic, he also leaned into it in ways that were more intense than ever. Weeks after he announced his 2024 bid for president, he took to Truth Social not only to double down on his claims that the 2020 election was stolen but also to claim that the US Constitution could be "terminated" to again install him as president.

"A Massive Fraud of this type and magnitude allows for the termination of all rules, regulations, and articles, even those found in the Constitution," he wrote. "Our great 'Founder' did not want, and would not condone, False & Fraudulent Elections."

His campaign's opening message was, in short, that the country should throw out the Constitution, a document revered by most conservatives. Trump was saying out loud that he would consider getting rid of the Constitution and using it as a key messaging point early in his campaign. It was that kind of talk that, at the time, was starting to turn off Republican voters who were crucial to having success in early primary contests and who wanted to hear more about conservative policies and less about election conspiracies.

Trump continued to hammer on the unfounded claims of a stolen election in stump speeches throughout the early stages of the 2024 election cycle. It remained a popular talking point that delighted his MAGA followers but was largely ignored by other Republicans, including DeSantis and others seeking the presidential nomination.

"It's got to be about issues," the South Carolina GOP chairman, Drew McKissick, said when I asked him in late 2022 about Trump's aggressive posture. "The more that candidates focus on issues, which are what Republicans in South Carolina care about, the more success they will have."

He pointed to a sign in his office that contained a quotation from Lee Atwater, a legendary GOP consultant who served as an adviser to both Ronald Reagan and George H. W. Bush.

Issues Win Campaigns, the sign read.

"It was true then, and it's true now," McKissick said.

Speculation about how a Trump-DeSantis showdown would play out defined the early stages of the 2024 primary race. Did Trump still control enough of the Republican base to fend off an ascendant DeSantis? Could DeSantis withstand the type of Trump World attacks that at that point he had yet to face? Could DeSantis perform in early primary states that require him to talk to individual donors and display a degree of down-home charm that seemed incompatible with his personality? And could Trump persuade the donors flocking to DeSantis's campaign to return to his side?

"If Ron winds up in a primary against Trump, there will almost likely be a civil war in the party," said Blaise Ingoglia, the state senator and former chair of the Republican Party of Florida. "We are already seeing some of that playing out in pockets throughout the state here. The challenge will be to get everyone on the same page for a general election."

He pointed to the 2022 primary challenge that veteran GOP congressman Dan Webster faced from Laura Loomer, a Stone-endorsed far-right agitator and self-described "proud Islamophobe." Webster won, but by a much narrower margin than expected, which was seen as a slight win for Trump-aligned forces in Florida.

The DeSantis-side optimism was at an early peak after the governor not only won his reelection by nearly twenty points but also led a Republican Party in one of the country's most diverse swing states. The victory gave his team the ammunition to frame DeSantis as someone who could win for the party in any state. It also gave them license to intensify their message to Republican donors, many of whom had already started straying from Trump.

"It was a referendum on what he did for the first four years as governor," said Scott Parkinson, who served as DeSantis's chief of staff when he was in Congress. "He always talked about building a bold agenda, and that was the mission of his 2018 campaign and transition. He delivered, and voters noticed."

After 2020, Parkinson continued, you could already see Trump's coalition shrinking a bit. This was a dynamic that hurt him in states that were key to his 2016 win, states that were of increasing importance to a Democratic Party that had largely turned away from Florida.

"I think for a lot of voters, DeSantis is appealing from more of an establishment Republican posture," said Parkinson, who went on to be a top official at the Club for Growth before launching his 2024 bid for the US Senate in Virginia. "Trump represented the forgotten Reagan Democrat in the Rust Belt. That's why his movement did so well, but a small number of those types of voters peeled off from him in 2020. He lost Michigan and Pennsylvania and Wisconsin."

Still, Trump remained a towering figure over the party, someone with a natural ability to take all the air out of the room. It's a challenge that DeSantis, who has largely operated within a right-wing echo chamber, has not yet faced. The overarching question remained: Would DeSantis fold under that level of pressure?

"The DeSantis guys are not ready for it," said Rick Wilson, a cofounder of the Lincoln Project, which opposes both Trump and DeSantis. "I'll loop back to the Florida debate. I promise you, Trump, with his feral cunning, was watching that debate, and when he saw Charlie Crist, who he views as weak and incompetent, get shots in, Trump knew right then he could take DeSantis."

One exchange in particular caught DeSantis off guard, or so it appeared. Crist had been using DeSantis's perceived presidential ambitions against him throughout the gubernatorial election, telling voters he was simply using the governor's mansion as a stepping stone for broader ambitions. During one exchange, Crist asked DeSantis to "look in the eyes of the people of the state of Florida and say to them, if you're reelected, you will serve a full four-year term." DeSantis did not give an answer, and an awkward silence ensued.

"I know how this is going to play out, and it does not go well for DeSantis," said Wilson, who has built a national reputation as a leading anti-Trump voice but who does not think DeSantis could beat him in a presidential primary. "Trump will just hit him with some nickname, call him Fat Little Ronnie or whatever, and he is not prepared for what it will do to him psychologically or what it will do to him in the Fox News ecosystem. The minute Ron DeSantis files, he will immediately become the number one Never Trump candidate in the country.

"He will get destroyed, and I don't think it's close," Wilson finished. "In the worst-case scenario, Trump still holds 15 percent of the vote in every early primary contest. And do you know what that means with a large field? Trump is the fucking nominee, that's what that means."

For months, DeSantis supporters did not think Trump's aggressive tactics against the Florida governor were smart or sustainable. Even as DeSantis built a reputation for being surly and fighting every battle, they sat on the sidelines. This was an intentional move.

"Governor DeSantis does not pay much attention to former president Trump's empty cannons of rhetoric," said Slater Bayliss, the veteran Florida lobbyist who advised and helped raise money for DeSantis's campaign, in April of 2023. "I expect you will see a long-haul approach. I anticipate the governor will…bait the former president [so he can] keep swinging at him until Trump has exhausted himself and primary voters are equally as fatigued."

Even after months of speculation and direct attacks from Trump, DeSantis advisers were insistent that the governor had not only refrained from talking about or addressing Trump in public but had also ignored the topic behind the scenes.

Be that as it may, the issue of DeSantis's seemingly inevitable collision course with Trump had been on the minds of Republican donors for months leading up to the 2022 midterms. DeSantis's reelection campaign raised more than $200 million, the most of any gubernatorial candidate in the history of the country, a number that included millions contributed directly by Trump donors—which some observers saw as a sign of eroded support for the former president. Although Trump continued to control a sizable chunk of the party's grassroots base, by the end of 2022, there was a clear sense that he no longer held sway with the monied bloc that helps fund messaging and voter outreach.

"I can't offer names because I don't want to get anyone in trouble with Trump," said a DeSantis adviser who openly acknowledged that beating Trump won't be a "cakewalk" and that donors might need to come crawling back to the ex-president. "I would say that, at this point, nine out of ten major donors want Ron DeSantis over Donald Trump. Trump would be a one-term president, [a] lame duck the day he gets into office. They want someone who can at least run for reelection."

By mid-2022, there were significant GOP donors saying not just that they would support DeSantis but also that they were simply done with Trump. The most notable of them was Ken Griffin, a hedge-fund billionaire who gave more than $60 million to Republican candidates during the 2022 midterms. During a 2022 interview, Griffin, who had just moved the headquarters for his firm, Citadel, LLC, from Chicago to Miami, told my POLITICO colleague Shia Kapos that he was all in on DeSantis.

"He has a tremendous record as governor of Florida, and our country would be well served by him as president," Griffin said during the interview.

Griffin, who has given DeSantis more than $10 million over the course of his political career, said that his reason for moving on from Trump is that he wants to try to cool down some of the culture war–infused fights that eroded the relationship between the GOP and the business community. He did not address how he thought that would be accomplished under DeSantis, who had branded himself as an anticorporate crusader willing to pick fights with some of the world's largest companies, including Disney; however, he said he thought DeSantis was a much better candidate for the task. Griffin has since dropped his support for DeSantis, citing in part his focus on culture war fights.

Beyond Griffin, major Republican donors who were also quick to say they would not support Trump included Ronald Lauder, heir to the Estée Lauder fortune, who gave DeSantis $10,000 during the midterms, and Andy Sabin, a New York–based businessman who gave DeSantis nearly $60,000 for his reelection bid.

The split screen between how DeSantis and Trump carry themselves publicly gives insight into why donors who had previously opened their checkbooks for Trump were beginning to move on. The day I met with Roger Stone, DeSantis held a press conference highlighting his administration's focus on "protecting our environment" and announcing $22 million in water-quality grants for Biscayne Bay, which lies just off South Florida's Atlantic coast.

During the press conference, DeSantis brushed off questions about Trump, who had become a Florida resident. "I've also got twenty-two million [other residents], and I've got to look out for everybody," DeSantis responded.

The same day, as I was dining with Stone in the Fort Lauderdale Italian joint, Ye went on *InfoWars,* a live-streamed show hosted by conspiracy theorist Alex Jones, who had to file for bankruptcy after a court ordered him to pay $1.5 billion in damages to families after he claimed that the Sandy Hook shooting was a setup. During the broadcast, which came just after his dinner with Trump and Nick Fuentes, Ye made positive comments about Hitler that went viral.

"The Jewish media has made us feel like the Nazis and Hitler have never offered anything of value to the world," Ye said. "I see good things about Hitler also."

Moments after West made the statement, Stone went quiet as we were finishing up our roughly hour-long interview. He stared at his phone, as if in disbelief.

"Kanye just said he likes Hitler," Stone said. "That's no good."

The longtime Trump confidant stood up and said, "I've got to deal with this," then quickly left the restaurant.

"At some point we need to make America like Florida," the radio broadcast said. "It is a wildly positive night for Florida if you are of the opinion, as you and I have been for some time, that the 2024 presidential contest in the Republican Party will eventually come down to two eight-hundred-pound gorillas, Donald Trump and Ron DeSantis, throwing punches, grappling with each other, rolling around. To me this is a really good night for DeSantis and not a great night for Trump."

These were the words of Clay Travis, one of the hosts of *The Clay Travis and Buck Sexton Show,* a self-styled heir to *The Rush Limbaugh Show* and one that could rightfully claim a piece of its mantle: the program was broadcast on four hundred conservative radio stations across the nation. Travis was hosting the show the day after the 2022 midterms, which had seen Republicans falter all over the country, except in Florida. And Travis, like other right-wing media stars, liked what he saw.

The massive win by DeSantis and the idea that Trump had tanked Republicans' hopes was washing over conservative talk radio, something I was listening to on my roughly four-hour drive home to Tallahassee from Charlie Crist's election night party, an event that felt much more like a funeral for a dead Florida Democratic Party.

"If you look at Ron DeSantis, forty-four years old, the successful governor...who has turned [Florida] red, you would think he is head and shoulders above the rest when it comes to running for president," said Fox News host Brian Kilmeade on his morning national radio show, echoing nearly every conservative talking head in the country.

DeSantis's massive win in Florida was immediately seen as proof of an ascendant Republican who'd officially broken through to the American public. Already he was being viewed as the unquestioned front-runner for the 2024 presidential nomination. On top of all that, the victory offered results Republicans had long dreamed of: DeSantis had won Miami-Dade County, Florida's largest county, where the GOP had not won since 2002. He'd won Palm Beach County by three points, a shocking outcome in one of Florida's bluest counties. He'd won the Hispanic vote by fifteen points. He'd tied Crist 29–29 among female voters under thirty. He'd won 52 percent of the female vote overall and 63 percent of the male vote. And he'd not only won rural areas with nearly 70 percent of the vote, he'd also won Florida's urban areas (55 percent) and suburban areas (58 percent).

DeSantis's ability to dominate the nation's most diverse state further elevated his status with national Republicans, who quickly saw him as someone who could appeal to a much larger set of voters than Trump ever could.

"If we would have had pedestrian results commensurate with everything else in the United States, then Ron would have a less compelling case," said Florida state senator Blaise Ingoglia, a former chairman of the Republican Party of Florida. "He already had a compelling case, but winning Florida by twenty points...I mean, he won Miami-Dade. That is the stuff the Republican Party has been looking for in a leader since Ronald Reagan."

Trump's team rejected the narrative that his involvement in key 2022 Senate and gubernatorial races had sunk the GOP ticket that year, but after DeSantis's dominant performance fanned the flames of insecurity and underappreciation, Trump grew restless.

Two days after election day, he caved to his instincts, which told him to attack. He released a rambling statement of nearly five hundred words written beneath his official "Save America" letterhead.

"Ron DeSanctimonious is playing games!" Trump wrote from Mar-a-Lago. "The Fake News asks him if he's going to run if President Trump runs, and he says, 'I'm only focused on the Governor's race, I'm not looking into the future.' Well, in terms of loyalty and class, that's really not the right answer."

DeSantis did not respond in any material way to the statement. His advisers quietly told reporters he was not taking the bait, a move they acknowledge was strategic.

"Do not fire until you see the whites of their eyes," one told me of the thought process.

It's an odd departure from a governor who likes to present the persona of an alpha male, but his team of advisers saw no benefit to a counterpunch.

Trump's team, meanwhile, had not supported their candidate's statement, feeling it had not been wise to attack a sitting Republican governor on the heels of a twenty-point reelection victory.

"He had been feeling underappreciated or disrespected, whatever you want to say, for quite a while. We, as in staff, said there will be time, there will be time, there will be time," said a Trump adviser who had tried to talk the former president out of making the statement. "I think he just did not want to hear it anymore. He had just had it. Literally just had it. He said, 'This punk'—that's my word, not his, but it's what he meant. The hubris [DeSantis] has…it just got to be too much.

"There was not a staff meeting per se to talk about the statement, but he did ask a lot of people," the adviser added.

As Trump's team had expected, the statement trashing DeSantis did not sit well with many Republicans. But at that point the damage had been done, and everyone was moving forward to Trump's announcement that he was officially running in 2024, a rollout held five days later at Mar-a-Lago.

It was an event that lacked the energy or size of the huge rallies Trump often has, such as the arena event he held in Orlando to announce his reelection in 2020. The announcement about 2024 came on the heels of an election cycle in which many in his own party blamed him for their massive losses. Further, a sense of "Trump fatigue" after endless investigations and legal woes was setting in among those in the party who were not MAGA evangelists.

Trump gave a lengthy speech to a group of die-hard supporters in tuxedos and fancy dresses, but the event had a strange atmosphere, even for staunch supporters.

"I mean, it was a good night. We are back, I guess," said a Trump adviser at the announcement. "It was all the true weirdos in attendance. It was kind of like, here we go again."

As Trump kicked off his 2024 bid for the White House, by far the first in the Republican field to do so, the situational awareness of the moment was not lost on his team. And though they were trying to project the idea that Trump remained the biggest, baddest kid in the schoolyard, quietly they knew they were fighting an uphill battle.

"Those in the room were a mixture of longtime loyalists, oper-atives, and some money people, but all very loyal to the president. There were some crazies, but many were not," another Trump adviser who helped plan the event said. "Everyone had a sober view, or at least the normies [did], of where we were. President Trump is under siege; DeSantis is ascendant. All of those things are true.

"But we knew Trump could overcome that. We just have to back him up and see where the chips fall."

CHAPTER FOURTEEN

THE INEVITABILITY OF RON DESANTIS

For those within Ron DeSantis's political orbit, it did not take long to pick up signals that he was running for president. In the early stages, his intention was never overt, but for anyone with even a novice's ability to read a room, the signs were clear.

Beyond the out-of-state fundraisers, DeSantis was leaning into national issues larger than those that affect Florida, enjoying near universal praise from conservatives not on Trump's payroll and embracing culture-war issues more than he ever had before. Headed into Florida's 2023 legislative session, which was expected to serve as a runway for his presidential launch, DeSantis used press conferences to hype proposals focused on ending diversity, equity, and inclusion programs as well as gender studies at state universities. He pushed for legislation that would erode laws protecting journalists from getting sued, make it tougher for undocumented immigrants to live in Florida, and allow Floridians to carry a concealed firearm without a permit.

At DeSantis's urging, the Republican legislature also filed no fewer than eighteen bills affecting the transgender community—a community that, prior to DeSantis, it had shown little interest in. DeSantis's brand of education reform was also a major part of the GOP agenda, an initiative that included expanding the state's infamous bill limiting the teaching of sexual orientation and gender identity (the Parental Rights in Education bill to supporters and the Don't Say Gay bill to opponents); restricting school employees from referring to students by their preferred pronouns; banning gender-affirming care, even as most professional medical societies endorse such treatments; and further cracking down on drag shows, including stripping liquor licenses from bars that host them—even when undercover state investigators found no evidence of "lewd" activity during the shows.

The daily news out of Florida's state capitol was a never-ending churn of far-right policy proposals easily sailing through the legislature. The proposals spun off endless protests, heated rhetoric, and a feeling that the compliant, Republican-dominated legislature would not dare cross the governor. It was energizing for the conservative political base and was ultimately seen as a way to further excite and prepare them for what now seemed inevitable: a DeSantis run for the White House.

At the same time, the rising cost of living in Florida was increasingly coming into view. The state was plagued by property insurance companies going belly-up, leading to spiking insurance rates even as lawmakers passed DeSantis-backed reform bills (written in large part by the insurance industry). These did little to lower rates. DeSantis, though, paid no attention to the issue, struggling to incorporate it into his culture war–centered platform. Trump, meanwhile, did try to capitalize on it, labeling DeSantis as something repulsive to America First Republicans: a globalist.

"Ron DeSanctimonious is delivering the biggest insurance company BAILOUT to Globalist Insurance Companies, IN HISTORY," Trump wrote in March of 2023, just as Florida's legislative session was kicking off. "He's also crushed Florida homeowners whose houses were destroyed in the Hurricane—They're getting pennies on the dollar."

Despite his now obvious distaste for his former protégé, Trump, at times, almost overtly followed in DeSantis's policy footsteps. During a March 2023 visit to Iowa, just days after DeSantis had visited the key proving ground for presidential aspirants, Trump slammed critical race theory, a hallmark of DeSantis's standard talking points, along with transgender sports bans and "parental rights" in education, issues DeSantis had emphasized in 2022. He also endorsed candidates in more than twenty local school board races, generally sleepy campaigns that do not usually attract top-of-the-ticket attention. In other words, Trump was starting to read the room—and wrap himself in the issues that spurred DeSantis's rise in the Republican Party.

"I basically said, 'Parents you have rights,' and the place goes crazy," Trump noted of the reaction he would receive whenever he touched on these topics. "Because our country has gone crazy with this nonsense."

During his visit to Iowa, Trump continued his assault on DeSantis, comparing him to Mitt Romney, who by that time was considered a Republican in name only, or RINO, by the conservative base. He chided DeSantis for voting to cut entitlement programs while in Congress—a mind-bending history rewrite, considering that Trump's own budget proposals included similar cuts to Social Security and Medicaid.

"That didn't matter to us," said a Trump adviser when pressed on this contradiction. "He took the votes. We were first out of the gate hitting him on it."

DeSantis had made early 2023 trips to states such as Nevada and New Hampshire, which are traditionally among the first to vote in presidential primaries. That move predictably increased chatter about his forthcoming run for president, which at that point he still hadn't announced—and that chatter, in turn, was making Donald Trump very angry.

But DeSantis clearly was loath to respond to Trump's growing rancor. Trump first took a direct shot at DeSantis during the November 2022 Pennsylvania rally, which came roughly five months before the dueling Iowa visits. When asked about Trump's continued attacks, DeSantis would say he was focusing on Florida and generally not engaging.

Even DeSantis's active communications and social media team sat on their hands. They continued their petty quarrels with reporters and concentrated on DeSantis's positions on social issues that conservatives felt were culturally defining battles, but they largely did not touch Trump. It was a silence that spoke volumes for a team that had developed a well-earned reputation for attacking anyone remotely perceived as an enemy to DeSantis. But even they sat on the sidelines during what could be loosely defined as the "meatball era"—the period when reports emerged that Trump was workshopping a new nickname for DeSantis: Meatball Ron, an apparent shot at DeSantis's weight—an ironic nickname considering Trump's own rotund appearance.

Trump was insistent that he would never call the governor of Florida a meatball. The *New York Times* reports that he was doing just that were fake news, Trump insisted in a Truth Social post. Yet he seemed to delight in the fact that his commenting on the issue would likely mean that the meat-based nickname would dominate a news cycle or two.

"I will never call Ron DeSanctimonious 'Meatball' Ron, as the Fake News is insisting I will," Trump wrote in February 2023 on Truth Social. "It would be totally inappropriate to use the word 'meatball' as a moniker for Ron!"

But DeSantis did not take the bait.

"Why engage? It reminds me of the old saying, 'Never wrestle with a pig in mud, because the pig likes it,'" explained one DeSantis adviser. "It's best to ignore the silly attacks. Talking on tough policy and social issues should be the focus, and if Trump wants to try and discredit a very conservative, popular governor, so be it."

Despite DeSantis's relative reticence regarding their feud, Trump was escalating his attacks, getting attention as he regained his campaign-trail footing. But all the while, his legal woes were resurfacing.

Trump shocked the political world in mid-March of 2023 when he posted on Truth Social that he was going to be arrested the following Tuesday. This, he claimed, was related to the infamous hush-money payments he'd made to Stormy Daniels ahead of his first presidential campaign. The allegations hinged on Trump's disguising hush-money payments as legal fees paid to his former attorney and fixer, Michael Cohen, who had long since flipped on Trump and was working with prosecutors.

Without giving much detail, Trump vaguely blamed "ILLEGAL LEAKS" in his comments on his pending arrest. His campaign later said it had been given no formal indication that his predictions would come true; however, Trump was going on the offense, so the historic nature of the moment—that a former president had paid hush money to a porn star—was drowned out amid a political tizzy.

The rambling Truth Social post—in all caps, of course—is hard to quote, as many of Trump's posts are. He rarely abides by anything resembling grammatical rules, even basic sentence structure, but the basic thrust of the argument is that the "highly political" Manhattan district attorney, Alvin Bragg, was coming after him based on a "fully debunked...fairytale" and that he was expecting to be "arrested on Tuesday of next week," which was in three days' time. Trump also told his supporters to "protest, take our nation back," in a message interpreted by many as akin to the signal he'd sent to his supporters ahead of the January 6 riots at the Capitol. Trump and his allies, of course, also linked Bragg to George Soros, the billionaire Democratic donor behind many conservative conspiracy theories, because his campaign had received money from a group Soros contributed to.

Trump was, in fact, not arrested that Tuesday, but by putting a huge spotlight on his own legal woes, he had put other potential Republican nominees—including DeSantis, very likely by design—in a difficult spot.

For the first few days after the message went out, a handful of national Republicans chimed in, largely blasting the potential indictment and arrest as politically motivated, but DeSantis stayed out. This drew criticism from Trump allies, who called DeSantis out by name for his early silence on the matter. For them it was all or nothing: if Republicans didn't buy into the narrative that the investigation was a political witch hunt manufactured by progressive Soros-funded organizations, they were weak and part of the cabal looking to take down Trump.

Three days after the initial Truth Social post, with the America First sharks circling, DeSantis finally waded into the freshly chummed waters. DeSantis tried a nuanced approach. He tried to go after Soros, the nation's largest Democratic donor and Republicans' favorite political bogeyman this side of Nancy Pelosi, but he did not throw a lifeline to Trump, who at that point had been relentlessly blasting him.

"I've seen rumors swirl; I have not seen any facts yet. And so I don't know what's going to happen," DeSantis told reporters during a news conference in Panama City, Florida. "But I do know this: the Manhattan district attorney is a Soros-funded prosecutor. And so he, like other Soros-funded prosecutors...weaponize[s] [his] office to impose a political agenda on society at the expense of the rule of law and public safety."

He then restated the accusations against Trump—effectively sliding a knife into the ex-president's back.

"I don't know what goes into paying hush money to a porn star to secure silence over some type of alleged affair. I just can't speak to that," he said.

DeSantis, then, did not go all in backing Trump, but he did refrain from outright attacking him. The same could not be said for Trump himself, whose subsequent retaliation was swift and fierce.

Trump posted a picture that had previously circulated of the governor when he was a teacher at the Darlington School, a high-priced private boarding school in Rome, Georgia, with the following caption: "Ron DeSanctimonious will probably find out about FALSE ACCUSATIONS & FAKE STORIES sometime in the future, as he gets older, wiser, and better known, when he's unfairly and illegally attacked by a woman, even classmates that are 'under-age' (or possibly a man!). I'm sure he will want to fight these misfits just like I do."

Trump was referencing a conspiracy circulated by DeSantis critics who claimed that DeSantis had had inappropriate relationships with his underage students. I interviewed a few of those former students, and each said that DeSantis would party with them, but only after the school year had ended. None I spoke to remembered anything sexual in nature.

This was politics, though, where perception is reality—a principle that had no bigger adherent than Donald Trump.

Donald Trump Jr. quickly jumped into the fray, too, calling DeSantis's half-hearted defense of Trump "weak." Meanwhile, Mike Cernovich, a right-wing social media personality who had previously been supportive of DeSantis, said he "blew it."

"Ron is patting himself on the back for not responding to Trump's attacks," a Trump adviser told me the day of the back-and-forth. "This is trench warfare. Death by a thousand cuts. What is happening is [that] Ron is being defined in real time to a national audience. Get in the race and man up, or don't."

In the face of renewed vitriol, DeSantis turned to his standard tactic: silence.

On his behalf, a DeSantis adviser pointed out that the governor had just suspended Andrew Warren, the state attorney who had pledged not to prosecute cases under Florida's new fifteen-week abortion ban and whose first campaign had gotten money from the same Soros-aligned group that supported Bragg's campaign.

Time and again, DeSantis has cited his investigation into Warren, and Warren's subsequent suspension, as a key win in his battle against "wokeness." It was a particularly useful defense in that moment because Trump's team was trying to paint DeSantis as weak in the face of what they framed as a progressive prosecutor coming after him. It was hard, the DeSantis team noted, to paint the governor as soft on progressive prosecutors after he'd suspended one, even if it was done under questionable circumstances.

DeSantis's attack on Warren turned out to be a great shield from Trump's retaliatory political attacks, but the Warren investigation actually started for very little reason. In late 2021, DeSantis had asked his public safety czar, Larry Keefe, a former Trump-appointed US attorney, to see whether the state had any "reform prosecutors," meaning progressive prosecutors. After a monthslong investigation, he announced Warren's suspension in August of 2022 amid the spectacle of a press conference and flanked by law enforcement. A fifty-nine-page ruling written by US district judge Robert Hinkle later eviscerated DeSantis for suspending Warren in a move he said was blatantly in violation of the Constitution DeSantis professes to hold dear.

"Florida Governor Ron DeSantis suspended elected State Attorney Andrew H. Warren, ostensibly on the ground that Mr. Warren had blanket policies not to prosecute certain kinds of cases," read the ruling.

"The allegation was false," Hinkle wrote, in a bluntly worded rebuke to the Florida governor.

Hinkle did, however, acknowledge that the court had no authority to reverse the suspension, so even though he felt that DeSantis violated the First Amendment when suspending Warren, there was nothing he could do to overturn the order.

A federal judge telling DeSantis in very clear terms that he violated the Constitution did not prompt any introspection or consideration of a reversal of course but rather a doubling down on both the decision and his ability to essentially use Florida's executive branch to do whatever he wants. Suspending an elected law enforcement official who did not violate any laws was an odd look for a governor who has tried to cultivate an image of a Paul Revere–type figure who warns others of the dangers of creeping big government. But his supporters didn't seem to notice.

To recap, after DeSantis failed to adequately defend Trump against the risk of arrest for allegedly paying hush money to a porn star, Trump tried to make him seem weak, framing him as

pandering to the left—even after DeSantis had taken the step of suspending a progressive prosecutor, thus violating that prosecutor's
First Amendment rights, according to a federal judge.

The entire episode captured the absurdity of the moment and
foreshadowed the even greater absurdity to come.

The inevitability of Ron DeSantis was very real—until it was not.

For months after the 2022 midterms, the rumor mill churned
with speculation that DeSantis would seek—and win—the Republican presidential nomination. All the while, in many political circles,
a sort of orthodoxy was built around the idea that Ron DeSantis was
next in line for the Republican throne. The man who transformed
the nation's largest swing state into a stronghold of the GOP, they
said, was a perfect fit to be the nominee of the party that had been
remade in Trump's image. DeSantis, of course, was Trump without
the baggage, or so the narrative went.

And there was no denying that DeSantis had real momentum.
By the spring of 2023, he and Trump enjoyed roughly 80 percent of
the Republican base's support in most public polling, and DeSantis
had become the incessant target of Trump's badgering and insults,
a sure sign that the former president saw him as the only real threat
to his reelection. But as DeSantis became more engaged with the
idea of running, and as there began to emerge both super PACs and
dark-money groups with the stated goal of getting him to run for
president, it did not take long for DeSantis's carefully burnished
image to become tarnished.

The first sign of trouble in DeSantis's presidential soft launch was
his misstep on Russia's invasion of Ukraine, the two-term governor's
first real foray into the dangerous political waters of foreign policy.
In March of 2023, in a written response to questions about Ukraine

from Tucker Carlson, he stated that continued "blank check" spending to help Ukraine fight the Russian invasion was not a "vital" national security interest, downplaying the situation as a "territorial dispute." This drew rebukes from several mainstays in the Republican Party's traditional, less isolationist establishment, including Marco Rubio.

That, however, was not the end of it. The news platform *Jewish Insider* quickly published a story titled "DeSantis' Ukraine Flip Alarms Pro-Israel Republicans," a particularly tough turn for DeSantis, who ran in 2018 promising to be "America's most pro-Israel governor." Former South Carolina governor Nikki Haley, who was trying to carve out her own lane in the GOP primary field, said DeSantis was simply "copying" Trump, who had a similar position on Ukraine. However, the former president was in no mood to throw his chief political rival a lifeline and instead told reporters, disparagingly, that DeSantis was just "following what I am saying."

As a wave of criticism began to dominate news cycles, DeSantis started to feel heat from those who mattered most: his political donors.

DeSantis is by far the most prolific fundraising governor in the history of the country. During his 2022 reelection bid, he raised well over $200 million, the most by any gubernatorial candidate in history. Much of this total, furthermore, came from the pockets of former major Trump donors who had flocked to the governor after tiring of Trump's brash personal and political style. They began filling the coffers of his state-level political committee, which by the end of February in 2022 had more than $80 million in the bank—a massive number that did not include the money that was flowing into other pro-DeSantis groups.

These influential donors prompted DeSantis to do something he rarely does: backtrack.

"There were a lot of people pushing back on him," one DeSantis confidant said. "It was not just one group of people: there were people who really got in his ear and let him know that calling it a 'territorial dispute' was not the right move."

So DeSantis put on his walking shoes and went backward. In a highly publicized interview with British TV personality Piers Morgan, DeSantis said he could have made his statements "more clear," saying his "territorial dispute" comment was focused on the eastern Donbas region and Crimea, which was seized in 2014 by Russia, although the international community still recognizes Ukraine's borders.

"There's a lot of ethnic Russians there. So that's some difficult fighting, and that's what I was referring to, and so it wasn't that I thought Russia had a right to that, and so I should have made that more clear; I could have done [that]," he told Morgan.

"That was all donor-inspired," said a DeSantis adviser of the backtrack. "He got a lot of pressure from key donors, a lot of them hawks. Those were the major supporters, many of them who used to be with Trump but came over, pushing back."

The Ukraine misstep came as public polling was simultaneously showing a decline in DeSantis's momentum. The governor was supposed to be picking up speed as he headed into a potential presidential campaign, but he seemed to be slowing down instead—and he couldn't seem to stop stepping on land mines.

"Over the last two months, we've gotten about a dozen polls from pollsters who had surveyed the Republican race over the previous two months," wrote Nate Cohn, the chief political analyst at the *New York Times*'s data journalism website the Upshot, who crunched the numbers in March of 2023, at the nadir of the DeSantis dip.

"The trend is unequivocal: Every single one of these polls has shown Mr. DeSantis faring worse than before, and Mr. Trump faring better," he concluded.

Of course, public polling is not always accurate. But trend lines can be instructive nevertheless, and after a tough few months in which Trump was in all-out attack mode, all these lines were headed in the wrong direction for the governor. And despite the fact that it was still very early in the election cycle, and although DeSantis's campaign did not yet technically exist, perception is a hard thing to shake in presidential races. DeSantis was fighting the proliferating narrative that he was a dud.

His ineffectual responses to Trump's frequent withering attacks only made matters worse. His silence in the face of social media insults, rounds of new disparaging nicknames, and taunts from Trump's supporters and family made him look weak to a conservative political base that values aggression and attack. It also left Trump with a media vacuum that he filled easily. The sugar high that DeSantis experienced after his huge reelection win was over, and it was clear to many that predictions of Trump's demise had been greatly exaggerated.

"Our strategy early with Ron was to kill him in the crib," a Trump adviser told me. "He will have too much money, more than us for sure, to actually end it early, but we are going to drag him down. We will be a weight around his neck, and if we pull him down far enough, it's over. No one else comes close to us. It's Ron or no one. That's why we are coming for his head."

Part of the problem for DeSantis at the time stemmed from the fact that the coalition he needed was almost impossible to build. He was pulling from two groups: Never Trump Republicans and the more persuadable voters who could be swayed in either direction.

And unfortunately for DeSantis, no matter what move he made, one of these groups would likely feel alienated, which left DeSantis sitting on the sidelines as Trump went on the attack.

"You can't hold on to all those groups," said a senior Trump adviser. "There is natural tension between them all, [and] his team is learning and seeing that firsthand right now. And the intensity of support with Trump voters is [at] a much higher level than [it is] for DeSantis. It's a problem for him."

In early 2023, as Trump went on the warpath and poll numbers continued to slump, DeSantis's team was still keeping its head down and trying to focus on building his political infrastructure.

DeSantis's team has always been small—notoriously so. The governor's hardwired mistrust, surly reputation, and penchant for firing staffers have kept his inner circle as insular as any national-level politician's could be. But as his shadow campaign took shape and things started to get real, it was clear it was going to need to expand—and fast.

The quest for political operatives in early voting states was led by Generra Peck, the woman who helped secure the governor's 2022 reelection, and Ryan Tyson.

Before joining DeSantis's campaign, Tyson had been one of the state's best-known Republican pollsters. He'd worked first for Associated Industries of Florida, a business lobbying group, but later went out on his own, setting up an independent firm that worked with politicians from both parties along with major corporate clients. Tyson, fittingly, has also long been one of Florida's most prolific practitioners of the political dark arts. As part of a multiyear legal fight, the group he'd founded, Let's Preserve the American Dream, was roped into an investigation involving a coordinated effort that took place during the 2020 election cycle in which Florida Republicans recruited "ghost candidates" who had no party affiliation in order to siphon votes from Democrats in high-profile state senate races. The scheme led one such candidate to plead guilty to campaign finance–related crimes and resulted in former state senator Frank Artiles facing charges that he bribed another candidate. As part of the case, Miami prosecutors successfully subpoenaed tax records from Tyson's organization, which offered a glimpse into its role in the scheme and its day-to-day operations. Neither Tyson nor his organization has been charged with any crimes.

Tyson, a fast-talking, überconfident political veteran from the tiny North Florida town of Chiefland, managed to dodge any material legal fallout from the scheme and shortly thereafter was absorbed into DeSantis's political machine. He became among its most important cogs and was one of a handful of staffers who briefed the roughly two dozen DeSantis donors and other dignitaries at the Tampa Convention Center for DeSantis's election night party in 2022.

"They were like kids on Christmas morning," said a donor who had been among those being briefed at the event by Tyson and Peck, the 2022 reelection campaign manager.

At the same time, a pro-DeSantis super PAC that promised to spend $200 million for the governor was being formed. Called Never Back Down, the group was initially led by Ken Cuccinelli, a Trump administration official who'd switched allegiances, a move that got him branded as a "snake" by irate Trumpers. The group coordinated events and paid for a huge collection of people to knock on voters' doors on DeSantis's behalf and funded generally negative messaging on a variety of Trump's alleged missteps: his failure to fire Anthony Fauci, his continued support of the COVID-19 vaccine, his generally brash manner, and the fact that he would only be able to serve one term—whereas Republicans, DeSantis's team argued, would need two terms to fix the damage that had been done during the Biden administration.

"The data we are seeing is the same as the Trump folks. They know they have problems, and we are going to try and kill [Trump] in the crib," said a DeSantis adviser, notably using the same infanticidal language Trump's advisers leveled at DeSantis.

"We will have to walk through the fire," the adviser added. "But this will be a two-person race, and that will be good for us. You won't see Nikki Haley or Mike Pence mentioned in any real way. This is Trump versus DeSantis."

In some ways, DeSantis was right where he wanted to be: in the ring with Trump, vying for the GOP presidential nomination. But he was struggling to throw a punch, much less land one.

By the time the 2024 election cycle rolled around, nearly all Trump's liabilities were out in the open, having been dissected and disseminated by publicly available court documents in several states. And while it was true that many donors had fled the turbulent waters of Trump World for the comparatively calm seas of DeSantis's Florida, base voters, as early poll after early poll showed, did not seem to care about Trump's shortcomings. In fact, debacles that easily could have ended other politicians' campaigns—for example, being indicted on thirty-four felony counts by a New York district attorney, which is what happened in early April of 2023—only boosted the intensity and ardor of his most loyal voters. Trump, it seemed, was like the Hydra of Greek myth: chop off one of his heads and watch two grow in its place.

This did not stop DeSantis and his allies from trying to find Trump's weak spots. At one point in early 2023, the organization

Club for Growth, an antitax business lobby with a dislike of Trump and seemingly unlimited resources, was actively working on opposition research, hoping to dig up dirt that had a chance at swaying the former president's loyal primary voters.

"They have been asking campaigns or potential campaigns, 'Hey, can you help us with some of your opposition research? We can't find a message that works,'" said a veteran Republican who was familiar with the search. "They are going to be on the front lines. They are going to try and beat the shit out of Trump, and they have all the money in the world. But one thing they do not have is a message that they know will work."

The overall feeling was undeniable: DeSantis's presidential ambitions were in trouble—and in danger of devolving into the chaos that had caused donors to flee Trump in the first place. DeSantis's onetime benefactor, surely, was savoring the irony.

CHAPTER FIFTEEN

"IT'S ON"

R on DeSantis has a hard time connecting with people.

This is something Florida watchers have known for years and something they predicted would be a problem for him on the national stage. At home, DeSantis could afford to pitch himself to voters through the relatively controlled medium of television: in Florida, where there are twenty-two million residents and ten expensive media markets, statewide races don't feel like they've begun until candidates get on TV. It is as much a statement about Florida as about DeSantis himself that he rose as far as he did without having to worry about retail politics such as baby kissing and glad-handing.

The same could not be said, however, of the race for the White House.

The awkwardness of the man whom conservatives heralded as America's Governor was on full display during his March 2023 visit to Iowa, a crucial early voting state where the as-yet-unannounced presidential candidate was testing the waters. Michael Bender, a former Florida Man who is now a national political correspondent for the *New York Times,* captured the dynamic in a story titled "A Glimpse of DeSantis in Iowa: Awkward, but Still Winning the Crowd."

Bender, who was at the event, opened the story with an anecdote about a woman in Iowa wearing a University of Florida sweatshirt, a gesture most people would see as a nice slice of home in unfamiliar territory. DeSantis greeted the interaction by making an awkward reference to the state's "grandparent waiver," which allows out-of-state college students to get breaks on tuition if they have grandparents who are residents in the snowbird-rich state. The woman, Bender wrote, looked confused, and DeSantis escaped to the next voter.

But DeSantis couldn't escape his own personality. Former staffers, many of whom have been unceremoniously fired from DeSantis World over the years, started opening up to reporters about the governor's awkwardness, fueling the narrative that DeSantis is as aloof and disconnected as many suspect.

There were stories of a 2019 meeting with some of the state's biggest business groups who were trying to push lawsuit reform. DeSantis briefly addressed the gathering of politically influential leaders in his private conference room, then sat in the corner on his phone as staff took over.

"It was very awkward and not how we expect governors to act in that space," said a business executive who attended the meeting.

"I think the man has ADD or something," said another veteran Florida lobbyist. "That's just his personality. I have been in meetings with him and groups of people, and it's just kind of weird. It's not really him—the staff just takes over, or he comes in briefly and just ducks back behind the curtain."

If the news cycle stayed stuck on the "DeSantis is too awkward to be president" message, that would have been bad enough. But it was starting to seem like DeSantis wasn't just awkward—he was also *weird*.

In one viral story, the *Daily Beast*'s Zachary Petrizzo and Jake Lahut reported that a former unnamed staffer had seen DeSantis using three fingers to eat chocolate puddingon a private flight to Washington, DC, in 2019. It was like a "starving animal who has never eaten before," the staffer recalled.

It's amazing what sticks and what doesn't during major political campaigns, but the mental image of DeSantis eagerly wolfing down pudding using just his hand caught fire, serving as fodder for late night TV show hosts, Democrats, and, of course, Team Trump, which was eager to grab on to any anecdote that could further fuel the perception that DeSantis isn't just vacant—an empty suit who would have been nothing without the former president—but also sloppy and strange.

The issue reached a climax when DeSantis was forced to answer a question about gobbling up the pudding during the much-publicized March 2023 interview with British journalist Piers Morgan, a moment that spun off a chyron that read, "Ron: I don't eat pudding with 3 fingers." It was an embarrassing look during what was supposed to be a friendly interview. To make matters worse, it aired on Fox News, which had long been DeSantis's safe space.

DeSantis said that he "didn't remember" wolfing down pudding with his hands, but that of course only handed the Trump campaign more ammo.

"We were having a good run with Meatball Ron," joked a Trump adviser. "Then they gave us Pudding Paws? Are you kidding me? That's gold. I think you'll see us come back to that."

(Since the initial *Daily Beast* reporting, I have learned that the method by which DeSantis wolfed down the pudding was by using his pointer, middle, and ring fingers as opposed to his middle, ring, and pinkie fingers. Believe it or not, this has been a topic of discussion from time to time among those who gather in Tallahassee watering holes to discuss high-minded issues, or so I am told.)

The perception that DeSantis was a weirdo was something his campaign knew it would have to address eventually, but getting overrun with an avalanche of stories and social media blowback even before the official launch made them look flat-footed. Worse, it fed the idea that the governor, who had come up in an insular, state-delimited bubble of his own creation, was not ready for prime time. The team tried to use the Morgan interview to soften those rough edges: DeSantis noticeably smiled much more than he ever had previously and even debuted a new belly laugh in response to a few Morgan one-liners—but it came off as so contrary to his usual demeanor that it was received as artificial.

In a sign of just how far he was willing to go to endear himself to voters, DeSantis also opened up to Morgan about the passing of his sister, Christina, who had died unexpectedly in 2015 at the age of thirty.

"It was just a shattering experience," DeSantis said during the Morgan interview, with tears in his eyes. "I remember my mom calling me. My wife and I were on our way back from church on a Sunday morning, and she said that Christina was in the hospital and she had a blood clot but was stable."

As it turned out, the respite was temporary, and his sister died of a pulmonary embolism several days later. After her death, DeSantis said, he sought comfort in his Catholic faith.

"You start to question things that are unjust, like 'Why did this have to happen?'" DeSantis added. "And you just have to have faith there there's a plan in place. Trust in God; there's no guarantee that you're gonna have a life without challenges and without heartbreak, and that's just a function of being human."

It was a rare moment of vulnerability for DeSantis, who had spent the better part of the two years building a reputation as a hard-charging culture warrior whose reservoirs of empathy had long run dry. Those who know him say that his reticence about his sister's passing was related to how close the two had been before her death.

"I've heard him talk about it privately before, and it's really hard when he does," said a longtime DeSantis confidant. "He has never been comfortable with talking about it; they were super close. She was the closest person in his life. He shut down for a bit after she died. I think his relationship with her was special and one I think he just wanted to keep as his own.

"I do think the campaign is going to have to talk about her more," the confidant added. "It humanizes him in a way that few other things can."

DeSantis's political rise had not included many references to his personal life, much less to Christina, whom he rarely mentioned, albeit for understandable reasons. Christina was even left out of his book. The fact that he was bringing her up now, some whispered, only underscored his desperation.

To their credit, DeSantis's team never panicked, even amid the mounting attacks from Trump World and their candidate's ineffectual attempts at defense.

In March of 2023, as the bullets really started to fly, DeSantis's top advisers and a handful of donors huddled to map out an early state strategy. It was one of the biggest meetings held by DeSantis advisers before his campaign formally launched, coming amid a news cycle dominated by the narrative that DeSantis could not take a punch from Trump, that his donors were losing confidence, and that the erstwhile assumed front-runner wasn't even going to make it past the starting line.

"We were never concerned. What that briefing made clear is that so much was already mapped out and coordinated," said a DeSantis adviser who was in the meeting. "There is no rush building infrastructure or identifying people; all the wheels are in motion. And on the donor front? We were not losing anyone. We were the preferred pick."

But even as the DeSantis team remained optimistic in the face of early missteps, there remained a single, looming concern: DeSantis on a debate stage with Trump.

Though DeSantis had run in two statewide Florida campaigns, there was a sense that when he stepped into the debate spotlight, he failed. Especially in the debates with Andrew Gillum and Charlie Crist.

In his three decades in politics, Crist prided himself on being a happy warrior. He took shots at his opponents occasionally, but no one could have confused his debate style with Trump's. Yet even the mild-mannered Crist landed a direct hit on DeSantis when, during their lone debate, he challenged his opponent—by then already rumored to make a bid for the White House—to "look in the eyes of the people of the state of Florida and say to them [that] if you're reelected, you will serve a full four-year term."

DeSantis had given no response. He'd simply stared silently at Crist, unable to muster an answer as the state looked on.

Although DeSantis went on to trounce Crist at the polls, the gaffe hadn't done much to inspire confidence. Now DeSantis was facing Trump, the primary obstacle to his presidential ambitions, who not only had more experience on the national debate stage but also seemed to delight in demolishing his opponents as the whole country watched. DeSantis's supporters couldn't help but dread the moment when their candidate would have to step into the bright lights of a presidential debate stage and face the fury of Donald Trump—their fear palpable months before the first presidential debate (which was planned for August of 2023) and even before DeSantis had formally announced his campaign.

"Charlie Crist was not even a challenge politically, but he still rocked him," said a DeSantis adviser. "I won't know any of this is real until he stands on the debate stage...with Trump, [when] Trump hits him with everything he has and Ron is still standing and is credible.

"The world is going to be watching. If he can go toe-to-toe with Trump, it's on."

In the months after DeSantis's historic reelection win, the assumption was that his obvious next move would be a run for president. Everyone knew it, and he was asked about it endlessly, for good reason.

But despite his staggering gubernatorial victory, DeSantis not only refused to acknowledge the prospect of a presidential run but also continued to blow off questions about the obvious. The early months of 2023 were instead dominated by a national tour to hawk copies of his book *The Courage to Be Free*, which outlined the policies of his first four years as governor and made the case that Florida offered a "blueprint for America's revival."

DeSantis spent much of the tour ignoring, if not openly mocking, questions about whether he was considering a run for president, something that by that point seemed inevitable. Further fueling the speculation was his list of tour stops: in addition to Florida, he hit nearly every early primary state, all while insisting that what everyone was seeing—essentially, a presidential soft launch—was not actually happening.

DeSantis's first order of business, or so he said, was to sell some books. Even before his debut book hit the *New York Times* bestseller list, DeSantis was far from broke, but he'd never had what many in Florida politics termed "real money." As of December 31, 2021, he was worth roughly $320,000, most of which came from a checking and savings account, and he still owed $21,284 in student loans. He was the governor of the third-biggest state in the country, but he did not own a house or a car. Consider these details in comparison to the lifestyles of his predecessor, the billionaire Rick Scott, and his political rival, Donald Trump.

DeSantis reported a $1.2 million book advance on his 2023 financial disclosure forms, meaning that the book gave DeSantis both a measure of financial freedom he had never previously experienced and a huge platform on which he could build his anticipated White House bid.

DeSantis was not exclusively doing quaint book signing events in suburban Barnes & Noble locations. Many of the events were huge and, even to the untrained eye, looked just like the political rallies he would soon hold in earnest. Each event, of course, focused on key themes of the book, a highlight reel for the policies DeSantis would lean into when he formally became a presidential candidate.

"We will fight the woke in government, but we will also fight the woke in our schools [and] our corporations. We are never going to surrender to the woke mob, because Florida is where woke goes to die," DeSantis said during a stop on Long Island, serving up his standard fare to the hundreds in attendance.

At most stops there were Trump supporters sprinkled in among the DeSantis readership. They weren't there in support, however;

on the contrary, they took the chance to openly heckle the man whom most of them had anointed America's Governor. For the most part, though, the events gave DeSantis a large platform from which to tout the right-wing policy reforms he'd ushered into Florida.

Trump's backers did drag DeSantis into a more direct conflict in March of 2023, when they went so far as to officially file a complaint with the Florida Commission on Ethics alleging that DeSantis was running a "shadow" presidential campaign that ran afoul of state law. This was based on a faulty reading of Florida ethics laws, but the team at Make America Great Again, Inc., or MAGA Inc.—the pro-Trump super PAC behind the complaint—knew that.

"This is just kind of his welcome-to-the-big-leagues-moment," one Trump adviser told me at the time, basically implying that the complaint would not stick (it didn't). It had simply been a way to muddy up DeSantis.

While DeSantis was playing the role of traveling book salesman, Never Back Down, the newly launched pro-DeSantis super PAC that would become home to several former DeSantis aides, was running soft-touch biographical TV ads across the country, an attempt to introduce the governor to a broader audience. The ads lacked the sharp edges that had come to define DeSantis's political and personal style. Instead, they focused on his time as a navy JAG officer, the fact that he'd worked his way through college, and the way he'd "fought the swamp" when in Congress. The ads, notably, did not use DeSantis's own voice at all, which aides at the time said was intentional: he has a nasally, whiny tone to his speech that does not make the best of first impressions.

Concurrently, DeSantis was trying to establish a palatable launchpad for his presidential campaign. In an attempt to appear like an everyman, though, his pitch to early state voters came off as corny pandering, an ill-conceived campaign-trail schtick more than anything else.

"I was geographically raised in Tampa Bay," DeSantis wrote in his book, "but culturally my upbringing reflected the working-class communities in western Pennsylvania and northeast Ohio—from weekly church attendance to the expectation that one would earn his keep. This made me God-fearing, hard-working and America-loving."

He then called Florida the "Iowa of the southeast," echoing a similar line he'd used in Utah. Later, in an interview with conservative talk show host Mark Levin, he explained that because of his western Pennsylvanian father and northeastern Ohioan mother, "Rust Belt values" raised him. He'd become the man from everywhere—or at least all the places that had some political relevance.

The intense level of pandering felt ripped from an episode of *Veep*. It was eye roll–inducing to almost everyone paying attention and slightly annoying to people who were actually from the states DeSantis was name-dropping—Ohioans and Pennsylvanians who had the gall to be proud of where they were from without the needless Florida comparison.

DeSantis, it seemed, was intent on making sure his staffers' biggest worries—about his appeal, about his demeanor, about his general *weirdness*—were well founded.

Their awareness of this fact was on display at a May 2023 event in Iowa, right before his formal presidential launch. DeSantis came onstage after Governor Kim Reynolds's introduction, then proceeded to forget her presence—and their scheduled one-on-one conversation—entirely, leaving her to stand to the side and rambling on for roughly thirty minutes until her polite interruption.

"Doesn't really have his sea legs yet," a DeSantis aide told me at the time. "He's never really needed these kind of sea legs."

As DeSantis was struggling to find his footing ahead of his highly expected presidential launch, Trump was already a boxer in fighting shape. And he had a single target in mind: DeSantis.

By early 2023, any notion that DeSantis was not running for president was functionally gone, even as he continued the laughable ruse that he had not yet made up his mind. Trump, very much aware of this, began to unleash a torrent of sometimes daily attacks on his rival. In vintage Trump fashion, though, he sometimes struggled to stick with a single message. Was DeSantis disloyal? Was he just a RINO? Or was he, in fact, a meatball? Nicknames got much of the attention in that moment, but Trump was just starting to cook.

"The media is covering up for Ron DeSantis," Trump said in a February 2023 speech at the Conservative Political Action Conference, a hilarious bit of framing considering DeSantis's hatred of the media and the way it reported about him. "He is a Trojan Horse; he is *the* Trojan Horse. Do not believe anything you're reading by the media about Ron DeSantis."

The CPAC event itself presented a notable snapshot of the political theater of the moment. DeSantis had opted out of the conference, an event at which he had spoken in the past, instead attending a private donor retreat hosted by the antitax group Club for Growth, with whom DeSantis is closely affiliated; his former congressional chief of staff, Scott Parkinson, was once the group's vice president of government affairs before launching his bid for the US Senate in Virginia. The group had not only long been allied with DeSantis, it had also had a falling-out with Trump, who said the group was disloyal.

DeSantis's decision to forgo the conference—especially in favor of the Club for Growth event—was perceived as a snub, especially because by then, virtually everything he did was viewed through the lens of his rivalry with Trump, who had enthusiastically made an appearance at CPAC. That dynamic was heightened when Club for Growth gave an internal poll to POLITICO showing DeSantis with double-digit leads in several key early states, numbers that proved to be preposterous shortly after DeSantis entered the race. Others thought DeSantis was steering clear of the event to avoid the scandal surrounding the CPAC host, Matt Schlapp, who had allegedly sexually assaulted a former strategist who worked for Herschel Walker's Georgia Senate campaign.

Still, despite Trump's looming presence—and the bewildering fact that DeSantis had yet to announce his presidential run—some observers held fast to the idea that the governor was the new face of the GOP.

"My view is that Ron DeSantis's success in Florida has created a model for how Republicans can fight and win. This is going to be an appealing message for Republicans after multiple disappointing elections," David Sacks, a Silicon Valley entrepreneur who supports DeSantis and contributed to his 2022 reelection, told me in early 2023. "The attempts by a competing camp to overparse his statement, even before he is a declared candidate, should indicate the perceived strength rather than weakness of his candidacy."

Still, DeSantis's attempt to pretend the sky is not blue eventually did lead to a series of awkward exchanges. No one, very much including the media, believed that he was not lining up a White House bid, so journalists would often ask him about the Trump attacks through the obvious lens of a brewing political rivalry. Despite the frequency of the inquiries, DeSantis never seemed to have an answer prepared. It got to the point where it seemed like borderline political malpractice not to have some basic throwaway line at the ready.

That was on full display in late April of 2023, when DeSantis was on a trade mission in Japan. The international trip came in his official capacity as governor but was widely seen as an attempt to beef up his foreign affairs bona fides ahead of a White House run.

Japan was his first stop of the trip, and right off the bat DeSantis, as usual, got a question about Trump and presidential politics, this one centered on polling that showed Trump leading a hypothetical DeSantis presidential campaign.

As if he were a malfunctioning robot, DeSantis's jaw dropped as soon as he processed what the question was about. With his mouth noticeably agape, the clearly rattled governor started waving his head wildly back and forth. It was a failed attempt by DeSantis, it seems, to remain calm and thus avoid fueling the already growing perception that he lacked interpersonal skills. But his attempt to stifle his primal instinct to lash out not only reinforced the "DeSantis is weird" narrative, it also provided its adherents the clearest example to date that they were, in fact, correct. As a result of the incident, DeSantis, during the first few days of his international trip, was among the most memed people on the internet, where the consensus among commentators was that he looked like a bobblehead.

He composed himself long enough to say, "I'm not a candidate, so we will see if and when that changes," but at that point the answer was hardly the point.

It was a less than ideal way for a wannabe president to make his introduction to the world stage.

DeSantis's first international test took him not only to Japan but also to South Korea, Israel, and the United Kingdom.

The stops came with varying degrees of feedback from both his own team and the international politicans and businessmen who were the focus of the trip. Some events, to his credit, went very well:

in late April, DeSantis gave a speech at the Celebrate Faces of Israel event at the Museum of Tolerance. As someone who had built his political career on being among the most pro-Israel politicans in the nation, DeSantis was in his element—and it showed.

"One moment where...his talent shined was in Jerusalem, when he gave a speech," said one adviser who was on the trip with DeSantis. "Like, he knows his shit."

On other parts of the trip, though, DeSantis's international inexperience shone so brightly that some people involved turned to POLITICO Europe to dish very candid assessments of what they'd witnessed. One told the outlet that DeSantis "looked bored" and "stared at his feet," an off-putting display that many Florida political insiders had endured for years.

DeSantis would also not say who paid for his international travel, which is the type of trip that governors who are *not* eyeing a bid for the White House generally do not make. Flight records show a private chartered jet making stops that coincide exactly with those on DeSantis's trip. But the governor's office, as it had in the past, would not answer questions about specific donors, only saying that the trip was funded by private donations through Enterprise Florida, the state's mostly taxpayer-funded economic development arm. Enterprise Florida has often played a controversial role in things like gubernatorial travel because it is not required to disclose names of outside donors who give to the organization.

DeSantis advisers who were on the trip downplay any idea that there was real tension or flubs. Some acknowledged, however, that at times there were moments of awkwardness because DeSantis was not a president or even an official presidential candidate but rather a state governor.

"I think it was an uncomfortable time to go because he is not an announced candidate," admitted an adviser who was on the trip.

"He was governor, but everyone knew he was running for president, so it was difficult to know how exactly to conduct yourself. If there was any awkwardness, I would attribute it to that."

Some of those who witnessed the trip, though, attributed the awkwardness to DeSantis himself. "It felt really a bit like we were watching a state-level politican," one UK businessman told POLITICO Europe. "I would not be surprised if [people in attendance] came out thinking, 'That's not the guy.'"

CHAPTER SIXTEEN

"WIN IOWA, WIN IT ALL"

B y May, speculation about whether DeSantis would run for president had largely run its course; the questions then turned to when and how he would launch his inevitable bid.

The governor had been falling in most public polling as Trump continued to unleash a torrent of assaults, in the process rebuilding his connection with the conservative base. However, outside a handful of laughable think pieces, no one seriously doubted that DeSantis was going to do what he was going to do.

Trump, in the meantime, had quickly racked up dozens of congressional endorsements, a stockpile that included nods from eleven of the twenty Republicans from DeSantis's home-state delegation. This groundswell of support for the former president in Florida, of all places, quickly created the perception that DeSantis's team was not yet ready for prime time.

The first two of Florida's congressional Republicans to endorse Trump, Matt Gaetz and Anna Paulina Luna, had been longtime Trump supporters and were not a surprise. But when Republican representative Byron Donalds backed Trump, it got a lot of attention, including from DeSantis's camp.

Donalds had introduced DeSantis at his reelection night party in Tampa, and the two had, until that point, been seen as allies. Further, Donalds's wife, Erika, is among the national leaders in the conservative push for more parental involvement in public education. She was heavily involved in the Florida school board races during the 2022 midterms, during which DeSantis endorsed most of her candidates.

The Donalds endorsement was seen as a blow to DeSantis and quickly led to wave of other Florida congressional Republicans backing Trump. In just a few days, seven Republican members of the Florida congressional delegation backed the former president in quick succession, and the sense that DeSantis was not prepared for the national stage only grew. This was not helped by the fact that the leader of the pre–presidential launch endorsement push for DeSantis was Ryan Tyson, the longtime Republican pollster turned DeSantis adviser, while Trump himself was making direct calls to members of Congress. This set up the split screen of a staffer whom many members of Congress had not heard of competing for endorsements with a former president and the current leader of the Republican Party.

"I had no idea who he was when I got the call. I wasn't quite sure what was happening," one congressperson told me of Tyson's endorsement effort.

The congressperson, who did not want to be named out of respect for DeSantis, said there was a general feeling that Trump's team was better prepared to compete on a national level. That moment was cemented when Trump invited his endorsers to Mar-a-Lago for dinner after they made their support public. A picture was tweeted showing them all gathered around a dinner table, a snapshot that served as a bit of salt in the wound for DeSantis's political team.

The picture was posted after DeSantis's team—specifically, Tyson—reached out to members of the Florida congressional delegation asking them to stop endorsing Trump in an effort to stop the bleeding. His calls, like the others, fell on deaf ears.

But the DeSantis team never panicked. Even as Trump reasserted himself and began to assume the mantle of clear Republican front-runner, there was a calm confidence within DeSantis's inner orbit. They were convinced that once they formally launched, they would get a bump that would close both the polling and momentum gap.

They did know, however, that they needed to start showing some urgency. At one point, they planned a presidential exploratory committee, a common step for any would-be candidate before entering the race. But as Trump began to pick up momentum, they scrapped the idea.

"Don't have time for stuff like that anymore," said one DeSantis adviser. "And Trump would probably just make fun of it. We don't need to give him anything else to talk about. It's time to just get in."

Some of the pressure eased in mid-May, when DeSantis was endorsed by ninety-nine members of the Florida legislature, a number that included each member of the legislative leadership team. There was an expectation that DeSantis would lock up most support from state-level lawmakers, mostly because it would send a devastating message had he not.

To nail down that support, the DeSantis team took a multistage approach. First, there would be a call from state senator Blaise Ingoglia, a close ally of DeSantis. If that did not get the job done, then the senate president, Kathleen Passidomo, and the Florida House Speaker, Paul Renner, would pick up the phone and try to seal the deal. If that didn't work, the few remaining legislative holdouts would get a call directly from DeSantis's office.

Another weapon DeSantis had at his disposal was the fact that he had not yet signed the state's $117 billion budget. This meant that DeSantis could use his veto pen to axe individual spending projects that were dear to members' hearts. (I interviewed several lawmakers at the time, and none said that overt threats were made, but anyone with even a modicum of political sense understood what the stakes were.)

"They didn't have to use vetoes or threats or anything directly," a Republican lawmaker told me. "It was just kind of understood."

Though none publicly said that DeSantis was threatening spending projects before he signed the budget, state senator Joe Gruters, the former head of the Republican Party of Florida, made the connection after the budget was signed and millions of his projects were vetoed.

"The governor is clearly upset I endorsed Donald Trump for president, and so he took it out on the people of Sarasota County," Gruters, a longtime Trump backer, told several media outlets at the time. "Simply because I support his political opponent, the governor chose to punish ordinary Floridians. It's mean-spirited acts like this that are defining him here and across the country," he added.

Running for president is hard. It becomes that much harder when you suffer a self-inflicted wound in the opening act.

That's exactly what happened to Ron DeSantis.

DeSantis had spent months working on a book tour that doubled as presidential campaign soft launch. His team raised tens of millions of dollars, and they thought they had the perfect person for the launch, one who could help them win back swaths of a Republican base that was clearly leaning toward Trump.

Then came Twitter.

"Anyway, thanks, everyone, for joining," said the Twitter CEO, Elon Musk, who was the cohost for DeSantis's long-awaited May 24 presidential launch on Twitter Spaces. "We are incredibly excited... to have Governor DeSantis on with us with this historic announcement. And then [we] look forward to live Q&A from the audience."

Those were the opening moments of a presidential rollout that was indeed historic—but for all the wrong reasons. It was a glitch-filled event that was at times impossible to hear and ultimately only fueled the perception that DeSantis was not ready for the big leagues. It was also an indictment of his appeal: as governor, he had built a communications strategy based on hiring staffers seen as "chronically online," a term describing those more focused on social media battlefields than on things normal people care about. Further, picking Twitter for his campaign launch also cemented the idea that he might struggle to gain traction with people not in tune with the daily churn of the social media outrage cycle.

The event, which was cohosted by Silicon Valley entrepreneur and DeSantis donor David Sacks, eventually settled into a consistent enough place for DeSantis to hit his normal talking points, though he did not really break any new ground.

DeSantis supporters did try to spin the glitch-plagued rollout by saying they "broke the internet" because it attracted so much attention, but their attempts fell flat for anyone not on the DeSantis payroll—and even for some who were.

"That was a disaster," a DeSantis adviser said days after the launch. "I don't really know how you can look at it any other way."

The Twitter flop got the most attention, but it was happening against the backdrop of another story that would turn out to be a big success for DeSantis. His formal campaign had organized a huge group of donors and fundraisers at the Four Seasons hotel in Miami so they could begin raising money for the campaign the moment it was legally official. The event created what was essentially a call center, but instead of underpaid workers mass-calling potential customers, it was staffed by wealthy political donors and fundraisers cold-calling their friends and asking them to max out for DeSantis's campaign.

"I was walking around, and I could literally overhear people calling others they had not talked to in years and asking them to give," said a person who attended the event. "It was the definition of all hands on deck."

The "dialing for dollars" event ultimately served its purpose. The nascent DeSantis campaign quickly announced that it had raised $8.2 million in twenty-four hours, a massive haul. It was an early victory for a campaign that desperately needed to flip the narrative.

However, as with so many things in the early weeks and months of DeSantis's campaign, what appeared to be a positive turned to a negative.

Rumors quickly circulated of a fundraising leaderboard in the main room at the Four Seasons where the DeSantis event had taken place. The list included the names of people who had raised the most money for DeSantis in the first few days of the campaign—and right near the top was James Uthmeier, the governor's former general counsel and current chief of staff of his official taxpayer-funded office.

Turns out Uthmeier had helped organize a program to get state employees to give to DeSantis's campaign. As part of the scheme, state employees were sent a special fundraising link that they in turn could text to lobbyists. Any contribution given through the link was credited to Uthmeier, which quickly made him one his boss's biggest fundraisers. He raised nearly $500,000 in the first twenty-four hours of the campaign, a number that almost certainly got bigger as time went on. The number is more impressive when you consider that these were contributions sent directly to the official campaign, which are capped at $3,300 per person.

As soon as the text message started going out to lobbyists, I was being alerted to the abnormality of the request. Political fundraising is part of the game, but to have taxpayer-funded state employees bundling political contributions directly from the lobbyists involved in the state government came off as unseemly to most who were aware of the scheme. There have been times in the past when the gubernatorial staff has solicited campaign money, but for staffers to be so brazen as to put those requests in writing and then become among the largest individual fundraisers was seen as unprecedented.

When I reported this at the time, there was an almost universal sense of bewilderment as to why the governor's team would so overtly enlist state employees in the effort to raise political cash. Everyone knew Uthmeier wanted to report a huge early campaign finance figure, but this didn't seem like the most prudent way to go about it—nor did it seem like a necessary risk. DeSantis was a prolific fundraiser as governor. He had access to a national network and had dozens of professional fundraisers and donors huddled in Miami trying to raise him quick cash. The use of taxpayer-funded staff in that effort just seemed like yet another misstep.

The campaign—and later DeSantis himself—defended the move, saying that staff could do whatever they wanted in their private time. But none of those explanations did anything to remove the tarnish from a use of government resources that was almost universally viewed as inappropriate, so much so that it eventually led to a formal ethics complaint.

"These allegations represent a gross violation of state laws and ethics, and we could not in good conscience ignore them," the Florida Democratic Party chair, Nikki Fried, said when filing the complaint against DeSantis over the fundraising controversy—and over

Joe Gruters's allegations that DeSantis had punished lawmakers for not supporting him politically. "If true, they are yet another example of Ron abusing his public office for personal gain."

By that point, though, there was no belief that state-level institutions would do anything to hurt DeSantis's rise or political campaign, a feeling that ended up being correct. The complaint, like the one filed by the pro-Trump super PAC, never amounted to anything.

Donald Trump stood onstage at a convention center in Columbus, Georgia, ready to fight.

It was just days after he had become the first president in US history to face federal indictment. Special counsel Jack Smith had unsealed a thirty-seven-count indictment alleging that Trump had not only kept classified documents from his time in the White House but had also orchestrated a scheme to hide those documents from federal investigators who'd asked about them.

"The ridiculous and baseless indictment of me by the Biden administration's weaponized Department of Injustice will go down as among the most horrific abuses of power in the history of our country," he told a packed convention center.

I attended the event, which featured an overwhelming collection of Trump supporters, some of whom waited for hours in the sweltering heat to get into the Columbus Convention and Trade center. They were galvanized by what they saw as the politicization of the federal justice system. In the days and weeks following the indictment, Trump supporters, from grassroots activists to US senators, dispatched a defense of Trump that largely ignored the underlying allegations of the indictment, instead focusing on the theory that he had been targeted because he was Biden's most likely general-election opponent. They also noted that other prominent politicians, including Biden, had been found with classified documents in their homes or offices and had not been raided or indicted. However, these comparisons always failed to mention that in those cases, there was a level of clear cooperation with federal investigators rather than attempts at obstruction, as was the case with Trump.

In arguably the most flagrant show of Republican avoidance, when pressed about the indictment, Iowa senator Chuck Grassley said he had not read it because he was not a "legal analyst." The admission is notable because, although he isn't an analyst, Grassley did chair the Senate Judiciary Committee.

Whenever Trump faces legal woes, it offers a clarifying glimpse into both his mindset and that of the Republican base. The federal indictment could land Trump in jail for the rest of his life, but he and many on his team didn't shy away from the legal fight—they welcomed it. In fact, they predicted—very accurately, it turns out—that Trump's being indicted would boost his poll numbers and further intensify his support with Republican voters, just as it had when he was indicted in New York over his alleged hush-money payments to Stormy Daniels and when federal investigators searched Mar-a-Lago as part of the classified-documents investigation.

The Trump indictment also paints Republican opponents into a corner. A Republican with ambitions of advancing in a what remains a Trump-dominated party cannot do anything but support the former president and attack law enforcement when he faces legal troubles. It doesn't matter whether they believe that the pro-Trump script they have been given is truthful; it is something they must follow to remain remotely viable in a party dominated by his sycophants. In fact, no candidate outside of former New Jersey governor Chris Christie, a top former Trump ally, was openly bashing the former president. Christie, for his part, had candidly acknowledged that his bid for president was a kamikaze-like mission to try to sink Trump's campaign.

In the early stages of the 2024 GOP primary, the other candidates were attempting a different tactic, leaning into the paradoxical notion that they could somehow defeat Trump while continuing to publicly praise him—or at least shy away from openly criticizing him.

The fact that this group includes DeSantis was doubly paradoxical, given that he'd worked so hard to build a national reputation for hawkishness and aggression. His super PAC, after all, is named Never Back Down.

But when it comes to Trump, DeSantis has almost always backed down.

"The weaponization of federal law enforcement represents a mortal threat to a free society," DeSantis said in the days after the early June indictment. "We have for years witnessed an uneven application of the law depending upon political affiliation. Why so zealous in pursuing Trump yet so passive about Hillary or Hunter?"

Predictably, though, Trump continued to hammer DeSantis, using his trademark nicknames and deploying his legions of online fans to trash the governor and his supporters—continuing the social media war that, ultimately, has likely never changed the mind of a single voter.

The closest DeSantis came at that point to laying a finger on Trump were his attempts to remind voters that, with Trump at the helm of the party, Republicans experienced humiliating losses in the 2018, 2020, and 2022 election cycles. These remarks are in line with the larger argument that Trump opponents have tried to build concerning his electability or lack thereof. Those losses, they say—which include Trump's failed reelection bid—are proof that Trump does not appeal to the swing and independent voters Republicans need in order to reclaim the White House and finally spur a red wave.

"None of this matters if we do not win," DeSantis said at the June 2023 gathering of the Faith and Freedom Coalition, an organization composed of Christian conservative activists. "There is no substitute for victory. We cannot continue with the culture of losing where we lose winnable races."

But this weekend event—which included every announced Republican candidate—was another shining example of the fact that Trump's mere presence had made it difficult for any other candidate to gain real momentum. At that point, Trump led DeSantis by between twenty and thirty percentage points, and the entire rest of the field was scrambling for single-digit crumbs. Each candidate got a turn on the stage that day, and they all were received with good vibes and golf claps—but Trump's presence hung over them like a gathering storm cloud. DeSantis himself was surely fuming that he had been given a day-one afternoon speaking spot, a significantly lower tier than the keynote slot Trump had been given.

And then Trump took the stage—and his speech was greeted with thunderous applause.

It was a capstone to a weekend that, like all other Republican events, was not just a conservative gathering but also an homage to Trump—the leader of the GOP.

"Win Iowa, win it all."

That was how a DeSantis adviser described the campaign's thinking heading into the summer of 2023. DeSantis had been on the campaign trail as an official candidate for more than a month, but after weeks of being verbally abused and strategically outmaneuvered by Trump, he had done nothing to reverse the former president's narcotic-like effect on the GOP base.

A Saint Anselm College poll of primary voters in New Hampshire released in late June of 2023 found that 47 percent of them supported Trump, up five points from a previous poll. DeSantis, meanwhile, was at 19 percent, down ten percentage points.

"Former President Donald Trump is consolidating support in the face of several candidates diluting his opposition," the New Hampshire Institute of Politics executive director, Neil Levesque, said at the time.

Levesque also stated the obvious: if DeSantis wanted to try to dethrone his rival, he would have to rip off the Band-Aid and "articulate a clear rationale for his challenge to Trump." This was bad news for DeSantis, who, like others, seemed to have an incurable allergy to attacking the man he was trying to beat.

In short, DeSantis needed to contrast himself with Trump in order to close the gap, something he had, up to that point, been afraid to do.

The poll was just the latest data point underscoring DeSantis's fading presence in a primary contest he had spent years preparing for. Trump was dominating all public polls, and DeSantis was facing an ever-shrinking window in which he could feasibly rewrite the narrative that the ex-president was the dominant figure in the race.

He wasn't off to a great start. DeSantis's first month had been a disaster; Trump had mauled him badly. But, as DeSantis's team tried to assure the media, donors, and longtime supporters, they had a silver bullet: Iowa.

National public polling, they said, was a poor indicator of reality, and if they could hold out until Iowa, their patience would be rewarded. The team was convinced that the numbers in the state were better than those being broadcast to the public and that a win there would bring new life to his campaign.

"The DeSantis strategy is to invest heavily in the early states and build long-term relationships with voters," said a DeSantis adviser in June of 2023. "If Governor DeSantis can pull a win in Iowa or New Hampshire, it resets the race and opens the map."

And indeed, a pro-DeSantis super PAC had created a $100 million Iowa-based training camp to educate door knockers and ground-game volunteers, signaling its commitment to the strategy. But it was also a sign of desperation: there was a clear idea that DeSantis's only chance to salvage his presidential run—built on years of pushing a right-wing agenda on Florida—was a win in Iowa or New Hampshire.

To DeSantis's credit, he was making some headway. In New Hampshire, most notably, he helped directly raise $132,500 during the state GOP's annual Amos Tuck Dinner, a huge amount for the small state party.

"In Trump's seven years of being president and not being president, he raised zero dollars," a longtime New Hampshire Republican consultant told me at the time for an NBC News story. "In one night, DeSantis got us $132,500. That's a guy who puts his money where his mouth is."

Exacerbating problems for DeSantis was that he was losing one of the biggest weapons that had helped him build his brand: Fox News.

The network's airwaves were no longer his exclusive domain, and when DeSantis did get on air, the questions asked of him were much less like the softballs he had enjoyed for the previous few years. Insiders at the network said the turn on DeSantis was no mistake and was, in part, orchestrated by Rupert Murdoch himself.

"They are transactional and can smell a loser a mile away," a Fox insider told *Rolling Stone*, referring to Rupert, who retired in September 2023, and his son Lachlan, who served as cochairman of News Corp and has since taken over for his father.

The loss of Fox News, which had been DeSantis's golden ticket to Republican stardom, was the latest in what at that point had been a set of stinging blows to his campaign—but it wasn't to be the last. In mid-July, his campaign fired twelve staffers, not exactly a move that signals forward momentum less than two months into a campaign.

For the remainder of DeSantis's first term, through the 2022 election cycle, and months into his 2024 presidential campaign, his team had maintained a brawling media style, debuting a new Twitter account—@DeSantisWarRoom, led by the newly named rapid response director, Christina Pushaw—and continuing the by then long-standing approach of spewing venom at anything that moved, be it the media or rival politicians.

But for the first time, the team seemed to have met its match. The social media and communications strategy had been unable to prevent Trump from quicky dominating DeSantis in early presidential polls. The online fights, predictably, did not move any votes, and in such a vast political ecosystem, the Pushaw-crafted social media strategy was getting drowned out after the team finally decided to go after Trump, whose grip on the party base was unaffected by DeSantis's troll army. In fact, DeSantis-aligned social media creatures attacking Trump only made Trump stronger: the former president's MAGA supporters saw DeSantis as disloyal for attacking the magnanimous man who helped him become governor and the leader of their political movement.

As DeSantis's poll numbers cratered and questions of his viability as a presidential candidate started to creep in, the social media fighters who had defined DeSantis's postpandemic persona sort of faded into the background. Their presence was much less noticed, and those who were noticed were mocked by national audiences who were seeing the act for the first time. But in general, DeSantis's online warriors were ignored by Florida-based media and political types who had long dealt with them and by that time were over it.

Things got so bad for DeSantis in mid-2023 that he had to return to the "legacy media" he so detested. He decided to sit down with CNN anchor Jake Tapper for an interview, an announcement that was scoffed at by many people eager to point out the hypocrisy of someone who had built a reputation as an antimedia crusader turning to a cable news outlet he regularly attacked when he needed to boost his struggling campaign.

Not only was it a slice of hypocrisy, it also cut into a core belief among DeSantis and his supporters: mainstream media had lost its juice and was no longer needed.

"Do most GOP primary voters watch CNN?" Pushaw tweeted in May of 2023 at Karoline Leavitt, a spokeswoman for a pro-Trump super PAC.

The Twitter back-and-forth came as DeSantis was just getting in the presidential race and the fight between the two camps was heating up.

Less than two months later, Pushaw changed her tune when the CNN interview with DeSantis was announced. She was apparently delighted that her boss would be joining the network she had previously expressed hatred for and used three exclamation points to prove it.

"Let's go!!!" she tweeted shortly after the CNN interview was announced.

During this difficult time, DeSantis's first financial disclosure form did offer some positive signs, as Never Back Down reported that it had raised $130 million, a number that included a more than $80 million transfer from his state political committee (so not new money), and that his campaign had raised $20 million in just six weeks. But just below the surface, even that positive news came with some caveats: in those same six weeks, DeSantis burned through $7.9 million, and roughly two-thirds of the money came from donors who had given the legal maximum and would not be able to give again. Only 14 percent of his first haul came from small-dollar contributors, which is generally seen as a barometer of approval among the party's grassroots.

Yet again, what had been a strength for DeSantis during his 2022 reelection now proved to be a weakness early in his White House bid.

As the walls closed in and questions began to swirl about whether DeSantis's long-hyped presidential run would go down as one of the biggest busts in history, his team was quietly reassuring donors to pay no heed to the noise of the moment and trust the process.

An internal campaign memo outlined what DeSantis's team saw as glimmers of light amid what had become dark news cycle after dark news cycle. Trump was winning, they conceded, but his support in early states was persuadable, they told donors who at that point were getting antsy.

"Early state voters are only softly committed to the candidates they select on a ballot question this far out—including many Trump supporters," read the memo. "Our focus group participants in the early states even say they don't plan on making up their mind until they meet the candidates or watch them debate."

The memo argued that Trump had a 25 percent "floor," which meant that the DeSantis team thought one-quarter of the GOP primary vote would always be with him no matter what, but they still tried to beam confidence and downplayed the idea that anyone other than DeSantis could take on Trump.

"As it has been for the last year, Trump and DeSantis remain the only viable options for two-thirds of the likely Republican primary electorate," it read.

The memo made the case that the campaign would not spend money in Super Tuesday states at the expense of New Hampshire, an early primary state that some thought DeSantis would largely skip because it is known for being home to a moderate brand of Republican less receptive to DeSantis's culture-war rhetoric.

The governor's team also made it clear that they would continue to stay away from aggressively going after Trump, only talking about their main primary rival if asked directly.

"Our campaign will make the contrast between Joe Biden and Ron DeSantis clear—but we won't avoid Trump's failings when asked," the memo read. "Our strategy? Question asked, question answered, then on to how we beat Joe Biden."

In a notable admission, the campaign also acknowledged it needed "earned media," a term used for free attention drummed up largely by news coverage. For a DeSantis political team that had denigrated the press and downplayed its significance, it was an acknowledgment of the media's continued importance.

"More earned media will result in increased standing on the ballot," read the memo. "We will aggressively pursue this formula in the next eight weeks as we understand that standing in the polls is directly tied to earned media—pro-DeSantis surrogates understand the importance [of appearing] on every possible news segment."

So that was the pitch DeSantis's campaign was making to project its long-term viability. Staffers had a plan, and they were going to execute it even when it felt like everything was going wrong.

The message was heard by early DeSantis supporters. Their confidence was shaken by the flameout that was DeSantis's first two months on the campaign trail, but many pressed on undeterred.

"This is not going like anyone thought," said a DeSantis donor in July of 2023. "But we are pros. We are in it for the long haul."

CONCLUSION

DAWN OF THE DEAD

FLORIDA FLORIDA FLORIDA.
A lot has changed since the year 2000. But some things remain the same.

Tim Russert's immortal words, scribbled on that whiteboard in the early morning hours of November 8, 2000, may have been about Florida's power as a swing state rather than the deep-red swamp it has become. But although the nature of the state's political clout has changed, it has not diminished in the intervening years. If anything, it has grown.

Today, of course, the contest between Al Gore and George W. Bush looks almost quaint compared to the rivalry between DeSantis and Trump. What are a few hanging chads and a quick concession speech compared to the political death match that spilled out of Florida and onto the national stage two decades later?

But now, as then, the country's fate is Florida's to decide.

The question, of course, is, Which fate will it be?

Ron DeSantis's rise to national prominence in 2021 and 2022 was a thing to behold. At a time when Trump's residue remained dusted all over the surfaces of the Republican Party, Florida had given conservatives a shiny new object—a talisman that, for many in the GOP, augured a new golden age for the party. Trump may have been a thing of the past, but with DeSantis, Make America Great Again might be the way of the future.

DeSantis was a new breed of carnival barker, one who was singularly focused on shouting down the libs. He embodied the right's hatred for Anthony Fauci and COVID restrictions. He conquered vast new frontiers in the ongoing culture wars. He inserted must-know terms such as DEI and CRT and ESG into the political right's lexicon, each of which was quickly transformed from obscure academic abbreviation into a metastasizing disease unleashed by people on the left onto people on the right, assaulting the culture that they, their parents before them, and their grandparents before them held so dear.

It was in this moment of DeSantis's political revival that the country was learning of his Ivy League education, his military background, and his telegenic family. He checked all the boxes of a conservative dream candidate and was the answer to the question increasingly infiltrating GOP political circles: How do we get Trump policies with less Trump?

DeSantis's growing political capital quickly marked him as a GOP front-runner in the popular imagination. He began to run neck and neck with Trump in straw polls whose earned media value far surpassed any real-life implications—but at that point, that *was* the point.

The mythology surrounding Ron DeSantis only grew after his dominant 2022 reelection campaign in a race that was never really a race. There is no way to downplay a nearly twenty-percentage-point statewide victory, and I won't pretend to do that here. And while Democrats essentially abandoned ship in Florida, allowing DeSantis to run virtually unopposed, his margin of victory still cemented his status as America's Governor among infatuated conservatives around the country.

That infatuation soon turned into a love affair. And the DeSantis team intended to take that love to the bank.

"I knew definitely before the midterms," said one adviser when asked at what point he knew DeSantis was running for president. "It was nothing ever really expressed. Everyone around the team just kind of knew. There was an inherent feel. The biggest indicator was just how much money he was raising."

And who can blame the team for its prognostications? Fueled, in part, by small-dollar donations that poured in by the tens of thousands from all fifty states, the campaign raised $200 million for the governor's reelection. It was not just a big number; it was *the* number, touted across the nation for the massive accomplishment it admittedly was.

"It was just [becoming] easier to raise money. Clients and prospective donors were bringing up [a presidential run]," said a longtime Florida GOP fundraiser. "Everyone was reading the room. Everyone knew what was coming."

As DeSantis vacuumed up the cash, he developed a noticeable swagger. The moment I remember most is when he knocked off Trump for the second year in a row in the Western Conservative Summit's straw poll, seen as a key weather vane of grassroots support—a vane that, by mid-2022, was pointing squarely at DeSantis.

"It did not surprise me DeSantis did well, but yeah, it kind of surprised me that he did better than President Trump again," Dick Wadhams, a longtime Colorado Republican consultant and former chair of that state's Republican Party, told me at the time. "I go to a lot of Republican events and have sensed for some time that… DeSantis has quite an appeal because of his success as governor of Florida."

As DeSantis continued to rise in Republicans' eyes, the overwhelming perception that Trump's influence had soured the GOP's performance in the 2022 midterms only exacerbated the idea that the ex-president was yesterday's news. Trump-recruited US Senate candidates almost universally lost, allowing Democrats to hold the Senate in surprising fashion and even pick up an additional seat.

And so, as the nation headed into 2023, Trump was on the ropes, and DeSantis was the guy who had put him there.

Trump announced he was again running for the White House one week after election day in 2022. However, far from the flashy affair he had hoped for, the event at Mar-a-Lago was rather ho-hum, attended by a small collection of supporters and advisers but without the GOP dignitaries who in the not-too-distant past would have flocked to Trump.

The former president didn't get a polling bump from his launch, and he noticed.

"This is the McLaughlin & associates POLL that just came out and which got it right in 2016 and 2020," Trump posted on Truth Social in mid-December of 2022, flashing his brand of holiday spirit, "unlike the WSJ, NBC Fake News, ABC Fake News, Fake Polling FOX NEWS, the dying and very sickly USA Today, and most others in the LameStream Media. In other words, it was REAL POLLING. As you can see, we are leading by a lot." McLaughlin, perhaps not so incidentally, is a firm that had previously worked for Trump.

The series of "fake" polls, of course, showed DeSantis leading or running very close to Trump, while the "real" polls had Trump up 58–36 to close out 2022.

Trump was flailing in the wind, seemingly set to tumble into the political dustbin of history. He would not fully acknowledge the gravity of the moment, but his haters sure did.

To kick off the new year, center-right writer Matt Lewis fantasized in the *Daily Beast* about "Trump's Reign of Terror" coming to an end. "Reports of Trump's political demise have been greatly exaggerated for years now. But this time feels different," Lewis wrote. "After years of falling upward, gravity finally reasserted itself in 2022. The chickens, it seems, have come home to roost. Whether a fellow Republican can successfully step into the void remains to be seen."

If anyone could do that, it was DeSantis—or so it seemed.

Even as DeSantis continued to talk about all the issues that made him a national political player, he refused to embrace the idea that he was aiming to launch a presidential campaign. The vacuum left by that silence was filled with stale stump speeches, all of which sounded identical.

By that point, I'd covered the DeSantis administration for five years, during which the running joke had long been that his speeches never change. He knew the talking points that worked for his supporters, and he knew they would never get tired of the rehashed jokes about the oddity of having young kids in the governor's mansion or the worthlessness of a "zombie studies" degree, something DeSantis often talked about when he was criticizing higher education. (Some universities do offer classes on the walking dead, but there are likely far fewer students who have taken them than the number of times DeSantis has tried to joke about them.)

The fact of the matter was, DeSantis knew how to excite his rabid base—but it was a method that left everyone outside it either asleep or increasingly turned off, especially in concert with his far-right policy pitches and cranky persona.

In March, just two months after he rode a wave of adulation into the new year, DeSantis's flawed strategy started to become apparent. In a Fox News poll taken that month, Trump had 54 percent of the GOP primary vote compared to just 24 percent for DeSantis, a huge margin when you consider that just two months earlier, DeSantis was riding a wave of momentum and had largely closed the public polling gap.

Trump, it seemed, had risen from the dead—a political zombie, staggering through the halls of Mar-a-Lago.

Except now, no one in DeSantis World was laughing.

DeSantis has, at the time of this writing, never been able to recover from his early stumbles and from Trump's reemergence. The former was DeSantis's own fault, and the latter he should have seen coming all the way from Tallahassee. Was the GOP's new golden boy really so golden after all?

On May 24, 2023, when DeSantis finally announced via Twitter that he was running for president, it already felt like he may have missed his moment—but perhaps the moment had never really existed. At the end of the day, Republicans still seemed to be more infatuated with Trump than with DeSantis.

Indeed, by mid-2023, some party members—even those ready to move on from Trump—seemed convinced that, outside of unthinkable legal circumstances, the former president was likely to be the GOP nominee.

It's a fatalistic perspective that some former DeSantis staffers have, in fact, embraced—some even with a sense of vengeance.
DeSantis had essentially spent more than three years running for
president, a process that involved building an allegiance with Trump
and then tearing it down in what became the defining relationship
of the modern Republican Party. In the process, dozens of staffers,
consultants, and confidants became discarded by-products of a cutthroat DeSantis political machine that cared much more about the
acquisition of power than it did about any individual ally.

Those who have been shoved aside eagerly await what they hope
will be the fall of the man who tried to end many of their careers.

"I can say without question there are those of us who are watching this gleefully," said a fired DeSantis staffer certain of the governor's political fate. "What goes around comes around."

Perhaps no one felt this more keenly than the members of Florida's media establishment. In an interesting bit of irony, one likely
legacy of DeSantis's combative approach to media—epitomized
by his pugnacious former communications director, Christina
Pushaw, and her merry gang of misfits—is the emergence of Florida-
based reporters with much larger followings and higher-profile
jobs than they had before. Pushaw's intense and very personal style
of attack helped elevate DeSantis in the eyes of media-hating conservatives and elevated the reporters who covered him and brawled
with her. As a result, I and many others were hired by national
news outlets and had our footprints greatly expanded. At the time
of this writing, the *New York Times*, CNN, NBC News, and the
Washington Post all have brought on Florida-based reporters they
would not have hired previously, helping ensure that the former
swing state stays in the headlines as the race between DeSantis and
Trump enters its terminal phase.

DeSantis's waxing and waning fortunes offer the best example yet of a Republican Party that sees Florida as the new aspirational ideal for the way a state should be run.

Florida is home to both Trump and DeSantis. DeSantis not only placed the state at the vanguard of conservative cultural change but also found new ways to spotlight issues—including critical race theory and equality and inclusion programs—that had never previously been on the forefront of the minds of even the most conservative voters. His taking the lead on these issues caused conservatives from other parts of the country to move to Florida and helped the state rapidly build a reputation as the most conservative in the country.

DeSantis's problem, at least in the early stages of the 2024 election cycle, was not his platform: being anti-China, anti-LGBTQ, and antidiversity, and focusing on culture wars over traditional GOP talking points—such as lowering taxes and reducing the size of government—are all stances that are overwhelmingly popular with Republican voters. In fact, DeSantis was on the front lines of the idea that government should not necessarily be made smaller but rather remade to inject right-wing conservative policy ideas into modern-day life. Those ideas are not going out of style with many Republican voters, and DeSantis's fervent support of them was a big asset.

No, DeSantis's biggest problem, beyond his personal unlikability, was Trump's complete and total dominance of the GOP.

DeSantis will have plenty of money moving into early 2024 to try to build out a strategy for getting back in the game. He will have a bigger team to execute the plan, and on paper, he will be in much better shape than Trump, who, though he has a circle of blindly loyal advisers, also seems unable to run a gaffe-free campaign.

DeSantis's stumble in 2023, then, does not spell the end of his presidential ambitions in 2024, nor does it write off his ability to affect the future of the nation's politics. His launch did not go as anyone on his team envisioned, but even in those darkest moments, most said that DeSantis is here to stay, and his presence in the national Republican Party remains closer to its beginning than its end, regardless of what might happen in 2024.

In this election cycle, though, it's hard to gain on Trump, someone who breaks all the traditional political rules yet suffers no negative consequences as a result. The sorts of things that would end political careers in the past, or at least offer ample ammunition for opponents—indictments, rhetorical screw-ups, and federal investigations—only strengthen Trump's political fortunes.

By the time Trump had resumed his place as the unquestioned front-runner for the GOP nomination, he had been indicted twice: once in New York for allegedly making hush money payments to porn star Stormy Daniels and once in a federal capacity for allegedly keeping confidential documents after leaving the White House and trying to cover up the fact.

The state of the new Republican Party is such that, as of this writing, the candidate facing indictments is the front-runner, a status that has only been boosted by the fact that he was indicted. The Deep State and its malicious agents were coming after Trump and would never let him return to the White House—or at least that's what emboldened Trump fans would tell themselves each time their leader faced well-deserved legal troubles.

No matter what DeSantis did, he could not move the needle. He supported Trump against the "weaponized" Department of Justice. He traveled to the border to boast about his record on immigration and said he would shutter several federal agencies, including the Department of Education and the IRS. DeSantis even added his own wrinkle, saying that if Congress would not let him close the agencies, he would use them to "push back against woke ideology and against the leftism that we see creeping into all institutions of American life."

It was the sort of messaging and focus that conservative voters loved. It was the sort of messaging that had brought DeSantis to the national political dance.

But none of it left a mark on Trump.

As Trump was fighting indictments, continued investigations tied to the January 6 insurrection, and allegations that he tried to overturn the 2020 election in Georgia, the idea grew that the only real thing that could help DeSantis—apart from landing his own indictment, it seems—was very unlikely to happen: a conviction that would leave Trump behind bars, unable to continue in the race.

The idea has crossed the minds of Team DeSantis, but no one ever took it seriously.

"It has never come up on a call that I have been on," said one DeSantis adviser in June of 2023, regarding the idea that Trump's legal problems could be their saving grace. "It's in the back of everyone's mind, but it's not really something you can game out. We are not thinking about it."

So there they sat. The man once dubbed America's Governor had spent years perfectly crafting a reputation geared to conservative primary voters who were turning their backs on him.

Even as things grew grimmer, DeSantis, in his characteristically arrogant fashion, has never thought he was making the wrong move. Any stumbles were always the fault of someone else, and he still views his ascendance to the White House as something preordained.

"He does not think he is getting his ass kicked," said a longtime DeSantis adviser in July of 2023. "Things are growing awful. Truly, truly awful. But he thinks he is doing fine, and the media and everyone else is getting it wrong."

That month, DeSantis started saying as much when questioned by conservative media about his fledgling campaign.

"Since we won reelection by so much last November, we have been the target of the corporate media. They clearly do not want me to be the nominee," DeSantis said during a July 10 interview on *The Clay Travis and Buck Sexton Show*. "But more importantly than that, they know that I will actually accomplish the big things that we know need to be accomplished in this country."

There is no clearer example of how DeSantis views the presidency than the one that emerged on his October 2017 trip to see Sheldon Adelson in Las Vegas—a trip that laid the groundwork for Adelson to head the finance committee of DeSantis's first gubernatorial bid. But the meeting was more than just an attempt to win over the long-time Republican megadonor.

"He told Sheldon in that first meeting that he would be forty when sworn in as governor and that it was not the last thing [he] will do," said a veteran DeSantis adviser. "Ron DeSantis has always believed he would be president. It's something he thinks he is destined for. In his mind, God and Casey DeSantis want him in the White House. No one can convince him otherwise."

There is much to be hashed out during the 2024 election cycle, and despite his rising troubles, it seems like DeSantis will have the grit to stick it out well through the early nominating contest. But whether or not he clinches the nomination that he sees as rightfully his, his advisers do not see him relinquishing his newfound place in the national Republican Party.

"No doubt," a longtime DeSantis adviser and supporter said when asked if DeSantis will run for president in 2028 if his 2024 run fizzles out.

Others feel that, had Trump been absent, things would have gone very, very differently. One DeSantis supporter summed it up with just the right amount of drama for what has been a sordid, mudslinging-filled affair.

"I don't think Trump is awesome; I support DeSantis. But every alpha has another alpha they can't beat. Unfortunately, it appears DeSantis has met the apex predator."

Even if DeSantis pulls off the impossible and wins the Republican nomination, that's unlikely to save him from Trump. The relationship between the two men has deteriorated to such a degree that, no matter where they go from here, it is likely that Trump will never cease to terrorize his onetime protégé.

"Trump is a vindictive motherfucker. He is a caveman. He either clubs it, eats it, or fucks it," said a former DeSantis adviser. "He's not going to eat DeSantis or fuck him, so he's going to always club him. It's all he knows how to do."

ACKNOWLEDGMENTS

I was sitting in the media gallery overlooking the floor of the Florida Senate—I'll never forget the feeling of dread.

At that point, in May of 2021, I had been working on trying to get a book deal for more than a year. The idea first popped into my head on December 31, 2019, a moment that sat on the precipice of wide-scale societal change. Over the following year, as the pandemic changed everything around us, I wrote and rewrote a draft manuscript, a task that itself seemed overwhelming. As I toiled away, I was blindly reaching out to potential literary agents, trying to find someone who would help me navigate waters that turned out to be much choppier than I imagined.

After more than a year of marinating in the fear and uncertainty of whether I was going to be able to get a book deal, there I sat in a room full of my fellow Florida reporters, overlooking the senate floor.

It was the first time in my career I can truly say I had impostor syndrome.

That unfamiliar sensation was washing over me in response to having just publicly announced—for the first time—that I was writing a book, which at that point was about Florida's transformation from the nation's preeminent swing state to a state that was functionally center-right. As the retweets of my announcement spiked and the (mostly) positive social media comments and text messages rolled in, I sat there in total terror as I tried to grapple with a question I had no idea how to answer: What now?

I had no idea how to write a book. At that point, a book deal was something I was trying hard to get, but I had not for one moment stopped to think about what would happen if I did indeed actually get one. I was the proverbial dog that caught the car.

If I were on my own, I never would have survived that moment or the earliest stages of the book-writing process. I'd have given in to my weaker instincts and walked away. It's only because of a small collection of people and supporters that I did not, and for them I will be forever grateful.

First and foremost is my wife, Ana.

No person had to deal with the brunt of my stress-induced frenzy more than she did. There is no way to fully prepare for what it's like to write your first book. Looking back over the past four years, I think I would do it all over again, but that sentence would not ring true without the word *think*.

It's a grind, and more than once I was the worst version of myself, but throughout, Ana never wavered in her encouragement and support or in picking up the life tasks that at times I was either unable to do because of work commitments or because I was simply mentally wiped. It's a debt I'm not sure I'll ever fully repay, but she offered support during this process with the sort of grace and patience I'm certain I do not possess.

Beyond her ability to navigate the bouts of anxiety, doubt, and occasional fear I had when I was sure I would never get across the finish line, Ana also lent a professional steadying hand. She is by almost any estimation the best journalist who lives in our home, and she made suggestions and additions throughout the process that unquestionably made the book better. She saw things where I did not and had expertise in coverage areas that expanded my thinking about a number of important passages.

This book would not be where it is today without her support, patience, and professional guidance. Period.

Any acknowledgment associated with anything I do professionally would be worthless without special mention of my family. My mom, Diane; my dad, Kevin; and my younger brother, Steven, form the bedrock of who I am and what I have, to date, accomplished as a journalist. Throughout my career, and this process, they have shown overwhelming support. From the moment my draft finally became an actual manuscript to the first time I was written about in our hometown paper, the mighty *Denmark News,* my family members have been huge advocates and sources of unwavering support, even when I was not sure I was deserving. In the middle of this process, I was completely focused on the work. Any spare time I had away from my day job was devoted to the project and fretting over whether I'd ever figure out how to get it done. It was in those moments that I would sometimes be hard to reach, even for my family, and be out of touch and distant. If I ever have the chance to write a book again, that is likely the thing I will focus most on improving.

Two extraordinary women deserve to be mentioned here: my grandmothers.

Both Cora Kerlinske and Shirley Dixon, who passed while I was writing this book, played huge roles in the person I am today. I could not have asked for more loving, supportive grandmothers. Cora to this day is the best cocktail-hour conversationalist I know, and Shirley's love for Chicago sports teams made her the epicenter of a loving lifelong rivalry between her and the rest of the family, which, thankfully, decided to settle in Wisconsin.

I could also not be more grateful to my literary agent, Matt Carlini, with the Javelin agency. He took a first-time author who sometimes expressed frustration with the process and expertly guided him through the good times and bad. When I started, I had no idea what I was doing or how an idea in my head can actually become a book (I still don't, really, to be honest), but he fielded my stressed-out concerns like the true pro that he is.

Alexander Littlefield and his team, most notably Morgan Wu, at my publisher, Little, Brown, also deserve huge credit for breathing life into a draft that occasionally needed a spark. I am immensely proud of most of the draft and the work I put into it, but as the 2024 election cycle really started to take shape and my time and attention were increasingly focused on my day job (which I do love), some of the late-stage writing admittedly came off as a bit flat and tired. But when I got back my final draft edits, I was delighted to find that Alex and Morgan had expertly taken the copy I was most self-conscious about and made it something I was proud to call my own (even if they deserve a great deal of the credit).

I'm not sure I would have been able to hit my deadlines so easily without my current employer, NBC News, and my stellar editor there, Amanda Terkel. When I was between jobs in March of 2023, I asked for and got three weeks off to finish my first round of edits, which were by far the most work-intensive and intimidating. It was my only book leave throughout the entire process, and I'm not sure how things would have landed if NBC had not graciously offered that time to me.

I would be remiss if I did not also mention POLITICO's great foresight in 2015 to expand into statehouses across the country. POLITICO's creating a Florida bureau likely helped keep me in the journalism industry. At the time, I still loved writing about politics, but the state of the industry made me think there was no way I could both remain in it and have a fulfilling personal life. POLITICO changed that when it hired me to lead its Florida bureau. The team there offered me an elevated platform and the sort of resources I never had access to while working for newspapers early in my career. I must also give POLITICO credit for motivating me to write this book. During my final few years at the company, the role of the states division, or at the least the Florida division, changed. These were changes I vocally disagreed with, and they prompted me to express my frustration. Without those moments, I'm not sure I would have looked so hard for a different path forward, which ended up being this book.

A huge thanks is also owed to the amazing Florida press corps, particularly those who have grinded it out while covering the DeSantis administration and the Florida legislature over the past few years, a time when it became increasingly difficult for journalists to do their jobs at the most basic level. This corps includes Gary Fineout, Mary Ellen Klas, Steve Bousquet, Marc Caputo, Steve Contorno, Arek Sarkissian, Andrew Atterbury, Bruce Ritchie, Lawrence Mower, Ana Ceballos, Emily Mahoney, John Kennedy, Kirby Wilson, Gray Rohrer, Jason Delgado, Jim Rosica, Jim Turner, Jim Saunders, Dara Kam, Ryan Dailey, Libbey Dean, Forrest Saunders, Romy Ellenbogen, Douglas Soule, Tom Urban, Christine Sexton, Brendan Farrington, Jeff Schweers, A. G. Gancarski, Jacob Ogles, and Ana Goñi-Lessan.

In 2013, *Tallahassee* magazine wrote a story titled "The Shrinking Capitol Press Corps." It lamented that news organizations were slashing or eliminating their capitol bureaus and that the media presence covering the Florida governor and the state legislature was not nearly as robust as it had been in years past. That was more than a decade ago, and since that time things have gone from bad to worse. Much worse. News organizations no longer value state government reporting as they once did or should, which is a shame, and states are worse off for it. The above talented journalists continue to work

ACKNOWLEDGMENTS

extremely hard amid shrinking resources, low pay, morale-draining newsroom leadership, and an increasingly hostile environment created by those we cover.

Their work is important and played an invaluable role in helping shape this book.

Finally, none of this would have been possible without the dozens of sources I cannot name here. I cannot overstate my appreciation for their stories, insight, and willingness to take a risk by talking to a writer who is not well liked by many powerful political players. Their allowing me to pester them time and again, making themselves available for numerous phone calls, lengthy interviews, and endless conversations over Tallahassee "fine" dining or a beer, helped provide the information needed to make a book like this one really work and helped me chronicle this historic moment in time.

NOTES

INTRODUCTION: FROM SWING STATE TO "FREE STATE"

2. *"not his brother's keeper":* "How Election Night 2000 Unfolded," NBC News, November 7, 2000.

2. *won him the nation:* Richard Roeper, "'537 Votes': How the Supreme Court and Irate People in Miami Picked a President," *Chicago Sun-Times,* October 20, 2020.

3. *"there weren't a lot of close elections":* Scott Stump, "'My Strongest Memory Is Chaos': A Look Back at Election Night 2000," *Today,* October 5, 2020.

3. *The impact of the 2000 recount:* Gary L. Gregg II, "George W. Bush: Impact and Legacy," Miller Center of Public Affairs.

4. *had long been written:* Election Results Archive, Florida Division of Elections, November 8, 2022, https://dos.myflorida.com/elections/data-statistics/elections-data/election-results-archive/.

7. *clinched the state's gubernatorial election:* Matt Dixon and Gary Fineout, "DeSantis Wins Big, with an Eye Toward 2024," POLITICO, November 8, 2022.

7. *everywhere but in Florida:* Matt Dixon and Gary Fineout, "'Going to Be Ugly': All Signs Point to Republican Landslide in Florida," POLITICO, October 27, 2022.

8. *more money in the bank:* Matt Dixon, "'De Facto Frontrunner': DeSantis' $200 Million Haul Positions Him for 2024 Run," POLITICO, November 3, 2022.

9. *318,855 people moved to Florida:* "Where People Moved in 2022," National Association of Realtors, January 30, 2023.

9. *"By keeping Florida free and open":* Brooks Barnes, "Disney to Lose Special Tax Status in Florida Amid 'Don't Say Gay' Clash," *New York Times,* April 21, 2022.

10. *"Trump's man on campus":* Joseph Guinto, "Trump's Man on Campus," POLITICO, April 6, 2018.

11. *no one else came close to:* "CPAC Straw Poll: DeSantis Top Choice for 2024 If Trump Doesn't Run," Associated Press, February 28, 2022.

12. *where they might have a fighting chance:* Brendan Farrington, "In DeSantis' Shadow, Florida Democrats Fight to Be Relevant," Associated Press, April 8, 2023.

13. *workshopping nicknames:* Margaret Hartmann, "Donald Trump's Nasty Ron DeSantis Nicknames, Ranked," *New York,* June 28, 2023.

14. *eyeing a White House bid:* Anthony Zurcher, "Ron DeSantis Still Hasn't Said He's Running for President. What's He Waiting For?," BBC, February 28, 2023.

CHAPTER ONE: THE WILDERNESS

17. *when Marco Rubio returned:* Manu Raju, Tom LoBianco, and Kevin Liptak, "Marco Rubio: 'I Changed My Mind,' Will Run for Re-Election," CNN, June 22, 2016.

17. *a lackluster GOP primary field:* Marc Caputo, "Poll Shows Wide-Open Senate Race, Murphy Strongest in General Election," POLITICO, March 1, 2016.

18. *in Iraq, as a legal adviser:* Michael Kruse, "Ron DeSantis Is Very Pleased with Himself," POLITICO, March 18, 2021.

19. *the result of Russian meddling:* Kyle Cheney, "Trump's GOP 'Warriors' Lead Charge Against Mueller," POLITICO, May 7, 2018.

20. *sow doubts about Donald Trump's legitimacy:* "DeSantis: Important to Note Voting Systems Were Not Hacked," Fox News, February 4, 2017.

21. *"not about slavery!":* Frances Robles, "Pranks, Parties and Politics: Ron DeSantis's Year as a Schoolteacher," *New York Times,* November 5, 2022.

22. *quarreled with their party's own leadership:* Lauren French, "9 Republicans Launch House Freedom Caucus," POLITICO, January 26, 2015.

22. *"not going to mess with" entitlement programs:* Yacob Reyes, "DeSantis Takes Different Tack on Social Security, Medicare Than When He Was in Congress," *Tampa Bay Times,* March 17, 2023.

24. *fund his 2018 gubernatorial campaign:* Drew Wilson, "NBC News Poll: Adam Putnam Clear GOP Gov. Front-Runner, Democrats Split," *Florida Politics,* June 27, 2018.

25. *"Bedouin tribes of Israel":* Matt Dixon, "The Presidential Race Florida Is Really Talking About," POLITICO, May 22, 2020.

26. *for this gubernatorial hopeful:* Mark Harper, "DeSantis Names Heavy Hitters on Finance Leadership Team," *Daytona Beach News-Journal,* December 29, 2017.

26. *"a true FIGHTER!":* Marc Caputo, Alexandra Glorioso, and Matt Dixon, "Trump Endorses DeSantis for Governor via Twitter," POLITICO, December 22, 2017.

29. *"brilliant cookie":* Max Greenwood, "Trump Touts DeSantis in Florida," *The Hill,* July 31, 2018.

30. *"America's pulse":* Rick Scott, "Donald Trump Has America's Pulse," *USA Today,* January 6, 2016.

30. *raised $20 million:* Ledyard King, "Gov. Rick Scott Chairing PAC to 'Rebrand' National Republican Party," USA Today Network, May 10, 2017.

33. *"Adam Putnam's 'Never Trump' attitude":* Matt Gaetz, "In FL Gov. Race, 'President Trump Knows He Can Trust Ron DeSantis,'" Breitbart, May 21, 2018.

34. *"my full Endorsement!":* Emily L. Mahoney, "Trump Tweets Full Endorsement of Ron DeSantis," *Tampa Bay Times,* June 22, 2018.

35. *"A day after Sarah Palin visited":* Matt Dixon, "Area Republicans Rate GOP Vice Presidential Candidate Sarah Palin's Sunday Rally," *Villages Daily Sun,* September 23, 2008.

37. *DeSantis went on to trounce Putnam:* James Varney, "Ron DeSantis Beats Adam Putnam in Florida GOP Primary," *Washington Times,* August 28, 2018.

37. *"The Ron DeSantis endorsement":* Matt Dixon and Marc Caputo, "Florida Governor's Race Shocker Sets Up Trump-Fueled Showdown," POLITICO, August 28, 2018.

38. *the Trump-worshipping TV spot:* Erin B. Logan, "'Build the Wall,' Florida Gubernatorial Candidate Tells His Young Daughter in Campaign Ad," *Washington Post,* July 31, 2018.

40. *157 miles per hour:* Jeff Masters, "Category 5 Hurricane Maria Hits Dominica," Weather Underground, September 18, 2017.

41. *A study conducted the following year:* Sheri Fink, "Puerto Rico: How Do We Know 3,000 People Died as a Result of Hurricane Maria?," *New York Times,* June 2, 2018.

41. *erroneously blaming Democrats:* Brian Naylor, "Trump Denies Almost 3,000 Died in Puerto Rico, Falsely Claims Democrats Inflated Data," National Public Radio, September 13, 2018.

41. *disagreeing with Trump:* Marc Caputo, "'Mr. President. SHUT UP.': Florida Republicans Pan Trump's Puerto Rico Conspiracy," POLITICO, September 13, 2018.

41. *represented a "divorce":* Alex Isenstadt and Marc Caputo, "Trump Rails on Top Florida Ally over Hurricane Maria Flap," POLITICO, September 18, 2018.

42. *"Ron is the most selfish person":* Dexter Filkins, "Can Ron DeSantis Displace Donald Trump as the GOP's Combatant-in-Chief?," *New Yorker,* June 20, 2022.

43. *his baseball manager at Yale, told POLITICO:* Michael Kruse, Matt Dixon, and Gary Fineout, "The Governor Who Holds Trump's Fate in His Hands," POLITICO, September 16, 2020.

43. *"Coach, he balked":* Michael Kruse, Matt Dixon, and Gary Fineout, "The Governor Who Holds Trump's Fate in His Hands," POLITICO, September 16, 2020.

CHAPTER TWO: THE PERFECT STORM

48. *Florida's future redistricting processes:* Jim Ash, "New Amendments Target Redistricting," *Florida Today,* November 7, 2010.

48. *After a multiyear legal battle:* "Florida Judge Orders Special Session to Redraw Congressional Map," Associated Press, August 1, 2014.

49. *Fortress of Democracy:* Matt Dixon, "Wealthy Liberal Donors in Florida Bypass Party, Fuel Covert Machine," POLITICO, May 2, 2016.

51. *supermajorities in the state legislature:* Brendan Farrington, "GOP Earns Supermajorities in Florida House, Senate," Associated Press, November 9, 2022.

51. *erase Fair Districts altogether:* Jacob Ogles, "Gov. DeSantis Takes Aim at Fair Districts Amendments," *Florida Politics,* March 15, 2022.

51. *twenty GOP-leaning seats:* Brendan Farrington, "Florida Gov. DeSantis Vetoes Republican-Drawn Congressional Maps," Associated Press, March 29, 2022.

52. *helping Republicans flip the US House:* Matt Dixon, "GOP to DeSantis: Thanks for Helping Us Flip the House," POLITICO, November 17, 2022.

52. *"compelling state interest":* Ryan Newman, memorandum to Ron DeSantis, March 29, 2022, https://www.flgov.com/wp-content/uploads/2022/03/SLA-BIZHUB22032912102.pdf.

53. *a 457,728-person registration advantage:* Election Results Archive, Florida Division of Elections, https://dos.myflorida.com/elections/data-statistics/elections-data/election-results-archive/.

55. *they spent only $2 million:* Matt Dixon, "How National Democrats Helped Pull Off a Surprise Win in the Jacksonville Mayoral Race," NBC News, May 19, 2023.

CHAPTER THREE: "IT DOES NOT HAPPEN WITHOUT TRUMP"

60. *naked on the floor of a Miami Beach motel:* "Here's What the Hotel Photos, Video Show from Andrew Gillum Miami Beach Incident," *Tallahassee Democrat,* April 22, 2020.

60. *Gillum was indicted:* Matt Dixon and Arek Sarkissian, "Former Gubernatorial Candidate Andrew Gillum Indicted on Federal Charges," POLITICO, June 22, 2022.

60. *In May of 2023, he was acquitted:* Jeff Burlew and William L. Hatfield, "He 'Can Resume His Life': Case Against Andrew Gillum Dropped," *Tallahassee Democrat,* May 15, 2023.

64. *Florida should not "monkey this up":* Julia Jacobs, "DeSantis Warns Florida Not to 'Monkey This Up,' and Many Hear a Racist Dog Whistle," *New York Times,* August 29, 2018.

64. *"the racists believe he's a racist":* Gregory Krieg, "Andrew Gillum on DeSantis: 'The Racists Believe He's a Racist,'" CNN, October 25, 2018.

66. *forever changed the state's political trajectory:* Stephanie Saul, Patricia Mazzei, and Jonathan Martin, "Ron DeSantis Reboots in Close Florida Governor's Race, After Early Stumble," *New York Times,* October 4, 2018.

67. *he'd "made a mistake":* @CNN (CNN), "Republican Ron DeSantis says he will be a 'governor for all Floridians' after being asked about his 'monkey this up' comment and not returning money from a donor that used a racial slur when referring to former president Barack Obama," Twitter, October 21, 2018.

68. *DeSantis won by roughly forty thousand votes:* Ledyard King, "With Florida Recount Over, Andrew Gillum's Last Chance to Become Governor Rests with the Court," *USA Today,* November 15, 2018.

CHAPTER FOUR: A MOVABLE FRAT HOUSE

71. *sentenced to eleven years in prison:* David Shortell, Jeremy Herb, Paula Reid, and Devan Cole, "Former Matt Gaetz Associate Joel Greenberg Pleads Guilty to Six Federal Charges," CNN, May 17, 2021.

71. *when she was a minor:* Marc Caputo and Matt Dixon, "New Details Shed Light on Gaetz's Bahamas Trip," POLITICO, April 13, 2021.

73. *building the early administration:* Matt Dixon, "How Matt Gaetz Helped Make Ron DeSantis," POLITICO, March 24, 2021.

73. *ties to the medical marijuana industry:* David Harris, "Who Is Jason Pirozzolo? Politically Connected Florida Surgeon Reportedly Tied to Gaetz Probe," *Orlando Sentinel,* April 10, 2021.

75. *a national MAGA-fueled Republican rock star:* Michael Kruse, Matt Dixon, and Gary Fineout, "The Governor Who Holds Trump's Fate in His Hands," POLITICO, September 16, 2020.

78. *in return for pictures of her breasts:* Greg Woodfield, "Prominent DeSantis Ally Who Shot Himself Dead Last Year Was Under Investigation for Using Sold Out Taylor Swift Tickets to Lure Teen to His Office," *Daily Mail,* April 18, 2023.

79. *in an attempt to tip the 2016 presidential race in Trump's favor:* "Giuliani Associate Lev Parnas Is Sentenced to 20 Months in Prison," Associated Press, June 29, 2022.

80. *"attempted to influence the 2018 elections":* United States Attorney's Office, Southern District of New York, "Russian Oligarch Charged with Making Illegal Political Contributions," press release, March 14, 2022.

80. *the "victory in Florida":* Ben Wieder, "Russian Pot Entrepreneur Tied to Parnas, Fruman Is Latest Charged in Campaign Finance Plot," *Miami Herald,* March 14, 2022.

80. *DeSantis met the men on six separate occasions:* Gray Rohrer and Steven Lemongello, "Office: At Least 6 Times DeSantis, Parnas Met. But Still Unclear What Businessman Sought from Administration," *Orlando Sentinel,* November 16, 2019.

80. *At DeSantis's swearing-in:* Steven Lemongello, "Photos Link DeSantis with Giuliani Indicted Associates Parnas, Fruman Attended Inauguration," *Orlando Sentinel,* October 26, 2019.

83. *break into Florida's medical marijuana business:* Arek Sarkissian and Natalie Fertig, "How 2 Giuliani Associates Failed to Break into Florida's Pot Industry," POLITICO, October 23, 2019.

CHAPTER FIVE: THE PURGE

84. *rejected his hand-picked candidate for party chairman:* Brandon Larrabee, "Republicans Reject Gov. Scott's Pick to Lead State Party," News Service of Florida, January 17, 2015.

86. *fundraising strategy for Friends of Ron DeSantis:* Steve Contorno, "Ron DeSantis' Political Team Planned $25K Golf Games, $250K 'Intimate Gatherings,' Memo Says," *Tampa Bay Times,* September 12, 2019.

87. *Wiles had officially been booted from Trump World:* Alex Isenstadt and Matt Dixon, "Trump Campaign Cuts Ties with Top Adviser in Florida," POLITICO, September 17, 2019.

87. *refrain from raising money for the Republican National Committee:* Annie Karni and Patricia Mazzei, "DeSantis Is Said to Quietly Hinder Fund-Raising for Trump Convention," *New York Times,* July 9, 2020.

89. *"probably won't be that involved":* John Kennedy, "On Eve of Trump Rally, DeSantis Announces He'll Spend More Money on Elections Security," *Panama City Herald,* June 18, 2019.

89. *"Hey Ron, are we gonna win the state, please?":* Sarah Toce, "Trump Says He'll Blame Governor If He Loses Florida: 'I'll Fire Him, Somehow,'" *Raw Story,* October 16, 2020.

91. *"Today I released my budget proposal":* "Governor Ron DeSantis Announces His Bold Vision for a Brighter Future Budget for FY 2019–2020," FLgov.com, February 1, 2019.

92. *former state representative Jared Moskowitz:* Sharon Aron Baron, "DeSantis Appoints State Rep. Moskowitz to Head Up Florida Division of Emergency Management," *Coral Springs Talk,* December 6, 2018.

92. *he pardoned the Groveland Four:* Jacey Fortin, "Florida Pardons the Groveland Four, 70 Years After Jim Crow–Era Rape Case," *New York Times,* January 11, 2019.

92. *issued a posthumous apology:* Ana Johnson, "Florida Says Sorry to 'Groveland Four,' Wrongly Convicted of Rape in 1949," CNN, April 19, 2017.

93. *"I am encouraged to see the governor's commitment":* Lawrence Mower, Emily Mahoney, Elizabeth Koh, and Samantha J. Gross, "Ron DeSantis Proposes Record $91.3 Billion Budget, More Spending on Students," *Tampa Bay Times,* February 1, 2019.

93. *"The Constitution requires a balanced budget":* Mower et al., "Ron DeSantis Proposes Record $91.3 Billion Budget."

95. *"President Donald Trump is leaving Washington":* Brendan Farrington, "Trump Will Find Friendly Florida Crowd Amid Impeachment Talk," WINK News, October 3, 2019.

95. *"today I'm issuing the Presidential Protection Fund":* "DeSantis Raises Money to Back Trump Amid Impeachment Inquiry," WESH News, September 27, 2019.

CHAPTER SIX: LOOKS CAN BE DECEIVING

97. *"I'm thrilled to be back in my second home":* Gary Fineout, Matt Dixon, and Isabel Dorbin, "Showtime in Orlando for Donald Trump," POLITICO, June 19, 2019.

99. *in three statewide Florida campaigns:* "Scott's Off-Key Pitch to Hospitals," *Daytona Beach News-Journal,* March 20, 2015.

103. *ranging from hurricane relief:* Amy Sherman, "Did Florida Gov. Ron DeSantis Get a 'Historic Commitment' from Trump for Hurricane Michael Aid?," PolitiFact, March 7, 2019.

103. *Everglades restoration funding:* Tyler Treadway, "President Trump's Proposed Federal Budget Now Has $200M for Everglades Restoration," *TCPalm,* May 14, 2019.

103. *to health-care reforms:* Sarah Owermohle, Sarah Karlin-Smith, and Gary Fineout, "Trump Plan Would Allow States to Import Drugs from Canada," POLITICO, December 19, 2019.

103. *during the March 2019 speech:* Mark Skoneki, "Gov. Ron DeSantis' State of the State Speech: Full Text." *Orlando Sentinel,* March 5, 2019.

CHAPTER SEVEN: PANDEMICS AND PRESIDENTS

108. *inappropriate comments to a group of veterinary medicine students:* Christine Sexton, "DeSantis' Surgeon General Faced Sexual Harassment Allegations at UF," News Service of Florida, April 2, 2019.

110. *when the Florida Department of Health announced two positive cases:* Louis Bolden, "When Did Coronavirus First Appear in Florida?," WKMG-TV, May 7, 2020.

112. *"But people of this country can rest assured we are ready":* "15 Suspected Cases of Coronavirus Cleared in Florida, 4 Currently Under Investigation," Associated Press, February 28, 2020.

113. *"In this moment of growing uncertainty and anxiety":* Carl Lisciandrello, "Biden Blasts DeSantis' Response to the Coronavirus Outbreak in Florida," WUSF Public Media, March 25, 2020.

113. *issued a statewide stay-at-home order:* Mary Ellen Klas and Steve Contorno, "Florida Gov. Ron DeSantis Issues Statewide Stay-at-Home Order," *Tampa Bay Times,* April 1, 2020.

113. *"At this point, even though I think there's a lot of places":* John Kennedy, "DeSantis Orders: Stay at Home," *Gainesville Sun,* April 1, 2020.

114. *Trump and DeSantis sat side by side:* Christina Wilkie and Kevin Breuninger, "Trump and Florida Gov. Ron DeSantis Meet at White House as States Start to Reopen," CNBC, April 28, 2020.

114. *"We are with the governor of Florida":* "President Trump Meeting with Florida Governor DeSantis," C-SPAN, April 28, 2020.

115. *"When you see the president up there":* Dan Merica and Jeff Zeleny, "Florida Gov. Ron DeSantis Cites Trump's Changed 'Demeanor' in Issuing Stay-at-Home Order," CNN, April 1, 2020.

118. *Kushner had just been elevated:* Adam Cancryn and Dan Diamond, "Behind the Scenes, Kushner Takes Charge of Coronavirus Response," POLITICO, April 1, 2020.

119. *other supplies, including ventilators:* Yasmeen Abutableb and Ashley Parker, "Kushner Coronavirus Effort Hampered by Inexperienced Volunteers," *Washington Post,* May 5, 2020.

CHAPTER EIGHT: "WE'VE GOT TO STOP WITH THIS COVID THEATER"

121. *upended long-standing cultural and political norms:* Dylan Scott, "How Ron DeSantis Transformed into an Anti–Public Health Crusader," *Vox,* April 27, 2023.

122. *necessary part of COVID-19 mitigation:* "A Timeline of the CDC's Advice on Face Masks," *Los Angeles Times,* July 27, 2021.

122. *"we've got to stop with this COVID theater":* "Florida Gov. DeSantis Berates Students for Wearing Masks," Associated Press, March 2, 2022.

123. *"He pretty much said take off your mask":* Rod Carter, "Mother Upset After Florida Governor Asks Students to Take Off Masks, Calling It 'Ridiculous,'" CBS 17, March 2, 2022.

124. *"Even when DeSantis finally did something right":* Lexy Perez, "John Oliver Slams Florida Governor and Jared Kushner on 'Last Week Tonight,'" *Hollywood Reporter,* April 2, 2020.

124. *"It wasn't the data or the scientists":* Adrian Horton, "Seth Meyers to Jared Kushner: 'You're Not Qualified to Do Anything,'" *The Guardian,* April 3, 2020.

125. *"How did you do this?":* "Hannity Praises Gov. DeSantis for Protecting Elderly Floridians as Covid-19 Cases Mount," *NewsHounds,* April 23, 2020.

127. *ultimately laid out a three-phase approach:* Amanda Batchelor, "Re-Open Florida Task Force Releases 3-Phased Plan to Reopen State," Local10.com, May 1, 2020.

128. *"He is going to be opening up":* "President Trump Meeting with Florida Governor DeSantis," C-SPAN, April 28, 2020.

130. *#FloridaMoron to trend nationally on Twitter:* A. G. Gancarski, "Ron DeSantis Pushes Back on #FloridaMorons Criticism," *Florida Politics,* April 22, 2022.

130. *"I was really disappointed to see a lot of folks":* Jilliam Olsen, "Gov. Ron DeSantis 'Disappointed' to See Northerners Taking Shots at Jacksonville's COVID-19 Response," Tampa Bay 10, April 22, 2020.

132. *Andrew Cuomo Wins Over Past Critics:* Jimmy Vielkind, "In Coronavirus Response, Andrew Cuomo Wins Over Past Critics," *Wall Street Journal,* March 19, 2020.

132. *Cuomo was having a "reputational renaissance":* Bill Mahoney, "Andrew Cuomo, Social Media Superstar," POLITICO, March 23, 2020.

132. *women finding Cuomo attractive:* Doree Lewak, "NY Women Are Coronavirus Crushing on Andrew Cuomo," *New York Post,* March 21, 2020.

132. *journalistic integrity:* Minyvonne Burke, "Gov. Andrew Cuomo and Brother Chris Banter as CNN Anchor Talks of His Coronavirus," NBC News, April 2, 2020.

132. *"Most importantly, the same question must be asked":* Ross Barkan, "Glowing Coverage of Cuomo Also Raises Difficult Questions," *Columbia Journalism Review,* March 27, 2020.

133. *tested positive for COVID-19:* Michael Gold and Ed Shanahan, "What We Know About Cuomo's Nursing Home Scandal," *New York Times,* August 4, 2021.

133. *sexual harassment allegations surfaced:* Marina Villeneuve, "Gov. Andrew Cuomo Resigns over Sexual Harassment Allegations," Associated Press, August 10, 2021.

135. *at odds with state law:* Matthew Peddie, "State Rep. Carlos Guillermo Smith Sues Florida DOH to Release COVID-19 Data," WMFV, September 2, 2021.

136. *"Only the Legislature can create":* Jim Saunders, "An Appeals Court Considers Whether Florida Should Provide Daily COVID-19 Data," WGCU, September 14, 2022.

137. *"We don't have a vaccine":* Matt Dixon, "Why DeSantis Yanked Florida's Surgeon General from a Coronavirus Briefing," POLITICO, July 17, 2020.

138. *loyalty and obedience were valued above all else:* Daniel Villarreal, "Florida Surgeon General Removed from Governor DeSantis' Coronavirus Briefing After Saying Social Distancing Necessary Until There's a Vaccine," *Newsweek,* April 12, 2020.

139. *nothing to do with a double-booking:* Matt Dixon, "Why DeSantis Yanked Florida's Surgeon General from a Coronavirus Briefing," POLITICO, July 17, 2020.

139. *"Some people suggest that severe COVID-19":* Scott A. Rivkees, "Setting the Record Straight About COVID-19 Vaccines for Children," *Time,* November 23, 2021.

139. *"Dr. Scott Rivkees has largely":* Casey Tolan, Curt Devine, Majlie de Puy Kamp, and Drew Griffin, "Putting 'Politics in Front of Lives': DeSantis Faces Criticism over Florida's COVID-19 Response," CNN, December 18, 2020.

CHAPTER NINE: THE KNIVES COME OUT

141. *manipulating COVID-19 data:* Rachel Martin, "Florida Scientist Says She Was Fired for Not Manipulating COVID-19 Data," National Public Radio, June 29, 2020.

141. *had grossly overstated her claims:* Steve Contorno, "Fired Data Scientist's Claims of Covid-19 Data Manipulation 'Unsubstantiated,' Florida IG Report Finds," CNN, May 27, 2022.

142. *against Matt Gaetz in a super-conservative district:* Patricia Mazzei, "A Former Coronavirus Data Manager Who Clashed with DeSantis Will Challenge Gaetz in Florida," *New York Times,* August 23, 2022.

142. *She lost badly:* "U.S. Rep. Matt Gaetz Defeats Democratic Challenger Rebekah Jones, Retains District 1 Seat," *Pensacola News Journal,* November 8, 2022.

142. *the next COVID-ridden Italy or New York City:* Mary Ellen Klas and Ben Conarck, "Thermometer Company: Florida Compares Only to NYC in Spike in Fever Data," *Miami Herald,* March 21, 2020.

142. *"Hell, we're eight weeks from that and it has not happened":* Matt Dixon, "As Pence Stands By, DeSantis Unleashes on Former Health Official," POLITICO, May 20, 2020.

143. *could cause heart issues for some patients:* "Caution Recommended on COVID-19 Treatment with Hydroxychloroquine and Azithromycin for Patients with Cardiovascular Disease," American Heart Association, April 8, 2020.

143. *POLITICO colleague Andrew Atterbury reported:* Andrew Atterbury and Matt Dixon, "Florida Ordered 1M Doses of a Trump-Touted Drug. Hospitals Didn't Want It," POLITICO, June 11, 2020.

143. *suggestions from Trump and national physicians ideologically aligned with him:* Cleve R. Wootson Jr., Isaac Stanley-Becker, Lori Rozsa, and Josh Dawsey, "Coronavirus Ravaged Florida, as Ron DeSantis Sidelined Scientists and Followed Trump," *Washington Post,* July 25, 2020.

144. *giving him sweeping authority:* Kathryn Watson, "Florida Governor Ron DeSantis Suspends All Local COVID Emergency Mandates," CBS News, May 4, 2021.

144. *outsource work tied to the state's effort to fight COVID-19:* Mary Ellen Klas, "Florida Committed $283 Million to Adding Hospital Beds. Then They Weren't Needed," *Miami Herald,* May 21, 2020.

145. *landed more than $50 million in state contracts:* Matt Dixon, "DeSantis Donor Got $50 Million in Emergency Pandemic Work," POLITICO, August 5, 2021.

145. *flowed in to the DeSantis administration from other vendors:* Matt Dixon, "DeSantis Rakes In Cash as Florida's Covid Wars Rage," POLITICO, August 10, 2021.

145. *universally praised—including by DeSantis:* Melanie Michael, "'Vaccines Are Saving Lives': DeSantis Stresses Importance of Shots, Criticizes Mask Mandates as Florida COVID Cases Spike," WFLA-TV, July 23, 2021.

145. *first wave was sent to hospitals and health-care facilities:* Samantha J. Gross and Ana Claudia Chacin, "'There's Just Too Many People.' DeSantis Pressures Hospitals as Vaccine Demand Grows," *Miami Herald,* January 5, 2021.

146. *especially the elderly:* "DeSantis Wants Hospitals to Vaccinate At-Risk, Elderly Floridians. Hospitals Say They Need Help," News Service of Florida, December 29, 2020.

146. *wealthy, predominantly white zip codes:* Douglas Hanks and Ben Conarck, "Miami-Dade's Wealthiest ZIP Codes Are Also the Most Vaccinated for COVID-19, Data Shows," *Miami Herald,* January 23, 2021.

146. *The vaccination site that got the most attention:* Jessica De Leon, "DeSantis Faces Criticism over Exclusive COVID-19 Vaccines," *Bradenton Herald,* February 18, 2021.

146. *"After all, '22 is right around the corner":* Jessica De Leon and Mary Ellen Klas, "DeSantis' Political Fortunes a Focus of Manatee Vaccine Event, Texts Show," *Bradenton Herald,* March 9, 2021.

146. *negative news about the pop-up vaccine sites in wealthy communities:* David Goodhue and Mary Ellen Klas, "Wealthy Keys Enclave Received COVID Vaccine in January Before Much of the State," *Miami Herald,* March 5, 2021.

146. *vaccinated a World War II veteran:* David Rutz, "100-Year-Old World War II Veteran Becomes 1 Millionth Florida Senior Citizen to Receive Coronavirus Vaccine," Fox News, January 22, 2021.

147. *As an adviser to the president of the independent republic of Georgia:* Isaac Stanley-Becker, "DeSantis Spokeswoman Belatedly Registers as Agent of Foreign Politician," *Washington Post,* June 8, 2022.

147. *In March of 2021, she wrote an email:* Kirby Wilson, "Ron DeSantis Impressed Christina Pushaw So Much, She Asked Him for a Job," *Tampa Bay Times,* July 27, 2021.

148. *DeSantis doubled down in his support for Pushaw:* Eric Daugherty, "DeSantis Slams 'Hit Pieces' of Christina Pushaw Registering as Foreign Agent for Public Volunteering in Georgia: 'Nobody Believes Their Garbage!,'" *Florida's Voice,* June 8, 2022.

148. *DeSantis administration's full embrace of COVID-19 conspiracy theories:* Allison Quinn, "Florida Guv's Press Sec Walks Back Rothschild-Dog-Whistle Tweet After Backlash," *Daily Beast,* November 18, 2021.

148. *the October 2020 Great Barrington Declaration:* "Great Barrington Declaration Scientists with Gov. DeSantis in Florida," American Institute for Economic Research, March 18, 2021.

148. *controversial document embraced by conservatives:* Apoorva Mandavilli and Sheryl Gay Stolberg, "A Viral Theory Cited by Health Officials Draws Fire from Scientists," *New York Times,* October 19, 2020.

149. *saying that the declaration would "sacrifice lives":* Jessie Hellmann, "Dozens of Public Health Groups, Experts Blast 'Herd Immunity' Strategy Backed by White House," *The Hill,* October 15, 2020.

149. *This collection of scientists:* Kiera Butler, "Meet Ron DeSantis' New 'Public Health Integrity Committee,'" *Mother Jones,* December 16, 2022.

149. *DeSantis moderated the event:* Kirby Wilson and Allison Ross, "YouTube Removed Video of DeSantis Coronavirus Roundtable," *Tampa Bay Times,* April 9, 2021.

150. *openly flirting with the antivaccination community:* Marc Caputo and Gary Fineout, "DeSantis Flirts with the Anti-Vaccine Crowd," POLITICO, September 15, 2021.

150. *forbade businesses from imposing vaccine mandates:* Lawrence Mower, Kirby Wilson, and Romy Ellenbogen, "DeSantis Signs Vaccine Mandate into Law as Florida Challenges New Rule," *Tampa Bay Times,* November 18, 2021.

150. *DeSantis had sidelined his own administration's health-care professionals:* Matt Dixon, "Why DeSantis Yanked Florida's Surgeon General from a Coronavirus Briefing," POLITICO, July 17, 2020.

150. *local officials' ability to implement mask mandates:* Mary Ellen Klas, "DeSantis Declares COVID 'State of Emergency' Over, Overrides Local Restrictions," *Miami Herald,* May 4, 2021.

150. *This enraged Democrats and delighted Republicans:* Valerie Crowder, "Democrats Criticize Banning Local COVID-19 Laws, Vaccination Proof Requirements," WFSU, May 4, 2021.

150. *the hiring of Joseph Ladapo:* Arek Sarkissian, "How a Doctor Who Questioned Vaccine Safety Became Desantis' Surgeon General Pick," POLITICO, October 7, 2021.

151. *gender-affirming care for trans youth:* Arek Sarkissian, "Florida Releases Guidance Clashing with HHS Advice on Transgender Kids," POLITICO, April 21, 2022.

151. *UCLA's David Geffen School of Medicine:* Jeffrey Schweers, "Records Identify UCLA Boss Who Called Ladapo Unfit for Florida Surgeon General," *Orlando Sentinel,* May 16, 2022.

151. *DeSantis was ordering lockdowns:* Mary Ellen Klas and Steve Contorno, "Florida Gov. Ron DeSantis Issues Statewide Stay-at-Home Order," *Miami Herald,* April 1, 2020.

151. *"Lockdowns Won't Stop the Spread":* Joseph A. Ladapo, "Lockdowns Won't Stop the Spread," *Wall Street Journal,* April 9, 2020.

152. *in a May 2023 speech:* Selim Algar, "DeSantis Hits Biden over COVID-19 Vaccine Mandates with 'Warp Speed' Play," *New York Post,* May 22, 2023.

152. *a pariah in the school's medical department:* Divya Kumar, "Surgeon General Ladapo's Views Caused 'Acrimony,' Former Supervisor Says," *Tampa Bay Times,* February 3, 2022.

152. *Ladapo told my POLITICO colleague Arek Sarkissian:* Arek Sarkissian, "Ladapo Fires Back at Former UCLA Supervisor Who Refused Recommendation," POLITICO, February 4, 2022.

152. *healthy children* not *get the COVID-19 vaccine:* David K. Li and Nicole Duarte, "Florida Surgeon General Recommends Against Covid Vaccination for 'Healthy Children,'" NBC News, March 7, 2022.

153. *attempt to limit free speech:* Kirby Wilson and Emily L. Mahoney, "Doctors Were Warned Not to Spread Pandemic Misinformation. DeSantis Has a Different View," *Miami Herald,* March 3, 2022.

153. *"defending freedom of speech for health care workers":* Marilyn Parker, "Governor DeSantis Pushes Bill That Protects Doctors' Free Speech," News4Jax.com, March 3, 2022.

153. *focused on "free speech" in January of 2023:* Jim Saunders, "DeSantis Vows to Protect Free Speech Rights of Doctors When Sharing COVID-19 Views," News Service of Florida, January 18, 2023.

153. *Ward has long been controversial:* Matt Dixon, "Florida Doctors Worried DeSantis Gives 'Fringe' Dermatologist a Platform," POLITICO, January 26, 2023.

153. *Ward later said he felt "regret" for the statement:* Allison Baker, "Doctor Says 'I Regret Making That Statement' After Suggesting Students, Parents Lie About Having COVID," WJHG-TV, August 30, 2021.

153. *"to face a firing squad":* Eric Hananoki, "Key Ron DeSantis Medical Ally: 'Fauci Should Face a Firing Squad,'" Media Matters for America, January 31, 2023.

CHAPTER TEN: THE GREAT CONSERVATIVE HOPE

155. *someone whose presence they fought to have:* Steve Contorno, "Inside Fox News, DeSantis Is 'the Future of the Party.' And He's Taking Advantage," *Tampa Bay Times,* August 13, 2021.

156. *in order to get on Trump's radar:* Marc Caputo, "How Ron DeSantis Won the Fox News Primary," POLITICO, August 29, 2018.

158. *"What good is it if Fox News":* Jack Dutton, "Trump Blasts Fox News over Anti-Trump Ads," *Newsweek,* October 25, 2021.

159. *the first ever climate-related state of emergency:* Louise Boyle, "Hawaii Makes History as First US State to Declare a Climate Emergency," Yahoo! News, April 29, 2021.

160. *Murdoch empire souring on the Republican politician:* Nicholas Nehamas and Maggie Haberman, "DeSantis Confronts a Murdoch Empire No Longer Quite So Supportive," *New York Times,* July 12, 2023.

161. *One of DeSantis's oldest friends:* Michelle Price, "Longtime Trump Ally Laxalt Joins PAC Supporting DeSantis," Associated Press, April 22, 2023.

162. *first at Tea Party rallies:* Kyle Munzenrieder, "Ron DeSantis, Tea Party Favorite, Becomes First Republican to Enter Senate Race," *Miami New Times,* May 6, 2015.

162. *cofounder of the Freedom Caucus in Congress:* Lauren French, "9 Republicans Launch House Freedom Caucus," POLITICO, January 26, 2015.

164. *easily won the event's 2024 straw poll:* Meridith McGraw and Natalie Allison, "Donald Trump Wins CPAC Straw Poll," POLITICO, February 27, 2022.

165. *"We need people all over the country":* "Florida Governor Ron DeSantis Draws Cheers at CPAC Amid White House Speculation," CBS Miami, February 24, 2022.

165. *DeSantis's repeated use of the phrase:* Ana Ceballos, "DeSantis' 'Full Armor of God' Rhetoric Reaches Republicans. But Is He Playing with Fire?," *Miami Herald,* September 13, 2022.

165. *that the leader of a state should condemn any Floridian:* Bianca Padro Ocasio, "DeSantis Responds to Neo-Nazi Rallies, Says Criticism Is 'Smear' Job by Democrats," *Miami Herald,* January 31, 2022.

166. *"He has autocratic tendencies":* Michael Kruse, "The One Way History Shows Trump's Personality Cult Will End," POLITICO, April 16, 2022.

167. *"Ron DeSantis is turning Florida into his own mini-autocracy":* Ruth Ben-Ghiat, "Ron DeSantis Is Turning Florida into His Own Mini-Autocracy," *Lucid* (Substack), March 15, 2022.

167. *antigerrymandering language in the state constitution:* Gary Fineout, "Florida Supreme Court Locks In DeSantis-Backed Redistricting Map," POLITICO, June 2, 2022.

167. *Florida's antidiscrimination laws:* Ana Ceballos, "Here's What State Universities, Students Should Know About Florida's 'Anti-Woke' Law," *Miami Herald,* April 22, 2022.

167. *"state-sanctioned racism":* Ana Ceballos, "DeSantis Attacks Critical Race Theory as State Looks to Change Teaching Guidelines," *Miami Herald,* June 7, 2021.

167. *"positively dystopian":* Andrew Atterbury, "Florida Judge Blocks DeSantis' Anti-Woke Law for Colleges," POLITICO, November 17, 2022.

167. *Arresting twenty people, mostly Black:* Lawrence Mower, "Police Cameras Show Confusion over DeSantis' Voter Fraud Arrests," *Tampa Bay Times,* October 18, 2022.

168. *charges against them dropped:* Lawrence Mower, "Florida Prosecutors Drop Case Against Man Accused by Gov. DeSantis of Voter Fraud," *Miami Herald,* November 22, 2022.

168. *granting the statewide prosecutor jurisdiction:* Maryam Saleh and Ese Olumhense, "DeSantis' Election Police Have Largely Flopped in Florida Voter Prosecutions. A New Law Aims to Change That," *Reveal,* March 9, 2023.

168. *those arrested started agreeing to plea deals:* Angie DiMichele, "Delray Beach Man Arrested in DeSantis Roundup Enters Plea Deal in Voter Fraud Case, Sentenced to Probation," *South Florida Sun Sentinel,* February 9, 2023.

168. *infamous photograph showing several in a bathroom:* Jacob Knutson, "Trump Stored Classified Documents in Mar-a-Lago Bathroom and Ballroom, DOJ says," *Axios,* June 9, 2023.

169. *"These agencies have been weaponized":* Matt Dixon, "DeSantis Comes to Trump's Defense After FBI Search," POLITICO, August 8, 2022.

169. *Florida Governor Ron DeSantis Endorsed by George Soros:* Isobel van Hagen, "Trump-Backed Kari Lake Appears to Turn on Ron DeSantis After Sharing Conspiracy Linking Him to George Soros," *Business Insider,* February 18, 2023.

CHAPTER ELEVEN: STORMING THE MOUSE HOUSE

171. *standing by his side:* Matt Dixon, "DeSantis Axes $3B from Legislature's Budget in Front of Republican Leaders," POLITICO, June 2, 2022.

172–3. *"unduly restricts the right to peacefully assemble.":* C. Isaiah Smalls II, "Florida's 'Anti-Riot' Law Infringes on Right to Protest, United Nations Says," *Miami Herald,* August 31, 2022.

174. *"things that happened two, three years ago":* Aila Slisco, "DeSantis Sidesteps Questions on Trump's Transfer of Power," *Newsweek,* June 27, 2023.

174. *charges related to January 6 than any other state:* Ryan Kruger, "Florida Residents Played Major Role in Violence on January 6th," Fox 4 News, May 5, 2023.

174. *"That was concerning":* Ana Ceballos and Sommer Brugal, "Teachers Alarmed by State's Infusing Religion, Downplaying Race in Civics Education," *Miami Herald,* June 30, 2022.

178. *"Disney thought they ruled Florida":* Brooks Barnes, "Disney to Lose Special Tax Status in Florida amid 'Don't Say Gay' Clash," *New York Times,* April 21, 2022.

179. *"However despicable, risible, or just merely irritating":* Liz Mair, "Here's How DeSantis Could Lose Every Legal Battle and Still Win His War," *Daily Beast,* April 22, 2022.

180. *"Parents, teachers, doctors":* "Human Rights Campaign on DeSantis's 'Don't Say Gay or Trans' Law Going into Effect, Targeting LGBTQ+ Youth and Turning Back the Clock on Equality," Human Rights Watch, June 30, 2022.

CHAPTER TWELVE: "JUST KIND OF SAD AND WEIRD"

186. *"the gravitational pull the Sunshine State now has":* David Reaboi, "Ron DeSantis Welcomes You to Florida, America's New Texas," *Newsweek,* January 17, 2022.

187. *his burgeoning shadow war with Trump:* Matt Dixon, "DeSantis Uses Conservative Lifeline as Trump Sours on Him," POLITICO, January 14, 2022.

188. *shortly after my story was published:* @ChristinaPushaw (Christina Pushaw), "BREAKING: Politico gossip columnist's feelings are hurt, because he was not and will not be invited to dinner at the governor's mansion," Twitter, January 15, 2022.

188. *"meat loaf night":* @Mdixon55 (Matt Dixon), "That night was meat loaf night at the Dixon-Ceballos house, whould not have missed it for the world": Twitter, January 15, 2022.

189. *then Democratic candidate for attorney general:* Scott Powers, "Gov. Ron DeSantis' Press Secretary's Tweet Suggests Denial of Nazi Protest," *Florida Politics,* January 21, 2022.

189. *"liberal media meltdown of the year":* Lawrence Richard, "Ron DeSantis Spokesperson Teases Major Announcement: 'Prepare for the Liberal Media Meltdown of the Year,'" Fox News, August 3, 2022.

189. *sue DeSantis over the move:* Zac Anderson, "DeSantis Suspends Democratic State Attorney He Accuses of Being 'Woke,' Not Enforcing Laws," USA Today Network, August 4, 2022.

189. *DeSantis's reelection campaign:* Matt Dixon, "DeSantis' Press Secretary Christina Pushaw Headed to His Campaign Operation," POLITICO, August 12, 2022.

190. *"Nation's most based comms director":* @docmjp (Matthew J. Peterson), "Nations most based comms director @ChristinaPushaw, lays out the path forward: cut off the mainstream press and treat them like the enemy they are. They need access for credibility. Remove it. Only grant access to whoever covers fairly. Raise up new media figures /ecosystem," Twitter, September 13, 2022.

191. *"I don't care what you or any liberal journalist think":* S. V. Date, "DeSantis Gives Interview to Jan. 6 Attendee Wearing 'Three Percenters' Militia Insignia," *Huffington Post,* October 6, 2022.

194. *among politicians who write books:* @realDonaldTrump (Donald Trump), "Some in the Fake News are falsely stating that Ron DeSanctimonious' book is doing as well as 'LETTERS TO TRUMP,' my new book. This is FAKE NEWS in that LETTERS

doesn't even come out until April 25th. Ron has groups buying his book in order to inflate sales and, in fact, on the first day, his book was already 30% discounted. LETTERS TO TRUMP has much different pricing and is a coffee table book. The so-called Stars corresponded with me, you'll love it," Truth Social, March 10, 2023.

197. *"Pushaw tried (wo)manfully":* Mac Stipanovich, "Mac Stipanovich to Christina Pushaw: Bye, Felicia," *Florida Politics,* August 16, 2022.

CHAPTER THIRTEEN: IT ALL FALLS APART

202. *Arizona gubernatorial candidate Kari Lake:* Michael Doudna, "Florida Gov. Ron DeSantis Rallies Support Around Lake, Masters in Arizona," 12News.com, August 14, 2022.

202. *Pennsylvania gubernatorial candidate Doug Mastriano:* Matt Dixon, "DeSantis Stumps for Mastriano in Key Battleground State," POLITICO, August 19, 2022.

202. *Ohio Senate candidate J. D. Vance:* Jeremy Barr, "Vance, DeSantis Rally Puts 'Highly Unusual' Restrictions on Press," *Washington Post,* August 16, 2022.

202. *GOP gubernatorial nominee, Tim Michels:* Rob Mentzer, "At Michels Rally, Florida Gov. Ron DeSantis Says Wisconsin Can Follow His State's Conservative Lead," Wisconsin Public Radio, September 18, 2022.

202. *gubernatorial candidate Lee Zeldin:* Anna Gronewold, "DeSantis Stumps for Zeldin, Painting Florida as New York's Future," POLITICO, October 29, 2022.

203. *"DeSantis won, but DeSantis-ism lost":* Michael A. Cohen, "DeSantis Won, but DeSantis-ism Lost," MSNBC, November 16, 2022.

204. *"better than I thought":* Mary Papenfuss, "Trump Comes Up with Mocking Nickname for Gov. Ron DeSantis," *Huffington Post,* November 6, 2022.

205 *has long been a huge Trump ally:* Jacob Ogles, "Joe Gruters Publicly Backing Donald Trump in 2024," *Florida Politics,* April 21, 2023.

208. *blamed the sugar industry for the ads:* Matt Dixon, "US Sugar's Fingerprints on $700K in Attack Ads Against Longtime Foe DeSantis," POLITICO, April 13, 2018.

208. *"in the history of American politics":* Cheryl Teh, "Roger Stone Cautioned Ron DeSantis That It Would Be 'Ingratitude and Treachery' to Run Against Trump in 2024," *Business Insider,* October 27, 2022.

208. *NBC News reported at the time:* Marc Caputo, "The Inside Story of Trump's Explosive Dinner with Ye and Nick Fuentes," NBC News, November 29, 2022.

210. *classified documents at Mar-a-Lago:* Dan Mangan and Kevin Breuninger, "Four Dozen Empty Folders Marked 'CLASSIFIED' Found in Trump Mar-a-Lago Raid, DOJ Reveals," CNBC, September 2, 2022.

210. *cochair of both Trump's Arizona campaigns:* Matt Berg, Marissa Martinez, and Matt Dixon, "Trump's 2024 GOP Rivals Rally Behind Him After FBI Search," POLITICO, August 9, 2022.

213. *slight win for Trump-aligned forces:* Michelle L. Price and Brendan Farrington, "GOP Rep. Dan Webster Narrowly Beats Far-Right Activist Laura Loomer in Florida," *Associated Press,* August 23, 2022.

215. *an awkward silence ensued:* Emily L. Mahoney and Kirby Wilson, "Will DeSantis Run for President in 2024? In Debate with Crist, He Won't Say," *Tampa Bay Times,* October 24, 2022.

216. *Griffin said during the interview:* Shia Kapos, "GOP Megadonor: I'm Ready to Back DeSantis for President in '24," POLITICO, November 6, 2022.

217. *included Ronald Lauder:* Brian Schwartz, "Trump Ally, Billionaire GOP Megadonor Ronald Lauder Won't Back Trump's 2024 Run for President," CNBC, November 12, 2022.

217. *gave DeSantis nearly $60,000 for his reelection bid:* Matthew Loh, "GOP Donor Who Gave Trump $120,000 in 2020 Now Says He Won't Give the Former President Anything," *Business Insider,* November 17, 2022.

218. *all over the country, except in Florida:* "The Day After: The Positives," *Clay Travis and Buck Sexton Show,* November 9, 2022.

219. *every conservative talking head in the country:* Jeremy Barr, "After Midterms, Ron DeSantis Eclipses Trump on Fox News," *Washington Post,* November 9, 2022.

220. *"Ron DeSanctimonious is playing games!":* Andrea Chu, "Trump Says DeSantis Is 'Playing Games' Amid Rumors of 2024 Rivalry," WTSP.com, November 11, 2022.

221. *a rollout held five days later at Mar-a-Lago:* Jill Colvin, "Trump Expected to Announce 3rd Campaign for the White House," Associated Press, November 15, 2022.

CHAPTER FOURTEEN: THE INEVITABILITY OF RON DESANTIS

224. *no fewer than eighteen bills:* Kathryn Varn, "A Rundown of Florida Bill Causing 'Massive Panic' in Transgender LGBTQ Communities," USA Today Network, March 15, 2023.

224. *limiting the teaching of sexual orientation and gender identity:* Ana Ceballos, "Florida Officially Limits Gender, Sexual Orientation Instruction in All School Grades," *Miami Herald,* April 20, 2023.

224. *referring to students by their preferred pronouns:* Ana Ceballos and Sommer Brugal, "Florida Bills Take Aim at Students' Pronouns and Restrict Lessons on Sex and Gender," *Miami Herald,* March 10, 2023.

224. *banning gender-affirming care:* Arek Sarkissian, "Florida Legislature Votes to Ban Gender-Affirming Care for Minors," POLITICO, May 4, 2023.

224. *further cracking down on drag shows:* Ana Ceballos and Romy Ellenbogen, "Restrictions on Drag Shows, Pride Parades in Question as Senate Approves Bill," *Miami Herald,* April 12, 2023.

224. *stripping liquor licenses from bars:* Ana Ceballos and Joey Flechas, "Another Drag Show Showdown: Florida Targets Prominent Miami Hotel's Liquor License," *Miami Herald,* March 15, 2023.

224. *investigators found no evidence of "lewd" activity:* Nicholas Nehamas and Ana Ceballos, "Florida Undercover Agents Reported No 'Lewd Acts' at Drag Shows Targeted by DeSantis," *Miami Herald,* March 20, 2023.

224. *property insurance companies going belly-up:* Lawrence Mower, "Florida's Latest Homeowners Insurance Crisis Is a Mess Decades in the Making," *Tampa Bay Times,* August 12, 2022.

225. *more than twenty local school board races:* Ana Ceballos, "DeSantis Endorses 30 School Board Candidates Across Florida. They Did Very Well," *Miami Herald,* August 24, 2022.

225. *"I basically said, 'Parents you have rights'":* Brianne Pfannestiel, "Trump Takes Aim at Ron DeSantis in First Iowa Visit of 2024 Caucus Presidential Campaign," *Des Moines Register,* March 13, 2023.

225. *comparing him to Mitt Romney:* Brett Bachman, "Donald Trump Issues Ultimate Insult to Ron DeSantis in Iowa Speech," *Daily Beach,* March 14, 2023.

225. *voting to cut entitlement programs:* Sarah Ewall-Wice and Aaron Navarro, "Entitlement Reforms Could Set Republicans Apart in a Potentially Crowded GOP Presidential Primary," CBS News, March 1, 2023.

226. *DeSantis would say he was focusing on Florida:* Steve Contorno and Kristen Holmes, "DeSantis Dismisses 'Noise' When Asked About Trump's Criticism of Him," CNN, November 15, 2022.

226. *new nickname for DeSantis: Meatball Ron:* Kierra Frazier, "Trump: I Won't Call DeSantis 'Meatball Ron,'" POLITICO, February 18, 2023.

227. *he was going to be arrested:* Luc Cohen and Karen Freifield, "Trump Says He Expects to Be Arrested on Tuesday, Calls for Protests," Reuters, March 20, 2023.

227. *disguising hush-money payments:* Erica Orden, Meridith McGray, and Kelly Garrity, "Trump Indicted in Porn Star Hush Money Payment Case," POLITICO, March 30, 2023.

228. *received money from a group Soros contributed to:* Linda Qiu, "Explaining the Ties Between Alvin Bragg and George Soros," *New York Times,* March 23, 2023.

229. *did not throw a lifeline to Trump:* Natasha Korecki and Jonathan Allen, "Ron DeSantis Breaks His Silence on a Possible Trump Indictment," NBC News, March 20, 2023.

229. *news conference in Panama City:* Jay Cridlin, "DeSantis Slams New York DA's Trump Investigation, Swipes at Trump Himself," *Tampa Bay Times,* March 20, 2023.

230. *had just suspended Andrew Warren:* Lawrence Mower and Emily L. Mahoney, "DeSantis Removes Hillsborough County State Attorney Andrew Warren," *Tampa Bay Times,* August 4, 2022.

231. *Robert Hinkle later eviscerated DeSantis:* Matt Dixon, "Judge Rules DeSantis' Ouster of Prosecutor Was Unconstitutional but Upholds Suspension," POLITICO, January 20, 2023.

232. *misstep on Russia's invasion of Ukraine:* Meg Kinnard, "DeSantis Walks Back 'Territorial Dispute' Remark on Ukraine," Associated Press, March 23, 2023.

233. *downplaying the situation as a "territorial dispute":* Meg Kinnard, "DeSantis Walks Back 'Territorial Dispute' Remark on Ukraine," Associated Press, March 23, 2023.

233. *"DeSantis' Ukraine Flip Alarms Pro-Israel Republicans":* Matthew Kassel, "DeSantis' Ukraine Flip Alarms Pro-Israel Republicans," *Jewish Insider,* March 15, 2023.

233. *a similar position on Ukraine:* Jeff Zymeri, "'A Mere Territorial Dispute': Nikki Haley Takes On DeSantis over Ukraine Stance," *National Review,* March 21, 2023.

233. *he raised well over $200 million:* Matt Dixon, "'De Facto Frontrunner': DeSantis' $200 Million Haul Positions Him for 2024," POLITICO, November 3, 2022.

234. *DeSantis said he could have made his statements "more clear":* Julia Musto, "DeSantis Says Ukraine Comments Were 'Mischaracterized,'" Fox News, March 24, 2023.

234. *"Over the last two months":* Nate Cohn, "DeSantis, on Defense, Shows Signs of Slipping in Polls," *New York Times,* March 17, 2023.

236. *roped into an investigation:* Ana Ceballos and Samantha J. Gross, "Dark Money Group Seeks to Block Disclosure of Donor Names in Ghost Candidate Probe," *Miami Herald,* January 10, 2022.

237. *Frank Artiles facing charges:* Ana Ceballos, Samantha J. Gross, and David Ovalle, "Former Senator Artiles Paid No-Party Candidate More Than $40K, Arrest Warrant Charges," *Miami Herald,* March 18, 2021.

237. *a glimpse into its role in the scheme:* Ana Ceballos, "Records Tied to $600,000 Money Transfer Subpoenaed in Miami 'Ghost' Candidate Case," *Miami Herald,* August 1, 2022.

CHAPTER FIFTEEN: "IT'S ON"

241. *"A Glimpse of DeSantis in Iowa: Awkward, but Still Winning the Crowd":* Michael Bender, "A Glimpse of DeSantis in Iowa: Awkward, but Still Winning the Crowd," *New York Times,* March 10, 2023.

242. *DeSantis using three fingers to eat chocolate pudding:* Dan Ladden-Hall and Zachary Petrizzo, "MAGA Attack Ad Rips into Ron DeSantis' Gross Pudding Habits," *Daily Beast,* April 14, 2023.

243. *"It was just a shattering experience":* Kimberly Leonard, "DeSantis Opens Up for the First Time About 'Shattering' Death of His Sister, Christina, at Age 30," *Insider,* March 23, 2023.

247. *still owed $21,284 in student loans:* Kimberly Leonard, "With $319,000 of Net Worth, Ron DeSantis Is the Anti–Donald Trump When It Comes to His Own Money, Records Show," *Insider,* June 15, 2022.

248. *the pro-Trump super PAC behind the complaint:* Matt Dixon, "Ron DeSantis Hit with an Ethics Complaint from Trump Super PAC," NBC News, March 15, 2023.
249. *"I was geographically raised in Tampa Bay":* Henry J. Gomez, "How Midwest Roots Shaped Ron DeSantis' Political Values and Perspective," NBC News, March 29, 2023.
249. *a similar line he'd used in Utah:* A. G. Gancarski, "Ron DeSantis Says Florida Is the 'Iowa of the Southeast,'" *Florida Politics,* May 13, 2023.
249. *"Rust Belt values" raised him:* A. G. Gancarski, "Ron DeSantis Credits 'Rust Belt' Values with Surviving Ivy League Liberalism," *Florida Politics,* February 26, 2023.
249. *the needless Florida comparison:* Henry J. Gomez, "Ron DeSantis Is Learning That Not Every State Wants to Be Florida," NBC News, May 22, 2023.
250. *"Do not believe anything you're reading by the media":* Andrew Feinberg, "'A Trojan Horse for the Left' and Fox News Trash Talk: At CPAC Trump Republicans Reveal Their Battle Plan for DeSantis—Will It Work?," *The Independent,* March 4, 2023.
251. *shortly after DeSantis entered the race:* Alex Isenstadt, "Club for Growth Steps on Trump Relaunch with Polls Showing DeSantis Beating Him," POLITICO, November 14, 2022.
251. *Herschel Walker's Georgia Senate campaign:* Natalie Allison, "Matt Schlapp Sued by Former Herschel Walker Aide over Sexual Assault Allegations," POLITICO, January 17, 2023.
253. *political insiders had endured for years:* Stefan Bosica, "Ron DeTedious: DeSantis Underwhelms Britain's Business Chief," POLITICO Europe, April 29, 2023.

CHAPTER SIXTEEN: "WIN IOWA, WIN IT ALL"

255. *DeSantis's home-state delegation:* Henry J. Gomez, Jonathan Allen, and Matt Dixon, "Trump's Endorsement Long Game Pays Off in Early Effort to Sink DeSantis," NBC News, April 21, 2023.
255. *Byron Donalds backed Trump:* Aiden Keenan, "Florida GOP Congressman Defends Endorsing Trump over DeSantis," NBC News, April 27, 2023.
256. *DeSantis's political team:* Ben Wieder, "Trump Uses Mar-a-Lago Photo Op with 10 Florida Congressional Members to Flex on DeSantis," *Miami Herald,* April 21, 2023.
257. *fell on deaf ears:* Matt Dixon, "Ron DeSantis' Team Tries to Stop Florida Republicans from Endorsing Trump," NBC News, April 12, 2023.
258. *"It's mean-spirited acts like this":* Jacob Ogles, "Joe Gruters Sees Retribution in Gov. DeSantis' Vetoes of Sarasota Projects," *Florida Politics,* June 15, 2023.
259. *"Anyway, thanks, everyone, for joining":* "Florida Governor Ron DeSantis announces 2024 Presidential Run on Twitter Spaces with Elon Musk Transcript," Rev.com, May 24, 2023.

259. *presidential launch on Twitter Spaces:* Dasha Burns and Matt Dixon, "Ron De-Santis Will Launch His Presidential Bid with Elon Musk," NBC News, May 23, 2023.

261. *When I reported this at the time:* Matt Dixon, "Ron DeSantis Administration Officials Solicit Campaign Cash from Lobbyists," NBC News, May 25, 2023.

262. *federal investigators who'd asked about them:* "Trump Is Charged in Classified Documents Inquiry," *New York Times,* June 8, 2023.

262. *he told a packed convention center:* Matt Dixon, "Trump Delivers Fiery Post-Indictment Speech: 'They're Coming After You,'" NBC News, June 10, 2023.

263. *Grassley did chair the Senate Judiciary Committee:* Steve Benen, "Several GOP Senators Haven't Bothered to Read Trump's Indictment," MSNBC, June 14, 2023.

264. *depending upon political affiliation:* Caitlin Yilek, Aaron Navaro, and Jacob Rosen, "Florida Gov. Ron DeSantis Indirectly Condemns Trump Indictment on Campaign Trail," CBS News, June 11, 2023.

265. *"None of this matters if we do not win":* Matt Dixon, "Faith in Trump Dominates Annual Gathering of Religious Conservatives," NBC News, June 24, 2023.

266. *down ten percentage points:* Julia Manchester, "Trump Widens Lead over DeSantis in New Hampshire: Poll," *The Hill,* June 27, 2023.

269. *"Do most GOP primary voters watch CNN?":* @ChristinaPushaw (Christina Pushaw), "Do most GOP primary voters watch CNN?," Twitter, May 24, 2023.

269. *after the CNN interview was announced:* @ChristinaPushaw (Christina Pushaw), "Let's go!!!," Twitter, July 16, 2023.

270. *"Early state voters":* Dasha Burns, Matt Dixon, Jonathan Allen, and Allan Smith, "Confidential DeSantis Campaign Memo Looks to Reassure Donors amid Stumbles," NBC News, July 13, 2023.

CONCLUSION: DAWN OF THE DEAD

275. *among infatuated conservatives around the country:* Gabriel Debenedetti, "The Agonizing Fall of Florida Democrats," *New York,* February 10, 2023.

275. *raised $200 million:* Matt Dixon, "'De Facto Frontrunner': DeSantis' $200 Million Haul Positions Him for 2024 Run," POLITICO, November 8, 2022.

275. *the Western Conservative Summit's straw poll:* Matt Dixon, "'Better Than President Trump': DeSantis' Clout Swells in the West," POLITICO, June 7, 2022.

276. *the ex-president was yesterday's news:* David Morgan, "After Final Trump-Backed Midterm Loss, Senate Republicans Bemoan Weak Nominees," Reuters, December 7, 2022.

276. *"the LameStream Media":* Caroline Vakil, "Trump Blasts Polling That Shows DeSantis Surging: 'Leading by a Lot' in 'REAL POLLING,'" *The Hill,* December 16, 2022.

277. *"this time feels different":* Matt Lewis, "Why Trump's Reign of Republican Terror Is Really Ending," *Daily Beast,* January 1, 2023.

278. *closed the public polling gap:* Victoria Balara, "Fox News Poll: Trump's Lead Grows in GOP Primary Race, Now over 50% Support," Fox News, March 29, 2023.

280. *DeSantis will have plenty of money:* Erin Mansfield, "Ron DeSantis Has More Campaign Funds Than Donald Trump Heading into 2024," *USA Today,* May 4, 2023.

281. *the "weaponized" Department of Justice:* Caroline Vakil, "Trump Indictment: DeSantis Blasts 'Weaponization of Federal Law Enforcement,'" *The Hill,* June 8, 2023.

281–2. *"push back against woke ideology":* Sam Levine, "DeSantis Says as US President He Would Eliminate IRS and Other Agencies," *The Guardian,* June 29, 2023.

283. *"accomplished in this country":* Paul Steinhauser, "DeSantis Commits to First GOP Presidential Primary Debate Regardless of Trump Participation," Fox News, July 7, 2023.

INDEX

ABOUT THE AUTHOR

MATT DIXON is a senior national politics reporter at NBC News and the former Florida bureau chief at POLITICO. He has been recognized for both his political and investigative work, winning a 2015 Green Eyeshade Award for investigative reporting. He has also been awarded the Gene Miller Award for Investigative Reporting and the Florida Press Club's top government reporting award. A Wisconsin native and graduate of Marquette University, he has lived in Florida since 2008, when he went to work for the *Villages Daily Sun* immediately after graduation.